The Story of
FREEDOM

TITLES FROM GENERATIONS

Family Bible Study Series
  Genesis: A Family Bible Study Guide
  Psalms I: A Family Bible Study Guide
  Psalms II: A Family Bible Study Guide
  Psalms III/IV: A Family Bible Study Guide
  Psalms V, Part I: A Family Bible Study Guide
  Proverbs I: A Family Bible Study Guide
  Proverbs II: A Family Bible Study Guide
  Proverbs III: A Family Bible Study Guide
  Matthew: A Family Bible Study Guide

Keep The Faith Series
  On Education
  On Family & Sexuality

Christian Discipleship Curriculum
  Worldviews In Conflict: A Study in Western Philosophy, Literature, & Culture
  Essential Writings on Church History
  Great Christian Classics: Four Essential Works of the Faith
  Great Christian Classics: Five Remarkable Narratives of the Faith
  Great Christian Adventures: Essential Literature for Christian Students
  Great Christian Stories: Essential Literature for Christian Students
  History's Heroes
  History of the World: The Transforming Influence of Jesus Christ
  What Does the Bible Say About That?
  Proverbs: A Companion Lesson Book for Children
  America In God's Providence: A Christian Worldview History
  American Faith

From Kevin Swanson
  Apostate: The Men Who Destroyed the Christian West
  The Tattooed Jesus: What Would the Real Jesus Do with Pop Culture?
  Upgrade: 10 Secrets to the Best Education for Your Child
  Taking the World for Jesus
  Family Life

LifeLaunch
  Kickstart: Launch Your Life

The Story of
FREEDOM

Kevin Swanson

Generations
PASSING ON THE FAITH

ISBN: 978-1-7327050-4-3

2nd Edition, 2019
Previously published as *Freedom*

Production Management: Joshua Schwisow
Cover Design & Typography: Justin Turley
Interior Layout & Design: Joshua Schwisow

Published by:
Generations
PO Box 1398
Elizabeth, CO 80107-1398
www.generations.org

For more information on this and
other titles from Generations,
visit www.generations.org

CONTENTS

PREFACE

Has freedom become a lost cause? Has the word itself been drained of all substantial meaning? Have we forgotten why brave men gave up their lives in a bygone era? I wonder. Christians, conservatives, and patriots have to a great extent lost the vision for freedom. There is less and less interest in liberty anymore, and the word is hardly mentioned in the political campaigns. Words like "tyranny" and "liberty" seem to have fallen into disrepute. The terms have come to feel a bit strange and unwieldy when used in common parlance.

One so rarely hears pastors preach against tyranny, as was common at other times in this nation's history. The passion for freedom that burned in the hearts of the Pilgrims, Presbyterians, and patriots has greatly diminished today. Some politicians seem reluctant to even invoke the word. When the word is employed, it is usually in reference to libertine behavior, or to some insubstantial freedom such as the possession of marijuana.

In the fall of 1994, I ran as a gubernatorial candidate in the State of Colorado. Basically, I wanted freedom from big government, a restoration of what our forefathers called "the right to life, liberty, and property." In my campaigning, I would display a graph of government spending as a percentage of the Gross National Income over the last 200 years. I showed the crowds the massive increase in the size of government since 1900 (rising sharply from 9 percent to 46 percent of the Gross National Income). I would point out that Republican and Democrat alike have contributed to this trend by increasing the purview of government in the nation, incrementally over 120 years. Then, I would follow up with a dramatic rendition of Samuel Adams' famous quote:

> "If you love wealth more than liberty, the tranquility of servitude better than the animating contest of freedom, depart from us in peace. We ask not your counsel nor your arms. May your chains rest lightly upon you, and may posterity forget that you were our countrymen!"

The crowd stared at me in shocked disbelief—not a single "hear, hear!" from the lot of them. It seems that the tranquility of servitude to the Social Security System, to Medicare and Medicaid, and to all the other bureaucracies, had fairly absorbed the populace. It was hard to find more than a few individuals across the state who had any genuine interest in freedom from big government. Suffice it to say that I walked away with less than 4 percent of the vote in the 1994 gubernatorial election. Since then, the purview of government has continued its steady growth.

Yet, I cannot believe that we are destined to a future of eternal slavery on earth. I cannot believe that all humans, believers included, are forever consigned to increasing levels of enslavement to their fellow man (and to the all-consuming state). As sure as I am of Christ's resurrection, I am certain that He will set the captives free in more ways than one. I am certain that if the Son will set us free, we will be free indeed (John 8:36).

FALSE PRETENSES

Though the word "freedom" is hardly used in our day, symbols of bondage are increasingly popular with the youth. One of the most popular movies of 2015 prominently features sexual practices that signify "bondage." Body-piercing, certain clothing styles, jewelry, and other symbols popular with the youth attempt to celebrate the accouterments of bondage and slavery. These things are cultural manifestations of a post-Christian era.

Nonetheless, slavery still retains something of a negative connotation in the mind of most Americans, at least with those who have been influenced by a Christian world and life view. The modern world, however, demonstrates itself to be shallow, inconsistent, and disingenuous when it preaches the freedom message. Feminists boast of their freedoms. Progressives promise to free women from their husbands, and then place them under fifteen layers of bureaucratic control (through socialist systems or highly-regulated capitalism). They liberate African Americans from slavery, only to deliver them over to the Washington welfare state by the millions.[1] "Liberals" fight for freedom to abort children and to use recreational drugs, while removing all other meaningful freedoms and constructing a police state. These examples are emblematic of the agenda of the Left in this country (and other socialist nations in the modern world).

There is no neutrality in the war of worldviews, and the first battleground forms over the definition of terms. Big Brother's "Newspeak"[2] will rush in to define "freedom" as slavery, and "peace" as war. The devil is not an idiot, and he knows that "he who defines, wins." Therefore, we must lay out our terms by clear biblical definitions from the outset, or we will lose this battle.

Part I

~

FREEDOM

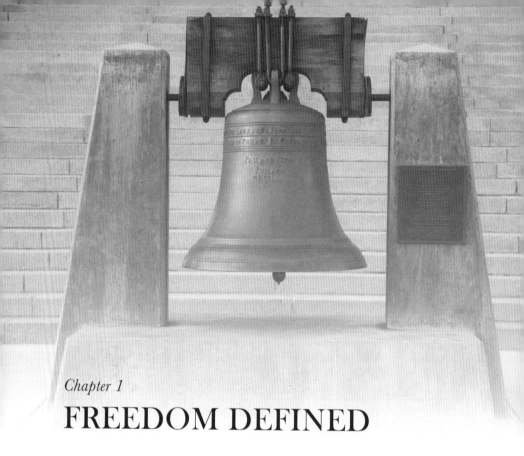

Chapter 1

FREEDOM DEFINED

"If the Son therefore shall make you free, ye shall be free indeed."
(John 8:36)

T he word "freedom" has a wonderful ring to the Western ear. If you were to ask the average person, "Would you like to be free?" doubtless he would still answer in the affirmative. However, based on the Google Ngram metric, frequency of usage in popular literature of the word "freedom" has dropped off by about 30 percent since the 1960s. The use of the word "liberty" has decreased in popular usage by 80 percent over the last century. Despite the wild revolutions and protests of the last century, people are far less interested in liberty than they were in previous centuries. But "freedom" is a problematic word, and it is generally avoided in conversations now. Widely differing values produce widely varying definitions of freedom, and the subject is best avoided in civil conversations. This value confusion has come about via the clever deception of the evil one.

The word "freedom" is a vital part of the Christian vocabulary. Above any and all others, Christians should speak often of freedom. No one should value freedom more, speak of freedom more, seek freedom, and exult in their freedom more than followers of Christ. In fact, the entire Bible is a story of redemption, and the very word "redemption" denotes freedom from slavery (Gen. 48:16, Ex. 6:6, 15:13, Lev. 27:28, 2 Sam. 4:9, Neh. 5:5, Ps. 25:22, 34:22, 44:26, 49:7,15, 72:14, 107:2, 130:8, Isa. 1:27, 35:9, 44:22, 50:2, 51:11, 52:3, 63:4, Hos. 7:13, 13:14). Nine psalms speak directly to Israel's deliverance from Egypt (Ps. 68, 78, 80, 81, 105, 106, 114, 135, 136). This historical event dominates the Old Testament consciousness. The exodus was the main event of the Old Testament story of redemption, and the psalmists and prophets repeatedly referred to it. It was the supreme act of God in the Old Testament whereby His people were delivered from bondage, and led into the Promised Land.

The Greek word for "freedom" in the New Testament is the same word used for "forgiveness," namely, ἐλευθερόω. It is translated "to obtain a release" or "to exempt from liability." Enslavement entails allegiance and obedience to the master. From passages like Matthew 11:30, we learn that while some level of servitude is inevitable in God's created order, some masters are better than others. The Hebrew word for "liberty" used in Isaiah 61:1 and Leviticus 25:10 is דרור (Deror). As is characteristic of the Hebrew language, the definition is better presented in pictorial form, as the release of a dam allowing water to flow freely without hindrance.

Modern English definitions betray a wrong worldview, by taking a humanist, absolutist view of these words. For example, the Google definition of freedom is "the power or right to act, speak, or think as one wants without hindrance or restraint."[1] Liberty is defined as "the state of being free within society from oppressive restrictions imposed by authority on one's way of life, behavior, or political views," or "the power or scope to act as one pleases."[2] The second definition especially illustrates the humanist approach to the word, as natural man does seek unrestrained individual license.

According to a Christian view of the world, all men by nature are enslaved by the devil who is the worst tyrant who ever lived (Eph. 2:2). The devil is the essence of that which is evil. He is deceptive and malignant, desiring nothing for mankind but misery and bondage. Therefore, wherever the Christian Gospel has not penetrated, slavery of all stripes dominates. Torture, unrestrained beatings, chattel enslavement, long-term confinement, pain, mass-murders, widow burning, infanticide, human sacrifice, forced separation of parents and children, the murder of pregnant women, and child sex slavery mark those pagan societies under the power of the devil and untouched by Christian influence. In our day, Muslims, pagan animists, humanists, and communists are all known for these horrific evils. As the Christian influence in the West has waned over the last fifty years, it should come as no surprise that child sex slavery, infanticide, and torture are coming back. The same phenomena was observed in communist Russia and the Eastern bloc during the twentieth century.

THE TESTIMONY OF JESUS CHRIST

Into this dismal world of tyranny and misery came the Lord Jesus Christ. He broke in on the scene in AD 30 pronouncing liberty for the captives from the very outset of His ministry (Luke 4:18). He spoke much of "freedom," as did His apostles. If these words were important to Jesus, they should of course frequent the working vocabulary of every follower of Christ today.

Now, one of the reasons why people in the time of Christ or people today are unlikely to use words like "liberty" is that they do not believe they are in bondage. When Jesus raised the matter with the Pharisees in John 8, they were stunned to hear that they too were enslaved. They rather insisted that they were Abraham's seed and consequently born free. Jesus however disagreed, responding emphatically, "Verily, verily, I say unto you, whosoever committeth sin is the servant of sin" (John 8:35).

The Pharisees thought of freedom in terms of political and cultural identity, and they could not think of it in the more fundamental sense. This is typical for natural man who is always more concerned with superficialities and externals. But Jesus Christ came to both reveal and resolve the core problems with which man is terribly plagued. The ultimate and most fundamental form of slavery is enslavement to sin. Given that sin is defined as the "transgression of God's law" (1 John 3:4), anybody who breaks God's laws is the slave of sin (according to Jesus Christ).

Christ followed up his discussion on slavery with those glorious words: "If the Son therefore shall make you free, ye shall be free indeed" (John 8:36).

Thus, Christ's redemption is fundamental as well. When Jesus Christ provides freedom, it will be no sham freedom, no temporary, superficial, pseudo-freedom as that promised by pseudo-liberal politicians. His freedom is the ultimate freedom, as free as a man can possibly be. Of course, absolute freedom as imagined by the humanist is impossible. Men may dream of complete autonomy, such as Jean-Paul Sartre's "authentic" life of freedom from all constraints. But that is an impossible dream. It can never happen. Men will either serve the devil or they will serve Christ.

> "Know ye not, that to whom ye yield yourselves servants to obey, his servants ye are to whom ye obey; whether of sin unto death or of obedience unto righteousness? But God be thanked, that ye were the servants of sin, but ye have obeyed from the heart that form of doctrine which was delivered you. Being then made free from sin, ye became the servants of righteousness." (Rom. 6:16-18)

Actually, the "freedom indeed" that Christ provides comes with another servanthood. When we come into His kingdom, we become servants of another King, the most benevolent King of all, and our relationship is characterized more by sonship (Gal. 4:7) and friendship (John 15:14,15) than by servantship. His yoke is easy and His burden is light compared to all others (Matt. 11:28-30). In essence, our Lord tells us to "choose your servitude." Either we can be enslaved to the most oppressive tyrant who ever lived, or we can be a servant, a friend, and a son in the family of God.

> "Wherefore thou art no more a servant, but a son; and if a son, then an heir of God through Christ." (Gal. 4:7)

"Ye are my friends, if ye do whatsoever I command you. Henceforth
I call you not servants; for the servant knoweth not what his lord
doeth: but I have called you friends; for all things that I have heard
of my Father I have made known unto you." (John 15:14-15)

THE LAW OF LIBERTY

God's law is described in the Book of James as the "perfect law of
liberty," (Jas. 1:25, 2:8-13). According to this text, the law of Christ
allows for maximum liberty because mercy overcomes judgment, and
releases us from bondage to sin (which is defined in Scripture as the
transgression of the law). Christian believers are freed from condemnation because of Christ's forgiveness (Rom. 8:1-3), and they are free
to keep the law because of His power working in them (Rom. 6:1-14).
Thus, Christians of all people are the most free. They are forgiven for
breaking the law and at the same time are enabled to keep the law,
thereby maximizing their day-to-day liberty under that law. They are
freed from the bondage of a guilt complex, and they are set free from
those sins and addictions that curtail true liberty. Additionally, they
are increasingly freed from extraneous man-made rules, regulations,
and fences that do not in themselves represent God's moral laws. Under the law of liberty, we receive mercy and we grant mercy. We bind
ourselves by judgment, and we bind others by judgment, a judgment
that must be ordered according to the boundaries of God's laws. According to the law of Christ, mercy triumphs over judgment.

When God commands, "Thou shalt not steal," (Ex. 20:15, Deut.
5:19, 19:14, Luke 18:20, Rom. 13:9), He defines maximum liberty for
ourselves and others. When men steal and kill, they curtail liberties (to
life and property) for themselves and others. When a man steals another man's wife, he tightens the slave bands of sin around his own wrists.
The libertine and antinomian are wrong when they define maximum
liberty as "doing whatever a man wishes to do." When men serve other gods and submit themselves to addictions (such as alcohol, drugs, or
pornography) they find themselves in the most severe bondage. These
earthly gods will beat them to death. In reference to foods, the Apostle Paul writes, "All things are lawful unto me, but all things are not

expedient: all things are lawful for me, but I will not be brought under the power of any" (1 Cor. 6:12-13; reference also 1 Cor. 10:23-25). To succumb to addictions is to walk into the cage and throw away the key. This is something Paul will not do, according to his own testimony. A nation has lost its interest in freedom when the populace gives way to addictions. From a recent collection of data published on addictions, it appears that most Americans are addicted to some form of destructive vice. For example, "Twenty-eight percent of young people between the ages of 18 and 24 binge-drink five times a month, putting away seven drinks in one sitting."[3] Add to this, the 9.2 percent of Americans who abuse drugs (this trend is on the rise).[4] Considering that there is an additional 66 percent of young men addicted to pornography,[5] with 10 percent clinically addicted to computer games, we now begin to get a picture of modern society. Above all, addictive behavior points to problems with slavery in a culture.

THE CONNECTION WITH POLITICAL LIBERTY

America's founding fathers understood an important axiom which was worked into the fiber of the national character from the beginning. Two of the most important figures in America's history state the same thing in different ways:

"Those who will not be governed by God will be ruled by tyrants"
- William Penn[6]

"Either you'll be governed by God, or by God you'll be governed."
- Benjamin Franklin

These men certainly understood the vital importance of self-government, the indissoluble connection between personal morality and political freedom. The principle is taken from the wisdom of Solomon:

"For the transgression of a land many are the princes thereof: but by a man of understanding and knowledge the state thereof shall be prolonged." (Prov. 28:2)

This should explain the modern leftist agenda, where government agencies are eager to see parents kill their own children, and they promote the most perverse sexual acts with tax dollars. From whence

comes their enthusiastic commitment to bring about the destruction
of the family? Fundamentally, they are committed to the establishment of tyrannical governments. Thus, as much as they break down
the moral fiber of the people, they grease the skids for more tyranny.
If there is a central principle that drives "the Gentiles," it is the thirst
for power over others.

> "The kings of the Gentiles exercise Lordship over them; and they
> that exercise authority upon them are called benefactors. But ye
> shall not be so: but he that is greatest among you, let him be as the
> younger; and he that is chief, as he that doth serve." (Luke 22:25-26)

This power motive drives the politics, the corporations, and the
non-profit systems controlled by "the Gentiles" or the heathen nations. These leaders are primarily focused on position and power, and
their systems will maximize servitude and minimize political freedoms
within their systems over time. Their educational systems, technology,
media, and organizations are always in the process of accumulating
and centralizing power.

Here then, is the connection with political freedom. At root, it is a
sinful people that provides the basis for political tyranny. Satan understands this, and all tyrants take advantage of it. But Christ solves the
problem, when He tells us, "If the Son will make you free, you will be
free indeed!" If sin is the transgression of the law, and if Jesus came to
save His people from their sins (Matt. 1:21), then we have the solution!
As more people enjoy the salvation that Christ brings, the seedbed for
tyranny disappears. The Israelites never quite learned this over 1,800
long years. You cannot solve the problem of Egypt, the Philistines,
Assyria, Babylon, Greece, and Rome, until you have addressed the
problem of sin. So Jesus Christ enters the picture to provide the world
a seedbed for freedom.

THE PRIMA FACIE EVIDENCE FOR THE CASE

Slaves who are locked into a slavish mindset will not be interested
in self-government. Both Scripture and history testify to this truth.
Those least likely to be interested in freedom from tyrants are usually already controlled by the idolatry of materialism, pornography

addiction, drunkenness, or the self-centered life. They would sacrifice nothing for a higher value than their own present comfort. This is the young man who plays video games while his empire burns even as the Romans sat in the games while the pagan hordes burned down the city. This is the man who is more interested in the Super Bowl than the elections. This is the father who puts more time into his golf game than in teaching his children God's Word or fighting for righteousness and liberty in the public sphere.

When men have embraced sin, they will usually embrace tyranny as well. They run to it, and they will "kiss the chains that bind them," to use Samuel Adams' words. They may even boast in their chains. They commend the systems that regulate them and recommend them to others. Such is the deception of the evil one. To hope that an immoral people would join the struggle for freedom is but a pipe dream. The leeks are better in Egypt (Num. 11:5).

The problem with the man who is too enthralled by pornography to battle the rising tyranny of the day is that he is blinded by sin. He loses all sense of his condition, and he loses a grasp on the distinction between good and evil. A Christian businessman was speaking to several coworkers about his interest in supporting ministries that rescued children forced into sex slavery. It was immediately obvious that the other men were uncomfortable with the discussion, and they changed the subject. Why weren't they as ardent in their opposition to tyrannical forms of evil as the Christian? We may not be able to identify the precise problem with these men. But it should be obvious that any man caught in pornography addiction will apply little or no enthusiasm towards ridding the world of child sex trafficking. Sin is the root of all tyranny, all blindness, all loss of perspective, and all evil in the world. Therefore, a man can hardly engage the battle for freedom elsewhere if he has yet to be set free from the shackles of sin in his own life. This can only happen by the powerful blood of Jesus Christ. The gospel, therefore, is basic to all forms of liberty.

> "For the weapons of our warfare are not carnal, but mighty through God to the pulling down of strong holds, casting down imaginations, and every high thing that exalteth itself against the knowledge of

God, and bringing into captivity every thought to the obedience of Christ; and having in a readiness to revenge all disobedience, when your obedience is fulfilled." (2 Cor. 10:4-6)

This text puts both the individual and the social responsibility together in the right order in a single passage. Every Christian is called to cast down every imagination that exalts itself against the knowledge of God, and bring into captivity every thought to the obedience of Christ (vs. 4, 5). However, we cannot avenge *all* disobedience, until our own obedience is matured or perfected (vs. 6). The man who is dealing with individual sin in his own life can hardly address institutional sin until his obedience is matured.

A CRUCIAL CONNECTION

Most Christians would readily agree that Christ came to "set us free from Satan's power and might." They seek freedom from sin by the redemption of Christ. However, many still do not accept the necessary implications which extend into the temporal, political, and economic settings. Or they do not regard them as important. The Apostle Paul makes this crucial connection in 1 Corinthians 7:

> "Let every man abide in the same calling wherein he was called. Art thou called being a servant? Care not for it: but if thou mayest be made free, use it rather. For he that is called in the Lord, being a servant, is the Lord's freeman: likewise also he that is called, being free, is Christ's servant. Ye are bought with a price; be not ye the servants of men." (1 Cor. 7:20-23)

While the Apostle Paul recognizes the inevitability of some manner of slavery in a sin-cursed world (whether to local slave masters, large corporations, banks, or governments), he is not content to leave it there. Specifically, Paul addresses the slave in the Roman economy of the day. On one hand, Paul does not recommend slave revolts and illegitimate revolutions. If there is no lawful way to extricate yourself from this condition, he says, "Abide in the same calling... don't be anxious about it." Nonetheless, he adds an important qualification: "If there is an opportunity to obtain freedom, take full advantage of it. Use it rather."

In case the reader is tempted to ignore this qualification, Paul concludes the paragraph with a sharp rejoinder: "Ye are bought with a price; be not ye the servants of men." This brief statement offers tremendous support for the cause of freedom from the unnecessary and illegitimate servitude of men. What more could he say? Is there any higher value we may attach to it than the price of the precious blood of the Son of God? Yes, the blood of Christ most certainly redeems us from sin. But that blood redemption also extends to the *effects of sin, including temporal slave-based systems of men.*

Thus, Christians will resist all forms of slavery, while still recognizing the inevitable consequences of sin in a sinful world. Surely debt, tyrannical governments, and varying forms of enslavement are as inevitable as divorce and disease in this world of sin. But we are not content to leave it there. We continue to value and believe in the efficacious power of the blood redemption of Christ. We cling to His promise: "If the Son will set you free, you will be free indeed." Where Christ works His redemption, He will make thorough work of it.

We will not take one form of slavery in exchange for another. Should the federal government attempt to enslave a nation in exchange for abolishing fiefdoms in the Southern states, we will not settle for it. We want an end to all forms of slavery, by legitimate means. We understand that revolution and war cannot accomplish what regeneration can do. Thus, we are primarily interested in the preaching of the Christian Gospel and the salvation of men from their sin. Should the humanists recommend alternate forms of slavery and revolutionary forms to bring it about, we will reject it. Should an ungodly president promise to set men free, we will suspect his agenda. However, whenever a nation seeks freedom by repentance and appeals to the Lord Jesus Christ, we are more hopeful.

When men cease looking to big governments and petty lords for their security and when they learn to trust in God for their daily food and their salvation, they will begin to value true freedom again. When they repent of their sins of pride, slothfulness, idolatry, and addictions, they will find less of a need for the chains of institutionalized slavery to form their social systems. The day they are more impelled by the power of love than the motive of power, they will spend more time preaching the Gospel and discipling men than enslaving them. They will walk away from the temptation to centralize power and wealth in fiefdoms large or small.

BIBLICAL LAW DEFINES LIBERTY

Actually the Bible does not speak of liberty or freedom apart from redemption from sin, which is the transgression of the laws of God. Thus, true liberty and human rights properly derive from the law of God duly respected and obeyed in all spheres of life including the political. If liberty is defined by the laws of God, then the freedoms to be defended and secured by human governments should be obvious for the Christian. The following offers several examples of these "rights" as defined by the laws of God.

A man and his family have a right to defend their home, if one breaks in at night (Ex. 22:2).

A man and his family have the right to own private property, protected from thieves (Ex. 20:15, Rom. 13:9). The civil magistrate should require thieves to work and restitute to the victims of theft (Ex. 22:1, Eph. 4:28). Governments have no right to eminent domain over a man's home (1 Kings 21:17-19).

A man has a right to possess appropriate weaponry to defend himself and others. Defense of others is preferred to self defense in Scripture (Neh. 4:14, Luke 22:36).

Christians ought to have the freedom to preach the Gospel in public forums, public parks, public beaches, and public streets without interference from the civil magistrate or the mob (Acts 5:29).

Christian parents ought to have the freedom to direct the education and make medical choices for their children (Ex. 21:16, 22:16, Num. 30:1-6, Deut. 6:7, Eph. 6:4).

A man has a right to set wages for his employees, free and clear of government control (Matt. 20:15). All must maintain their verbal or written contracts made in the marketplace.

Governments that take more than 10 percent of the people's income are tyrannical (1 Sam. 8:15-18).

When it comes to public projects, the rich shall not pay more and the poor shall not pay less (Ex. 30:15).

The state has no right to dictate the worship of the church (2 Chron. 26:17ff). However, the state may interfere when a cult engages in human sacrifice or possibly even animal sacrifice (Ex. 22:20). The limits of religious liberty in any nation must be carefully considered. Jesus Christ tolerated the idea of multiple denominational strains (Mark 9:38ff), and the parable of the wheat and tares prohibited any kind of religious jihad for Christians (Matt. 13:29-30).

A man may not be convicted of a crime without at least two or three witnesses (Deut. 17:6, 19:15, 2 Cor. 13:1). Severe penalties must be meted out on false witnesses in a court of law (Deut. 19:16-19).

If a baby in utero is killed accidentally (when subjected to hazardous conditions by careless men), at least a fine must be imposed on those responsible (Ex. 21:22-23). The civil magistrate must protect the right to life.

This is a sampling of very basic laws that establish liberty, as determined by the God who is the very definition of justice. True Christians then must and will seek justice by the incorporation of the general equity of these laws with the civil magistrate. Above all people in the world, they will recognize the bounds of true liberty and defend them rigorously.

WESTERN LIBERTIES FORMED BY CHRISTIANS

Over the last two thousand years, great men have appeared on the scene—heroes of the Christian faith who have identified this connection between Christ and the blessing of liberty, and they have brought freedom to the world. If history provides us any heroes at all, these real freedom-fighters are worthy of our admiration and appreciation. These heroes did not appear in Muslim countries or in pagan nations, nor do they come from Mexico, Africa, or China in the 18th, 19th, and 20th centuries. These true Christian leaders did not take men out of the hands of one tyrant only to deliver them into the hands of another (as in the case of Marxist revolutions and slave revolts). These great men came from Ireland, Scotland, England, the Netherlands, and America. To this day, these are the countries which remain the most free in the world (according to the Heritage Foundation Freedom Index). Of the most free nations in the world, each of the top ten have roots in the Protestant Reformation which took place in the 16th and 17th centuries.[7] The battle for freedom played out in Scotland with William Wallace, in England with Oliver Cromwell, in Ireland with Patrick, and in America with Patrick Henry and a host of others. The effect of this work is evident in the Freedom Indexes produced some centuries later. While England, America, and Scotland have had their tyrants and turncoats, they have also been blessed with an unusual number of courageous freedom heroes who have secured liberty by their blood and by their faith. This is the only explanation for what little economic and political liberty this world has ever experienced. It is history's unfolding story of Christ and His followers.

It is one thing to tell the stories of pastors and missionaries who brought a good message, and these are all very encouraging. Yet it is quite another thing to look at the fruits of other courageous men of faith who did something with their faith in other spheres. They secured something of lasting value with their faith—they brought liberty to millions of oppressed peoples. That is what makes this story so compelling. In the present day these great lessons from history provide us an inspiring vision for the future. The Western heritage of freedom is quickly fading as I shall explain later. Many enjoy the fruit of liberty, but few are doing anything to cultivate the tree that produces it. Might there be more opportunities to see liberty retained and expanded throughout the world? May God bring more freedom heroes to every nation in the world, should Christ tarry (over the centuries to come). Christ's kingdom proclaims the jubilee, and where His kingdom scratches the surface of this earth's systems, there will be more opportunities to bring about temporal freedoms.

"And ye shall hallow the fiftieth year, and proclaim liberty throughout all the land unto all the inhabitants thereof!" (Lev. 25:10)

Part II

~

TYRANNY

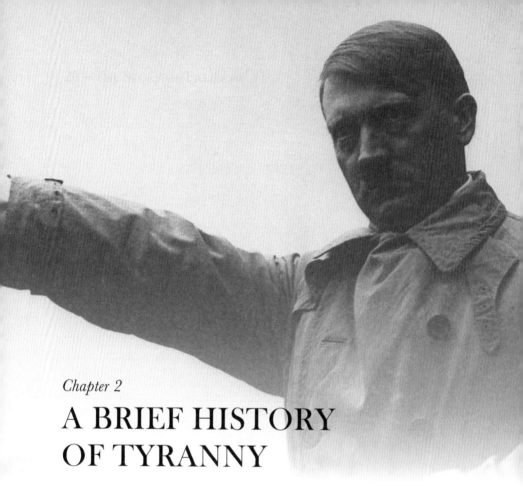

Chapter 2

A BRIEF HISTORY
OF TYRANNY

"When the righteous are in authority, the people rejoice: but when
the wicked beareth rule, the people mourn." (Prov. 29:2)

Human leaders have quite the capacity to make the lives of
their people miserable as shall be demonstrated in this chapter. The evil deeds performed by tyrants will challenge the
limits of the imagination. This in itself proves the devil is real. He
is the father of all tyrants and wicked men take their cues from him.
Government is not neutral, and the policies advocated by leaders are
not amoral. Given that rulers are the ministers of God (Rom. 13:1,
4), and God has directed His rulers to praise the good and avenge
evil, they violate His law when they do just the opposite. Wicked rulers then, are those who disobey God's laws in highly egregious ways.
Tyranny may be defined as powerful men and powerful systems which
oppose God and His just law. If men are to be free from tyranny, they

must know something of the laws of God. It is only the law of God which provides maximum opportunity for liberty among men (John 8:35, Jas. 2:12). If tyranny represents the violation of God's laws in the corporate body (sometimes led by individual dictators), anarchy ensues when individuals engage in egregious violations of God's laws.

Noah Webster captured something of a biblical view of tyranny when he defined a tyrant as

> "A monarch or other ruler or master, who uses power to oppress his subjects, a person who exercises unlawful authority, or lawful authority in an unlawful manner; one who by taxation, injustice or cruel punishment, or the demand of unreasonable services, imposes burdens and hardships on those under his control, which law and humanity do not authorize, or which the purposes of government do not require."[1]

Tyrants attempt to supplant God's sovereignty by opposing His laws and imposing their own pseudo-sovereignty over the hearts and behavior of men. Actually, man-centered preaching does the same thing when church leaders strive to manipulate people into "decisions" for Jesus. This is justified by the intent to save souls from eternal damnation. At root, the inquisitions of previous centuries were concerned with the same sort of thing. The road to hell is paved with good intentions, as the saying goes. Under the pretense of religious care for human lives and souls, political or religious tyrants enforce their programs in an effort to change men's hearts, produce certain outward behaviors, and get them to heaven. What they may not realize is that they have replaced the sovereignty of the Holy Spirit of God with the sovereignty of man. This makes for a very bad religion indeed. The sovereignty of man is the very beginning of tyranny in all its forms. God must do the regenerating work in the hearts of men, by the sovereign Spirit.

When governments deny the sovereignty of God, they inevitably cross the line into tyranny in a desperate attempt to dominate the minds and actions of men. These are the fundamentals with regard to the battle against tyranny. This revolutionary power-grab often occurs deep in the hearts of leaders, evading detection. In such cases it is only by their fruits that they are known (Matt. 7:20).

TYRANNY ADDRESSED BY GODLY MEN IN HISTORICAL RECORDS

The words "tyranny" and "tyrant" were formerly part of the common parlance of the day, and great Christian pastors and writers did not hesitate to address this critical topic. John of Salisbury (AD 1120-1180), while serving as Secretary for the Archbishop of Canterbury, wrote on this subject in his Magnum Opus, *The Policraticus*. Such labors certainly would have had an effect on the nobles at Runnymede 35 years after he died (in 1215). John of Salisbury defined tyranny as "the abuse of power entrusted by God to man."[2] In regards to the responsibility of the lower magistrates, he wrote,

> "Loyal shoulders should sustain the power of the ruler so long as it is exercised in subjection to God and follows His ordinances: but if it resists and opposes the divine commandments, and wishes to make me share in its war against God, then with unrestrained voice, I answer back that God must be preferred before any man on earth."[3]

Martin Luther's major complaint before the Diet of Worms concerned ecclesiastical tyranny. His defense before the princes of Germany and Charles II, the Holy Roman Emperor, could very well be viewed as the inception of the great Reformation of the Christian Church that would transform the world over successive generations. At the Diet, Luther explained,

> "For universal experience and world-wide grievances are witnesses to the fact that through the Pope's laws and through man-made teachings the consciences of the faithful have been most pitifully ensnared, troubled, and racked in torment, and also that their goods and possessions have been devoured (especially amongst this famous German nation) by unbelievable tyranny... if I recant... the only effect will be to add strength to such tyranny."[4]

In his writings Luther argued that capital punishment for murder was a legitimate function of the state on the basis of Genesis 9:6, Exodus 21:24, and Matthew 5:19. However, he restricted the purview of government from forced subscription to the teachings of the church. He stated, "Heresy can never be prevented by force. That must be taken hold of in a different way, and must be opposed and dealt with otherwise than with the sword. Here God's Word must strive; if that does not accomplish the end, it will remain unaccomplished through the secular power, though it fill the world with blood."[5] He described most princes as "the worst knaves and the greatest fools on earth." In his paper *On Secular Authority*, he recommended disobedience and resistance to tyrants using the strongest possible words: "In Meissen, Bavaria, in the Mark, and other places, the tyrants have issued an order that the New Testaments be delivered to the courts everywhere. In this case their subjects ought not deliver a page or a letter, at risk of their salvation. For whoever does so, delivers Christ into Herod's hands."[6]

THE SWISS REFORMERS

The Swiss Reformer John Calvin also soundly condemned both ecclesiastical and civil tyranny in his monumental work, *The Institutes of the Christian Religion*. He used the word "tyranny" 94 times throughout the four books (compare this to 106 mentions of "predestination," which is thought by many to be his major theme). He described true heroes as those who deliver men and women from the oppression of tyrants.

> "Herein is the goodness, power, and providence of God wondrously displayed. At one time He raises up manifest avengers from among His own servants, and gives them His command to punish accursed tyranny, and deliver His people from calamity when they are unjustly oppressed; at another time He employs, for this purpose, the fury of men who have other thoughts and other aims. Thus He rescued His people Israel from the tyranny of Pharaoh by Moses; from the violence of Chusa, king of Syria, by Othniel; and from other bondage by other kings or judges."[7]

John Calvin further warned tyrants that "the Lord takes vengeance on unbridled domination."[8] While he cautioned private citizens not to take up arms against tyrants, he clearly left the door of resistance open for the "popular magistrates" or lower magistrates such as sheriffs, governors, or parliaments.

"For when popular magistrates have been appointed to curb the tyranny of kings (as the Ephori, who were opposed to kings among the
Spartans, or Tribunes of the people to consuls among the Romans,
or Demarchs to the senate among the Athenians; and perhaps there
is something similar to this in the power exercised in each kingdom
by the three orders, when they hold their primary diets). So far am I
from forbidding these officially to check the undue license of kings,
that if they connive at kings when they tyrannize and insult over the
humbler of the people, I affirm that their [the kings'] dissimulation is
not free from nefarious perfidy, because they fraudulently betray the
liberty of the people, while knowing that, by the ordinance of God,
they are its appointed guardians."[9]

Pierre Viret, another influential Swiss reformer, also defined tyrants as those "who do not reign according to [God's] word or recognize Him as their sovereign Ruler (as appears with Pharaoh, Sennacherib, Nebuchadnezzar, and Saul)..."[10] Viret reminded rulers of
the Old Testament requirement that "the book of the Law be read
before the king after he was elected, that he might know how to lead
and govern according to its teaching...(Deut. 17:18-20).[11] Viret also
allowed for the interposition of the lower magistrates when he wrote,
"If such a people possess a lawful means to resist the tyranny of such
tyrants by their legitimate magistrates, and are able by this means to
avoid slavery, they can follow the counsel of Paul (which we previously
spoke of) who said...'For he that is called in the Lord, being a servant,
is the Lord's freeman.' He adds, 'but if thou mayest be made free, use
it rather' (1 Cor. 7:21)."[12]

JOHN KNOX

Scotland yielded a powerful reformation, and it could not have
been done without the aid of the nobles. The mighty Reformer John
Knox (ca. 1513-1572) wrote his appeal to the nobles, in which he ex-
horted them to defend the cause of liberty from the tyrannical church
and political leadership in Scotland. He told them to "defend your
brethren and subjectes whome he hath putt under your charge and
care. Now if your King be a man ignorant of God, enemie to his true
religion, blinded by superstition, and a persecutor of Christes mem-

bers; shall yee be excused, if with silence yee passe over his iniquitie? Be not deceaved, my Lordes, ye are placed in authoritie for another purpose then to flatter your King in his folie and blind rage."[13]

Knox instructed these lower magistrates that God has raised them up, "to be as bridels, to represse the rage and insolencie of your Kinges, whensover they pretend manifestly to transgresse Goddes blessed ordinance."[14]

A century later, Samuel Rutherford (1600-1661) emerged as an important leader among the Scottish Presbyterians. Rutherford may be looked to as the ecclesiastical apologist for the founding of this country. Certainly the American Presbyterians who supported America's War for Independence en masse, and secured the victory in the key battles in the South, well understood Rutherford's points. He wrote his masterpiece, *Lex Rex,* in 1644 in which he placed the King under the authority of God's law. Rutherford's efforts warranted him the charge of high treason under King Charles II. He died before facing trial, at which point the English authorities proceeded to burn his book. Tyrants do not like books on tyranny.

In the opening paragraphs, Rutherford described tyranny as "a work of Satan, not from God, because sin, either habitual or actual, is not from God."[15] Thus, Rutherford equated tyranny with sin and the transgression of the law of God. He also pointed out that "the magistrate is good in the nature of his office, and the intrinsic end of his office (Rom. 13:4), for he is the minister of God for thy good."[16]

Rutherford's view of kingdoms gained solely by conquest was tentative, even condemnatory. He wrote, "We cannot think that a tyrannous and unjust domineering can be God's lawful means of translating kingdoms; and for the other part, the conqueror cannot domineer as king over the innocent and especially the children not yet born."[17]

Further on in the work, Rutherford addressed the "law of the tyrant" as that which stands opposed to the law of God.

> "God can give no moral power to do wickedly; for that is license, and
> a power to sin against a law of God, which is absolutely inconsistent
> with the holiness of God; for so the Lord might deny himself, and
> dispense with sin. God avert such blasphemies."[18]

He considered slavery in all of its forms, an unnatural state of being; originating in the fall: "Slavery should not have been in the world, if man had never sinned, no more than there could have been buying and selling of men, which is a miserable consequent of sin and a sort of death, when men are put to the toiling pains of the hireling..."

Rutherford also allowed for resistance to kings "when the power is abused to the destruction of laws, religion, and the subjects."[19] However, he did add the important qualification that this resistance by defensive wars be administered only "at the commandment of the estates of the kingdom."[20] These estates are the lower magistrates such as sheriffs and county governments. Rutherford made an important distinction here between revolutionary anarchy and acting under the existing order that is ordained by God to resist tyranny.

A BRIEF HISTORY OF TYRANNY

From the earliest biblical records, we read the stories of tyrants such as Nimrod, Pharaoh, Herod, and Ahab. Their most serious sins included forced infanticide, abortion, and the confiscation of private property. King Ahab's eminent domain exercised against Naboth was the very act that brought about God's judgment upon him (1 Kings. 21:17ff). The very worst crime committed by nations and governments is the persecution of Christians (Rev. 13:7, 14:8-9). Whether the beast of Revelation is a single man, a particular government, or a series of persecuting powers, doesn't really matter. For the purposes of this study, the beastly principle consists of powerful tyrants who support sexual perversions and persecute the people of God (Rev. 17:4-6). It doesn't take much effort to identify where this has happened in history. Herod married his brother's wife and killed John the Baptist. Nero introduced homosexual marriage for the first time in recorded history and launched the first major Roman persecution against the church of Christ (killing Peter and Paul in the bloody purge). Today, most Western countries are embracing Nero's agenda. They wish to institute homosexual marriage everywhere and persecute any Christian that stands against it. The beast lives on.

THE PROTOTYPICAL TYRANT

The first tyrant in the history of the world according to biblical record surfaces in the form of Lamech, Cain's great great great grandson (Gen. 4:19ff). He was a murderer and a vengeful man who promised to kill seventy-seven men, if anyone should attempt to hurt him. Lamech set himself against the standard of God's justice when he proclaimed, "If Cain shall be avenged sevenfold, truly Lamech seventy and seven fold" (cf. Gen. 4:14 and Gen. 4:24). Harking back to God's sentence on Cain, Lamech ups the ante. If God's justice would demand a seven-fold retribution for any person who should touch Cain, Lamech's vengeance would exceed that in severity by a factor of eleven-fold. The tyrant is one who is more assiduous and aggressive in the execution of his personal vengeance than even God would require according to His standards of justice. Whether these tyrants be drug lords, petty dictators, emperors, bureaucrats, legislators, or presidents (Republican or Democrat), they all follow in the footsteps of Lamech, the truly original tyrant.

The roots of the modern tyrants such as Adolf Hitler and Josef Stalin may be found in Friedrich Nietzsche or Karl Marx—modern apostates who abandoned the Christian faith and became the powerful "Nephilim" in the modern world.[21] The remarkable influence of these powerful, ungodly men over nations and empires is due in part to their robust character which they inherited from a Christian past. Their virulent wickedness may be traced to their rejection of Christ. Thus, the spiritual roots of these giants may be compared with the prediluvian giants found in Genesis (6:4,13). They were called "the Nephilim," having appeared out of an unholy synthesis between the sons of God (God-fearers) and the daughters of men (humanists). They were in a real sense, the original line of tyrants that brought tremendous violence and mass-murder to the earth.

Then came the tyrant Nimrod after the flood, who masterminded the kingdom of Babel (Gen. 10:9-10). Nimrod was known for his commitment to the power principle or "master morality" embraced by the Gentiles, condemned by Christ, and defended by Friedrich Nietzsche.[22] Every force that presses towards centralizing power may be traced back to Genesis 11:4, when Nimrod's men said, "Go to, let build us a city and a tower, whose top may reach unto heaven; and let us make us a name." This statement bears witness to the strong inclination towards pride, autonomy, and wickedness. It is the very basis of the humanist empire, and the Lord quickly dismantled the project (Gen. 11:8). Now, this "Babel Principle" has surfaced repeatedly throughout the annals of human history. Man instinctively turns towards centralizing power, as one poet put it, "The burnt fool's bandaged finger goes wabbling back to the Fire." As a result, great and mighty empires have formed throughout the world over the last 5,000 years. Following is a list of the major empires that have given way to the Babel instinct.

- Akkadia in the twenty-third century BC (Sargon)

- Egypt in the sixteenth century BC (Hatshepsut and Thutmose III)

- China in the thirteenth century BC (Wu Dynasty)

- Babylon in the twelfth century BC (Nebuchadnezzar I)

- China in the twelfth century BC (Shang Dynasty)

- China in the eleventh century BC (Zhou Dynasty)

- Assyria in the eighth century BC (Sennacherib)

- Babylon in the sixth century BC (Nebuchadnezzar II)

- Persia in the sixth century BC (Darius)

- Greece in the fourth century BC (Alexander)

- India in the fourth century BC (Maurya)

- Rome in the first century AD (Augustus)

- The Muslim Empire in the eighth century AD (Al-Walid)

- The Mongolian Empire in the thirteenth century AD (Genghis Khan)

- Spain and the Holy Roman Empire in the sixteenth century AD (Charles V)

- The Ottoman Empire in the sixteenth century AD (Suleiman)

- France in the seventeenth century AD (Louis IV)

- Britain in the eighteenth and nineteenth centuries AD (George III, Victoria)

Egypt, Assyria, Babel, Persia, Greece, and Rome took their turns working the Babel project from 2000 BC until 475 AD. Then for a thousand years, the empire-building effort waned while missionaries discipled most of the nations throughout Europe.

In some cases, the god-state is self-consciously realized, and the king is taken as representative of god (or gods) on earth. This was the case for the Egyptian Pharaohs, the Japanese Emperor, the Byzantine Emperor, the Indian Raja, and the Aztec Montezuma. In some cases with the medieval European kings, they considered themselves as God's vice-regent on His absence and refused subservience to His laws. Ordinarily, the kings of men worked hard to centralize power and to wrest control over vast resources and lands.

The god-state was revived in the modern world by humanist philosophers like Rousseau, Hegel, and Marx—this time it is the democracy that worships itself. G.W.F. Hegel sermonized on this new religion, when he wrote, "The state is the march of God through the world... We must worship the state as the manifestation of the Divine on the earth."[23] Regrettably, men like Lenin, Stalin, and Hitler took Hegel seriously.

Any resistance to a dictator or to the power state is perceived as the ultimate crime for which these Lamechs would demand requital to seventy-seven fold. This becomes a reality when every conceivable method of torture is employed by these power centers against Christians in particular. The horrific Roman tortures recounted by Eusebius and Foxe included searing with hot irons, dipping in hot oil, ripping limbs apart, stretching on racks, and so on. The Nazis and Communists perfected these demonically-inspired methods of torture over the last century and used them generously on Christians and others considered as enemies of the state. Stories from Russia, North Korea, China, and Romania have provided ample evidence of the depravity of the human heart and the vile evil of which men are capable. Modern humanist governments have made significant strides towards recovering the legacy of pagan Rome. China has imposed forced abortion and infanticide on its people from the early 1980s to the present day. The Soviet Union, China, and North Korea have used slave prison camps for political and religious dissidents over the last century. Hundreds of millions of citizens have been murdered at the hands of their own governments. Untold millions starved to death by government policy (at the hands of centrist dictatorships).

THE DEVELOPMENT OF THE MODERN POWER STATE

The modern age of empire building commenced again with several important power grabs—first, the Norman Conquest of England in AD 1066, and then the Treaty of Meaux in AD 1229. This was the point at which the Northern Kingdom of France wrested control of Southern France from Raymond VII. The Vatican assisted in the effort at a time when a significant portion of the Christian church was capitulating to political power games. There were religious concerns with the Cathari in the south of France to be sure, but the political aims were preeminent in the hearts of men. Natural man has a hard time resisting the accumulation of power, and the subsequent centuries would tell the sad story of empire-building and the rise of tyranny.

Similar power struggles followed in Ireland and Scotland in the fourteenth century, Germany in the sixteenth century (and briefly under the Nazis), and the United States in the nineteenth century. The only major "accomplishment" of the "Holy Roman Empire" was the persecution of the Protestants. And the major impediment for the empire building was that there were some 10,000 castles in Germany, none of which supported the empire with much enthusiasm. The Reformation also thwarted the empire's intentions. The Spanish Empire produced the Inquisition, and came to a quick end shortly after the defeat of the Armada. The French Empire persecuted the Huguenots, and the French Revolution quickly put an end to its aspirations. In the early years of the nineteenth century, Napoleon attempted to salvage the empire but failed. Finally, the British Empire had its start in the seventeenth century with the colonization of America. By the eighteenth century, Britain overwhelmed France as the new world power, and the sun did not set on the British Empire until the end of the nineteenth century. After World War II, America became the heir apparent in this sequence of world empires. In their efforts to build empires, Britain and America each participated in the slave trade in the eighteenth century, and England joined the French and Spaniards in their persecution of certain Protestant sects in the sixteenth and seventeenth centuries.

POWER HANDOFF

Babel first offered the opportunity for the centralization of power and the abuse of it. This is the lesson to be drawn from Genesis 11. Thus, the rise of the tyrannical state in the modern age may be traced to the centralizing impulse, beginning with the papacy.

Well before William Wallace appeared on the scene, the Synod of Whitby took place in AD 664. This church council held in Northern England and officiated by King Oswy, addressed the minor differences between the Irish and the Roman churches. The debates centered on the supremacy of the Roman papacy and the Roman interpretation of Matthew 16:18. In the end, the Northumbrians (the Irish church in Scotland) were forced to submit to the Pope on the matters of debate. Even the Venerable Bede acknowledged that the Irish church better replicated the teachings of Christ than the Roman church, so there was no debate as to the legitimacy of this Christian work in Scotland and Ireland.[24] Nonetheless, this power grab did not wrest complete control of the Scotch-Irish Culdean church. It wasn't until the twelfth century that the Pope had complete ascendancy over the Culdean churches. This paved the way for King Edward's political control over all of Scotland, although he did run into the "little" problem of Robert the Bruce. Certainly there would have been no Scottish War for Independence had it not been for the powerful machinations of the Roman Church employing the power principle centuries earlier.

The twelfth through the seventeenth centuries were consumed with power struggles within the papacy. It is the greatest tragedy of all when the church turns towards the political power game. The power principle began to dominate within the Western church when the pope threatened excommunication of leaders on the basis of political issues (rather than clear moral or doctrinal matters). There is nothing wrong with Christian kings and nations opposing the rising threat of Muslim world domination. Kings have a duty to protect their nations from threats of invasion. But when the church drives military missions as in the case of the Crusades, roles are reversed and bad things happen. The church was both centralizing power and usurping political power during these dreadful centuries. Power struggles within the papacy at this time produced what is now known as the Babylonian Captivity of the church (during the 1300s and 1400s). In time the Pope became exceedingly powerful, arguably the most powerful person in the world. Not only did he control all of the church in a pyramidic, centralized manner, but he came to control the political states as well. This was a far cry from what Christ in the Gospels had defined as the Kingdom of God. This Kingdom acts as yeast and grows silently and inconspicuously. It comes by regeneration and reveals itself in culture and politics, not by bloody revolutions and political force.

FROM POPE TO PRINCE

Political power centralized in Rome until the Protestant Reformation. Although much of the Reformation was commendable, we must be careful not to look at history through rose-colored glasses. In every great reformation, sinful men will plant a few seeds that bring about destructive results. It should be obvious that England's Henry VIII had little interest in the Christian faith. But what was he to do when he found himself at personal and political odds with the Pope? The Protestant Reformation came at a good time for Henry VIII, who was unhappy with the Pope's view of his marriage(s). He found the perfect arrangement with the new ecclesiastical order. The King supported the Reformation, swapped wives, and took possession of lands belonging to the Roman Church. This enriched the King and his agents, while the transfer of control of the English Church to the King served as an added benefit. The new arrangement also removed competition for political power out of the hands of the Church. This was a major step for the consolidation of power with the monarchy in the 16th and 17th centuries.

The Roman Church's involvement in the political power game backfired. Between 1520 and 1820, the Church in the West lost almost all its political power in Europe. The state took that power for its own, with scarcely a "thank you very much" to the Church, and consequently the Pope became more or less irrelevant in European politics and in European society during the centuries that followed. The power game is not Christ's game, and the real church had better learn this lesson. The Church's weapon is the sword of the Word of God, and it is only by the powerful preaching of that Word that societies are transformed and the nations are discipled. Thankfully, preaching did return to the pulpits of the lands during the Protestant Reformation and much progress was made for the Kingdom of Christ during that time.

FROM PRINCE TO PEOPLE

How does one solve the problem of the rising power of the state? How do the people bind the hands of the tyrant king? These are the questions addressed by the French and the English enlightenment philosophers between the 1690s and the 1760s. Two competing answers to these questions vied for ascendancy during the French and American "revolutions." The first answer came by way of Samuel Rutherford's *Lex Rex*. We bind the king's hands by the standards of God's laws and written constitutions based on divine command. The second answer came by way of Jean-Jacques Rousseau. We bind the king's hands by eliminating the monarchy altogether and replacing it with democracy—the will of the people. Although the French revolution advocated the latter position, the American War for Independence allowed for a mixture of the two. This was the exception to the rule, however. Most of the Western world transferred all the power from the Prince to the People, and then aggrandized these new governments with ten times the power. Never has the world seen such powerful governments as those constructed by "The People." Of course, the People are usually manipulated by a small group of elite social planners who gain control of the vast education and media systems of the nation. The People are led to believe that they are the source of all power, and that they can advocate any laws and advance any representative to advocate those laws as they deem appropriate. Unwittingly, they subject themselves to more tyranny while believing that they are the true source of authority and power. Even as there was no law to restrain the Pope or the Prince, now there is no law to restrain the People, according to this revolutionary humanism (especially when the People learn that they are the very source of law). When the People discover that they can spend other people's money by government fiat, there is henceforth no end to the feeding frenzy. Every democracy has turned into a socialist country with a penchant towards redistributing wealth and destroying the character of the nation. The wealth of the nation is redistributed until there is nothing that money can buy. (As of 2014, about 63 percent of the American population were receiving a regular check from the government, including welfare recipients—49.5 percent, and government employees—13 percent).[25] The modern socialist nations have finally arrived at the commencement of their own deconstruction, both economically and socially.

The unprecedented growth in government under democracy is worthy of note. A Cambridge University study found that Roman taxes never exceeded 13 HS (sestertius) per year for the average citizen, well under 5 percent of the average household's annual income.[26] The study points out that the tax load on the Romans was greater than that imposed by the monarchies in England and France during the 1500s. However, the tax load for the mighty Roman Empire did not approach the tax load borne by the populace of the modern democratic states (which averages upwards of 40-70 percent of the Gross Income of the respective nations). As we shall learn, the power to tax includes the power to regulate and the power to control the masses.

In order to better grasp the power shifts that have occurred between AD 1100 and the present day, the following table illustrates the rough distribution of the money in the economy among the spheres of family, church, and state:

	Before The Reformation	After The Reformation	Today
State	4-5%	10%	50%
Church	30%	5-10%	2-3%
Family	65%	80%	45-50%

The Biblical limit for the state's portion of the economy is 10 percent (1 Sam. 8:15ff). The church should also receive a tithe of 10 percent. Thus, directly after the Reformation, the percentages shifted in the right direction only to move towards a dis-empowering of the family and church over the succeeding centuries.

WHO IS THE SOURCE OF LAW?

The fundamental battle for liberty is fought over the source of law. When one of the Roman priests stated at Knight Walsh's house in the presence of William Tyndale, "We were better to be without God's laws than the Pope's," Tyndale gave the memorable response, "I defy the pope and all his laws! If God spare my life ere many years, I will cause a boy that driveth the plough to know more of the Scripture than thou dost!"[27] When Samuel Rutherford wrote his book *Lex Rex*, he struck a blow for liberty that resounded for centuries afterwards. Someone had informed King James I that he was "under God and His law." James flew into a rage and gave his famous retort: "The King is above the law... even by God Himself [we] are called gods." Rutherford's response came in the form of *Lex Rex*, or literally: "God's Law is King." This countered the King's arbitrary approach who would rather put himself in the place of God insisting that the King is law ("Rex Lex").

Therefore, the great advocates for freedom in history will first argue over this matter of the source of law. Either it will be the law of liberty (God's law), or the arbitrary, tyrannical, wicked laws of men. Throughout the rising tyrannies of the last millennium, the source of law shifted from the Pope to the Prince to the People. Only God's men, Christ's true disciples, argued for liberty. They fought for the authority of God's laws (as communicated through written constitutions, the Bill of Rights, and the Magna Carta) over man's laws. The progress of humanism over the last millennium unfolds according to the following timeline:

- Pope Lex, "The Pope is the Law" (1100 - 1550)

- Prince Lex, "The Prince is the Law" (1550 - 1750)

- Populi Lex, "The People are the Law" (1750 - Present)

We would rather stand with Samuel Rutherford. Lex Rex. God's Law is King. Sadly, most of the world is living under statist tyranny, characterized by arbitrary laws, exorbitant taxation and regulation, corruption and bribery at high levels, and abuse of innocent citizens at the hands of evil dictators (or capricious petty bureaucrats). Tyranny is the default condition until the Gospel of Christ and the righteous laws of God have absorbed into the fabric of these nations. Moreover, the Western world has recently turned its back on Christ and the Christian worldview opening the way for increased tyranny. The work of discipling the nations is long and arduous, and we cannot expect immediate success. But as the centuries pass, there will be more breakthroughs in other countries, even as the Lord Jesus Christ has already impacted many of this world's nations over 2,000 years.

There is a slight difference between humanist Russia and China, and the humanist West. Throughout the twentieth century, Russia went to hell in a casket of thorns, while America went to hell in a casket of velvet. Russia and its communist allies established big government tyranny by bloody revolutions; America and the Western nations did it with fifty elections. China killed one-third of its population by forced abortion. South Korea killed one-half of its babies by voluntary abortions and abortifacients, and made far more progress with imploding its birth rate. Which country has curried the favor of God?

It is the duty of all Christians to love mercy, seek justice, and walk humbly before their God (Mic. 6:8). Therefore, stalwart advocates for liberty in this era must (1) define justice by God's law, and (2) oppose tyrants who refuse to acknowledge God's laws and who abridge human freedoms by violating God's laws. Those who claim to oppose tyranny and support freedom while failing to define liberty by the laws of God, cannot possibly make the list of the great heroes of liberty.

Let us identify tyranny wherever it exists, and expose the unfruitful works of darkness. Tyrants murder innocent citizens. Tyrants confiscate land. Tyrants centralize control of banking, economies, and education. Tyrants torture people. Tyrants kill women and children. Tyrants engage in scorched earth policies (violating biblical law clearly stated in Deut. 20:19-20). Both Josef Stalin and General William Tecumseh Sherman (in the Civil War) employed a scorched earth policy in warfare. These men were tyrants.

Tyrants break treaties as President Andrew Jackson did when he signed the Indian Removal Act of 1830. Historical evidence indicates that the Georgia Legislature may have played a part in this perfidy as well.

Tyrants also employ offensive warfare in order to expand their rule, as in the case of Adolf Hitler, Napoleon, Julius Caesar, Alexander the Great, and others throughout history. Tyrants break the sixth and eighth commandments on a regular basis without remorse.

Good leaders, on the other hand, will quell civil unrest within their own countries. They will execute criminals who break the law (as defined by God), and they will defend their land from marauders. The Apostle draws a careful and clear distinction between good leaders and bad leaders in Romans 13:3-4:

> "For rulers are not a terror to good works, but to the evil. Wilt thou then not be afraid of the power? Do that which is good, and thou shalt have praise of the same: for he is the minister of God to thee for good. But if thou do that which is evil, be afraid; for he beareth not the sword in vain: for he is the minister of God, a revenger to execute wrath upon him that doeth evil."

TYRANNY IN GOD'S PURPOSES FOR HUMAN HISTORY

We do not live in a perfect world and we never will until the great redemption at the end, when all things are made new. No doubt, we will continue to see tyrannical injustices prevail here and there. It was by God's purpose that the wicked hands of human tyranny crucified Christ (Acts 2:23). By God's predetermined plan, the tyrannical Roman Caesars unleashed ten bloody persecutions upon Christians over the first three centuries of the Church. However, each successive persecution further strengthened the Church until God finally crushed the Roman Empire. In a similar manner in the Old Testament, God raised up Babylon to address Israel's disobedience, and then he crushed that evil empire as well (Isa. 46:10-11).

The priority in history will continue to be the health and the growth of the Church of the Lord Jesus Christ (Eph. 1:21). Nonetheless, the kings of the earth must be called to account as well (Ps. 2). We have the duty to seek justice, and disciple the nations. In the meantime, God will use the wrath of men to praise Him, and to build His Church (Ps. 76:10). Through the centuries tyrants will come and tyrants will go, but always we believe, "He must reign til he hath put all enemies under His feet" (1 Cor. 15:25).

Part III

~

A BRIEF
HISTORY
OF FREEDOM

INTRODUCTION

"The Spirit of the Lord is upon me, because he hath anointed me to preach the gospel to the poor; he hath sent me to heal the brokenhearted, to preach deliverance to the captives, and recovering of sight to the blind, to set at liberty them that are bruised," (Luke 4:18)

All freedom is a gift from God. Redemption from the bondage of sin is nothing more or less than the supernatural work of the Spirit of God applying the sacrificial, atoning work of the Son of God to individual men and women. Political and economic freedom is rooted in the sovereign, powerful work of almighty God, secured through long and arduous human struggles, and catalyzed in dramatic historic turn-abouts that continue to amaze historians through the ages. Lamentably, so much of human history is sunk in the dreary malaise of slavery produced by the harsh constraints of regulative governments, despotic tyrannies, local fiefdoms, corporate institutions, and creditors of all stripes. Though tyranny be the default in a sinful world, there have been significant moments in history in which Christian liberty catalyzed within certain nations, and the world was better for it. To miss these moments is to marginalize the work of Christ who paid the price with His own blood. These are truly remarkable occurrences, what George Washington would refer to as "remarkable interpositions of Divine Government." They are manifestations of the common grace of God, rooted in special grace. And, they come about in the most remarkable way. Historians often miss the true story, because they are not looking for it. A true hero is seldom recognized. He is the poor wise man who saved the city, as Solomon put it. But alas, no one remembered him (Eccl. 9:13-15).

I first propose that there are actually great men of history, the "good guys," in stark contrast with the "bad guys" of history. There are righteous kings who bring great blessing and joy to their people; and there are also wicked, tyrannical kings who bring curses and mourning to the land (Prov. 29:2). There are true heroes, who have accomplished remarkable and important deeds in God's redemptive story. Their accomplishments resulted in great blessings for millions who came after them. It is the story of freedom, and it must be told.

Considering these great heroes, we must first point out that even these men were sinners at their best, and they had their faults. But a true hero will unite the genuine Christian character traits of humility and courage. He will be a man who fears God, a man of great faith, and a man who is careful with power (Ex. 18:21, 2 Sam. 23:3). He will not seek to centralize, colonialize, or aggrandize the power centers. When others are drawn towards mercantilism for the benefit of the mother country, or manipulation of money supplies for the benefit of the few via fractional reserve banking, the leader for liberty will repudiate these power moves. He will do his utmost to curtail all murder and the slaughter of the innocents in his realm. He will submit himself to the 6th commandment and all the requirements and limits which God's law imposes upon himself as a civil leader. In short, a true hero is a leader in submission to God, in the fear of God, and he keeps himself (and repents) according to God's laws.

There is no other way to distinguish good leaders and bad leaders. The secular historian may find some way to view Nero or Hitler as good leaders, but the question still remains—what is the *standard* by which to judge good and evil? Only God's laws can provide that objective standard. Did they subject themselves to the laws of God? Nero was a tyrant, because he violated God's laws in more ways than one. He put the Apostle Peter to death, and never repented of it. Moreover, it should also be pointed out that Peter was not a man guilty of death, as defined by God's laws. Quite the opposite, he was a faithful Apostle of the Lord Jesus Christ. Good guys don't murder good guys. It is true that some good leaders fail at points. For example, King David of the Old Testament was guilty of a tyrannical action when he arranged for the death of Uriah the Hittite. Yet, David humbled himself, accepted the correction from Nathan the prophet, and before God, repented of his great sin (Ps. 51). We do not expect perfection from others or ourselves. What we are looking for is a positive direction that by the grace of God produces more liberty in the land, not less.

There is something irresistibly attractive about these stories of liberty. They make the best action films for their representation of human courage and sacrifice in the face of overwhelming odds. What Hollywood producers forget to do is credit these great stories of liberty to the Christian heritage. They also fail to spell out the Christian definitions of liberty for which these men fought. At the end of the film, no one has acquired any vision for liberty, nor is anyone motivated to engage the battle for real and substantial liberties in the present day.

For us however, the stories are reminiscent of Hebrews 11. These are real heroes, who fought for righteousness, subdued kingdoms, and loved not their lives to the death. They are worthy of note, in the book that God wrote. Their stories will be told well into eternity. They acted in Christian faith, and they secured liberties that yielded blessings for millions. Because their stories are inspirational to us, we long to see more heroes in these ignoble times as well. Perhaps there is something we may learn from them which we may replicate in our lives.

Chapter 3

FIRST HEROES FOR THE CAUSE OF FREEDOM

We must start in Hebrews 11 with the biblical accounts. The first heroes who spearheaded the struggle for freedom are found in the ancient accounts of the Old Testament.

The Exodus and the book of Judges contain many interesting stories of men who led God's people out of various conditions of bondage. There was left-handed Ehud who submerged a dagger deep into the belly of the fat tyrant, and Samson who pulled off an amazing act of faith at the very end of his life, bringing the whole house down on a thousand Philistines. For the purposes of this survey however, we will content ourselves with four great examples: Moses, Gideon, David, and Esther. Each of their stories provides an amazing picture of faith, recorded in Scripture for our example (1 Cor. 10:11).

With the Old Testament stories, we are not to miss the story—the story of God's redemption from the tyranny of sin, fulfilled in the Lord Jesus Christ. Nor are we to miss the courage and faith of these great men and women of faith. They were willing to take gigantic risks here because their hopes were placed firmly upon a future inheritance beyond the boundaries of this life (Heb. 11:14-16). Thus, they did not shrink back from the battle for righteousness and liberty (Heb. 11:33). The here and now is not entirely unimportant. And, the problem of tyranny is just as egregious as the problem of sin. Much may be learned from the battles waged in the Old Testament era.

MOSES AND THE TYRANNY OF EGYPT

Great empires are typically known by their architectural accomplishments—the towers, ziggurats, and pyramids they leave behind. Based on the sheer size of the towers, Egypt is the only empire from the second millennia before Christ that left evidence of its power. These pyramids were built on the back of slave labor.

The children of Israel were part of this slave force. Exodus 1:11-14 describes the affliction they received at the hands of the Egyptians.

> "And they made their lives bitter with hard bondage, in mortar, and in brick, and in all manner of service in the field: all their service, wherein they made them serve, was with rigour." (Ex. 1:14)

Indeed this was "hard bondage" and lasted for generations as the Hebrews increased their numbers by birth. Fearing that the Israelites would one day outnumber the Egyptians, the Pharaoh ordered the infanticide of all male children born to Israelite women (Ex. 1:15-16). Thankfully, the midwives refused to obey the order of the king because they "feared God" (Ex. 1:17). Conscientious objection and disobedience to the orders of the magistrate is an important first step in opposing tyranny.

The pro-life movement in early Israel will be a testimony to all tyrannies until the end of the world. Here we detect the first movements towards freedom, and often it is courageous, God-fearing women like Puah and Shiphrah who lead the way. Moses' mother also exhibited the same faith when she opposed Pharaoh's command and hid her baby son in the bulrushes.

The tyranny was so severe, we read, that "the children of Israel sighed by reason of the bondage, and they cried, and their cry came up unto God by reason of the bondage" (Ex. 2:23).

During his early adult years, Moses witnessed firsthand the evils of human tyranny when he came upon an Egyptian beating an Israelite slave. His reaction tells us something about his character and his deep revulsion towards this evil. Young Moses proceeded to kill the Egyptian. Whether this was a lawful killing may be debatable, but suffice it to say the Bible does not condemn him for it. Politically speaking it was a tenuous move. His political power came from his position in Pharaoh's household, but the killing may not have stood up in court if he had been reported. Regardless, the incident resulted in his self-imposed exile from Egypt.

THE EXODUS

The story of the Exodus is a phenomenal account and the most dramatic escape story of all time considered worthy content for several major motion pictures over the years. It is the archetype for the most spectacular redemption of all. It serves as a pattern for Christ's redemption, and for the continuing saga of the monumental battle that continues to play out against tyranny.

From biblical accounts we know that the man Moses was remarkably meek, but supremely courageous. From the outset of his adult life, he appears willing to give up fame and fortune in the empire for the more ignominious and inglorious task of leading a reluctant (and at times ungrateful, rebellious, slave-minded) people to freedom. He confessed his own incompetence to the lead the people (Ex. 3:11, 4:10), but he was not afraid to confront Pharaoh on ten separate occasions with threats of plagues and fresh demands to release the people of God. Moses received rather weak support from his own coalition. It is not unusual to find a slave-minded people full of fear, adverse to risks, and generally faithless. Often they will see little use for freedom, even when surviving under minimally acceptable conditions. Though Pharaoh's reactions demonstrated increased levels of hostility on ten separate occasions, Moses courageously pursued his visits. Between chapters 7 and 11 in the Exodus account, there are fourteen references to Pharaoh's hardening of the heart. All the while, the Egyptians were intensifying the burdens on the people, which produced an even more untenable position for Moses. Nonetheless, he doggedly pursued his demands with the Pharaoh. "Let my people go!"

When the children of Israel made it to the coastline of the Red Sea, it appeared to be the worst of all situations. There they were pinned between a mountain on the north and a mountain on the south, the Red Sea on the east, and the Egyptian armies approaching from the west. At the head of the armies of the greatest empire on earth was the most angry and vengeful monarch imaginable. After suffering through all the plagues, each household in Egypt (including Pharaoh's household) had lost an eldest son to the avenging angel. The Israelites had no army, no weapons, and no military training. They were slaves. Moreover, mutiny from the ranks was a real threat for Moses. Under these extremely trying circumstances, Moses exhibited remarkable faith, and his words to the people would secure his place in the hall of fame for the greatest heroes of faith of all time.

> "And Moses said unto the people, 'Fear ye not, stand still, and see the salvation of the LORD, which he will shew to you today: for the Egyptians whom ye have seen today, ye shall see them again no more forever. The LORD shall fight for you, and ye shall hold your peace.'" (Ex. 14:13-14)

Positively astounding. Highly irregular. A seemingly incongruous response. Indeed, this must be faith.

What political leader has ever faced such an impossible physical situation? Moses had no army, no weapons, and no reasonable hope for any victory whatsoever. Never has a leader been faced with the certainty of a total loss of a nation like this. Never has a leader been forced to look to God for the total solution as Moses was here. He had no military plan and no human-derived solution for the problem at hand. Prior to verse 13, he had received no instructions and no explanation as to how God was going to achieve the victory at the Red Sea.

Then, in verse 16, God tells him to raise his rod in the air. Now typically that is not the sum-total of a military strategy that would produce a victory. Usually, there is more to it than that. But Moses obeyed.

As he raised the rod, what was he thinking? What would you think? "I sure hope this works!" A good deal was hanging on this single moment. And then, the waters begin to surge, in both directions! Miles of ocean water parted ways, God saved His people and destroyed the enemy without any more involvement on the part of humans in this contest.

Obviously, the great lesson to be gleaned from this deliverance is faith in God. Moses is very much the prototypical deliverer. Every true deliverer from human slavery must be a man of stalwart faith. He is more interested in what God will do than in his own contribution in the great struggle for liberty. He fully understands the impossibility of the task before him. He doesn't shrink from the task, and he does all within his capacity, always looking forward to the spectacular deliverance that God will provide in the end. Although final deliverance may be delayed to the last possible second, his faith does not subside while he raises the rod. He is in this first and foremost to see what God will do.

GIDEON

The period of the Judges followed quickly upon the taking of the promised land in Canaan. Within a generation, God's people rebelled. They refused to serve God and quickly found themselves enslaved by the small city states and roving nomadic tribes from the surrounding area. The Midianites were especially known for their scorched earth policy, pillaging the land and consuming all the seed and the available economic capital. Mass poverty and starvation are almost inevitable with such military methods. According to Scripture, the clear intent of these invaders was total destruction (Judg. 6:5). The tyranny was so utterly vicious, that the Israelites were pressed into hiding in caves in the mountains (Judg. 6:2). These are the conditions in which God raised up an unlikely hero in the form of Gideon.

When the angel of the Lord appeared to Gideon, he referred to him as a "mighty man of valor" (Judg. 6:12). Therefore, Gideon was sure that the angel must have mistaken him for somebody else. He explained to the angel that he was a nobody in a no-account family tucked away in the weak tribe of Manasseh. A leader must be able to rally the troops, and Gideon was rightfully concerned in that he had no troops to follow him into battle with the Midianites.

Why should God choose Gideon, given his weakness of faith? The answer is simple—God can use anyone, and His grace is sufficient for the weakest of them. Gideon is also a man who grows in faith through the process. He may start out with just a mustard seed of faith, but that seed grows into something mighty as God works with him, and this is where we find Gideon as the story unfolds.

Upon his commission to the task, Gideon promptly requested several signs from God. This itself is indicative of a weakness of faith (Matt. 12:40). However, God was gracious, and the fire sent from heaven burned the little offering on the stone. The fleece was dry, and the fleece was wet on two successive tests. Thankfully, these exercises really did grow his faith. Where signs fail to grow faith, but only inspire more doubt and unrelenting demands for more signs, God will refuse to provide them.

The first challenge laid upon Gideon was to instigate a generational repentance. Evidently, Israel's root problem was idolatry, and this was the thing that brought the curse of slavery to the nation. But God's leaders must set the example in this matter of repentance. Before God will bring a blessing to the nation, the leaders must first lead in repentance. So Gideon moved ahead on shaky knees with this challenge to destroy his father's idol grove (Judg. 6:27). In the middle of the night, he took a group of friends and burned the Baal altar to the ground.

Gideon's father's reaction offers a remarkable element to the story. It seems that he was impressed with Gideon's courage and defended his son's decision before the elders of the city. In memorial of his son's actions, he renamed Gideon "Jerubbaal;" a name which casts disrepute on the Baal god. For the rest of his life, Gideon's name served as a perpetual taunt in the face of the Baal and to anyone who served this false god. This presented a clear example of generational reformation that began in the life of a young man and was then shared by his father retroactively. When a father or a grandfather rejoices in the repentance exhibited in the lives of sons and grandsons, there must be generational repentance developing, and this then becomes the seed of freedom.

Gideon's major lesson in faith came when God began to whittle down the numbers assembled to fight the Midianites. Out of millions of Israelites, Gideon was able to assemble a paltry 22,000 to fight the 140,000+ Midianite warriors. After allowing the "fearful and the cowardly" (Deut. 20:8) to return home in accord with biblical law, he was left with a mere 10,000 men. Evidently, these were not courageous times. Not many were interested in fighting for their liberties. After this, Jehovah God challenged Gideon to bring the numbers of his army down even lower. "The people are yet too many" (Judg. 7:2). Using something of an arbitrary sorting method (based on how men drink water from a brook), Gideon was left with the 300, a ratio of 500 to 1 against the Midianite army. With that, Gideon was ready to engage the greatest battle of his life.

However, Gideon's faith was still weak, so the Lord sent him incognito into the camp of the Midianites. There he received a little insight into the enemy's faithlessness and fear. He realized that the enemy was more certain of the power of Jehovah at this point, than were the tribes of Israel! This boosted the faith of our man Gideon a good bit. He returned to his camp with a true sense of God's sovereign power, and then he "gets in the game." He announced to his men, "Arise, for the Lord has delivered the camp of Midian into your hand!" His expectations of victory were certain at this point. The premonition of "what God was going to do," sent chills down his back and he could hardly wait to engage the battle. This is the point at which he invented the rather unconventional military technique of pitchers and trumpets.

> "And he divided the three hundred men into three companies, and he put a trumpet in every man's hand, with empty pitchers, and lamps within the pitchers. And he said unto them, Look on me, and do likewise: and, behold, when I come to the outside of the camp, it shall be that, as I do, so shall ye do. When I blow with a trumpet, I and all that are with me, then blow ye the trumpets also on every side

of all the camp, and say, 'The sword of the LORD, and of Gideon.'"
(Judg. 7:16-18)

In the history of military science, this strategy has not proven successful. However, technique is not of essence here. The lesson for the Christian warrior is total faith. Self-confidence can only take him so far. In the battle for freedom, nothing less than God-confidence will take him the distance. Although Gideon started with no confidence, he was tutored in God-confidence in preparation for the battle.

Gideon took what resources he had at hand, strategically positioned three companies and commenced battle with the trumpets and pitchers. Instantly, Midian's armies were put into a state of chaos, and the battle was a complete rout, as Israel slaughtered some 140,000 of the enemy force.

The battle for freedom is usually waged against unspeakable odds. The majority of the "faithful" whom we would hope to stay in the battle walk away disheartened. The loyal opposition to tyranny often turns out to be less loyal than first expected. As modern apostasies spread through the Western world, the Christian pool of men and women who stand for righteousness and fight for liberty shrinks. The temptation to throw in the towel is unrelenting. Many Christians come up with eschatological or theological explanations for giving up. Others water down the antithesis and avoid assessing the state of affairs by the standard of God's law, and they will do anything except believe. What is needed in times like these are men and women of indomitable faith and unflagging courage.

We set out to build a movement from 400 to 10,000, and then we find that God cuts it back to 400 again. No doubt this happened to many leaders within the Christian church over the centuries. However, the man of faith must come to realize this is a battle of faith. When things appear to be at the very worst, we should be even more encouraged. During the most cowardly and faithless times of all, we can expect the greatest things of all. When the opposition rises to the very highest levels, and the resistance appears the weakest it has ever been, we are only that much closer to the most amazing victory ever seen. The battle is well in our hands! Let us advance. Faith best shows itself strong when facing giants, and when the odds are 300 to 140,000. This is God's modus operandi. First we look for the presence of faith, and then we expect the victory (1 John 5:4).

DAVID AND THE MIGHTY MEN

After 400 years of slavery and brief moments of liberation during the period of the judges, the children of Israel finally reach their "glory days" under the military conquests of David and his mighty men.

As a young man, probably no older than 17 years of age, David was given the task of delivering food to his brothers who were fighting with Saul's army against the Philistines. David came upon the Valley of Elah, where the Israelite army was hunkered down, cowering before the threats of the giant Goliath. The man was almost ten feet tall; a true giant and a powerful champion for the Philistine army. David's first response to the giant is instructive: "Who is this uncircumcised Philistine, that he should defy the armies of the living God?" (1 Sam. 17:26). Others were cowering in fear, but David was overcome with what his brothers thought to be youthful arrogance and foolishness. However, David explained his thinking to King Saul in 1 Samuel 17:36-37, harking back to his confrontation with a lion and a bear:

> "Thy servant slew both the lion and the bear: and this uncircumcised Philistine shall be as one of them, seeing he hath defied the armies of the living God. David said moreover, The Lord that delivered me out of the paw of the lion, and out of the paw of the bear, He will deliver me out of the hand of this Philistine."

First, young David had great confidence in God whom he believed helped him kill both a lion and a bear. These were smaller, but nonetheless difficult challenges previously encountered, and he was confident that God had brought about victory in each confrontation. Faith remembers what God has done in the past and builds on that record. Faith will hold on to those stories and recall previous encounters with the living God.

Secondly, David spoke out of his rock solid conviction regarding certain truths by which he interpreted the situation at hand. It is one thing for a lion to threaten the life of a lamb. It is quite another for uncircumcised Philistines to defy the armies of the living God. Later we read that David ran at the enemy without hesitation (1 Sam. 17:48). Why would young David take one look at this giant, completely ignore his formidable size and strength, and challenge him in this way? Others thought him out of his mind or carried away with youthful bravado. But his words did not ring of egotistical youthfulness. The problem, as David saw it, was that this tall fellow had defied the armies of the living God. David believed what he had been taught about God, about the people of God, and about the vision God had laid out for His people. As a young boy, David had listened to what his father and grandfather taught him from God's Word, and he believed it. Those truths became convictions that ran in his bloodstream. Convictions press a man to courage, and courage leads to action. Thus, David ran at the giant, let loose a stone from his sling, knocked him to the ground, and cut off his head with the giant's own sword.

In this dramatic event, David saw the Giant standing behind the giant. His overwhelming sense of the power of God and the truth of God's Word defined his reality more than the visible enemy. This is another tremendous picture of faith.

THE MIGHTY MEN

King David's forty year reign comprised the glory years of Old Testament Israel. The remaining centuries were filled with more idolatry and the accompanying slavery that characterize wicked nations. With David however, something of a foothold was gained for the kingdom of God. 2 Samuel 23 presents an inspirational telling of the story.

Since the days of Samson, the Philistines had maintained "dominion" over Israel (Judg. 14:4), and David and his mighty men were instrumental in re-securing Israel's independence from these oppressive powers. There is something commendable about these men that God's Word considers important enough to include in the canon. These are, in a real sense, "God's heroes," and they possessed traits we would do well to emulate.

What we notice in these men, first and foremost, is the quality of strength and resilience. Their military feats as related in 2 Samuel 23 are nothing short of staggering.

The stalwart warrior named Shammah (vs. 11) was abandoned by the rest of the army in the field of lentils and stood his ground. He took on the entire host of the Philistines and singlehandedly obtained the victory that day.

Adino the Eznite (vs. 8) took out 800 men at one time.

Eleazar (vs. 9-10) fought until the sword clave to his hand.

Abishai (vs. 18) took down 300 men at one time.

Indeed, these were powerful men of war, perhaps unmatched by any other men in the history of warfare. What supernatural energy must have been employed to take out 800 men at one time! Adino would have had to kill at a rate of 80 an hour for 10 hours straight. Such perseverance is truly remarkable. The average man is easily discouraged when abandoned by his comrades and left to fight alone in a field of lentils. He becomes disheartened after the third and fourth assault from the enemy. It takes a special faith and courage to continue in the battle alone, day after day, week after week, and year after year, facing new enemies all the time. When the battle is joined, the man of faith stays in the fight until the brutal end.

Men like Benaiah, the son of Jehoiada, the son of a valiant man of Kabzeel (vs. 20), are willing to make a total commitment to the battle. He leaped into a pit on a snowy day and killed a lion in hand to paw combat. Of course, he must have known that only one of them would come out alive. When a man commits to the battle, he is all in. He will fight to the death.

Another important characteristic to be found in these mighty men was a diehard loyalty to each other and to their captain. Three of David's men fought through a garrison of the Philistines to retrieve a cup of water from the well of Bethlehem. When David received the gift, he threw it to the ground and in essence, says, "I don't drink blood. This is the blood of the men who risked their lives to quench my thirst from the well of Bethlehem" (2 Sam. 23:16-17). This picture of loyalty is unforgettable, poignant and powerful. Some men are willing to die for the truth, for a principle of theology or for a cause like freedom. But would they give their lives for their brothers? Most of our coalitions are torn apart by minor differences and intramural quarrels because men are willing to die for the truth—but they are not willing to die for their brothers. This will never do. I am thankful that there are a few men who are willing to die for something, but the Christian must be willing to die for his brothers. In so doing, he follows in the footsteps of his Master (1 John 3:16).

ESTHER

Esther also played a part in the struggle for freedom at a critical juncture in the history of Old Testament Israel. The nation was facing its most precipitous challenge at the hands of the largest empire in the history of the world up to that point—the Medo-Persian Empire. A bloody genocide was in the making, threatening total extinction for the Israelites. The wicked man Haman joins the ranks of other wicked rulers like Hitler, Nero, and Herod. These tyrants are dangerous men, and they work their way into the highest echelons of power where they can do the most damage.

At the beginning of Esther's story, the future of God's people was hanging by a thread. However, God providentially raised up Esther as the wife of the King of Persia for a very special purpose—to preserve His people.

When God's people are marginalized and have zero influence politically speaking, there is one public policy item that takes first priority. Based on Old Testament records of Joseph, Daniel, and Nehemiah, the preservation of God's people trumps all. This is the last line of defense for liberty. If the magistrate kills all the Christians, the possibility of righteousness and liberty prevailing in that society is removed. There is no more salt, and the light is extinguished. The Gospel may not return to that people for centuries.

As the story goes, Esther intercedes for her people with the King, at the risk of her life. "If I perish, I perish," she says (Esth. 4:16). Esther's respect for her uncle Mordecai's advice, and her love for her people are commendable, but it is her courage and faith which sets her apart as a great heroine in the age old battle for liberty.

THE APOSTLES

The Roman powers and local magistrates in the empire began persecuting the Christian faith almost immediately upon Christ's crucifixion and resurrection. Two themes emerge out of the Acts of the Apostles: the persecutions and the consequent expansion in evangelism and the church.

The Jewish authorities incarcerated Peter and John (Acts 4:3), and they were back preaching in the public forum the next day (Acts 4:31). Again, the authorities arrested them (Acts 5:18), an angel released them, and they were back in the temple preaching the next day (Acts 5:25). Herod killed James and arrested Peter (Acts 12:2-3), an angel released Peter, and "the word of God grew and multiplied" (Acts 12:24). When asked why they persisted in disobeying the magistrates, Peter and John candidly responded with, "We ought to obey God rather than men" (Acts 5:29). God's law trumps man's law, and this becomes the basis for civil disobedience where there is direct conflict.

The Apostle Paul is imprisoned and beaten in almost every city to which he brings the Gospel. On the one hand, he accepts his tribulations with a contented, positive frame of mind. When arrested at Philippi, he sings in the prison, witnesses to the jailer, and baptizes the man's household (Acts 16:25-31ff). Then, he insists on his rights as a Roman citizen, requesting a formal apology from the local authorities (Acts 16:37). Christians are not doormats. They will fight lawfully for just dealings with the integrity of the Apostle Paul. At the same time, they will treat their enemies with respect, compassion, and mercy. This is the Spirit of Christ. We preach the Gospel, and we insist on just treatment as defined by God's laws. This provides a balanced perspective for Christians in our day who face tyrannical persecution on all sides, from Pakistan to Pennsylvania.

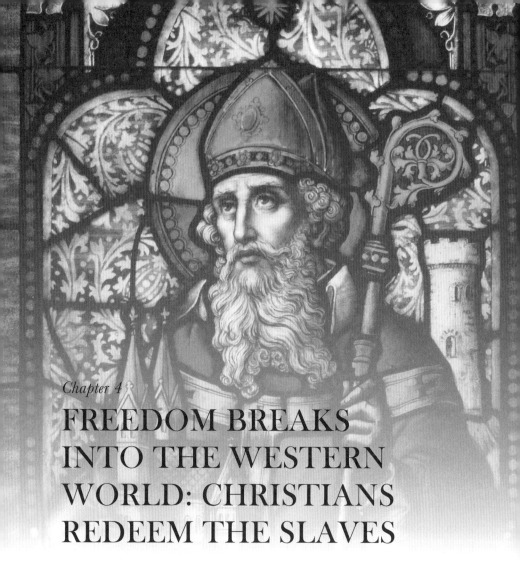

Chapter 4

FREEDOM BREAKS INTO THE WESTERN WORLD: CHRISTIANS REDEEM THE SLAVES

Chattel slavery was a common practice in the ancient world. The Greek philosopher, Aristotle, claimed that some people are born to be slaves. "Some men are by nature free, and others slaves, and that for these latter slavery is both expedient and right."[1] Of course, Christless pagans ultimately settle for the inevitability of eternal slavery. Friedrich Nietzsche attempted to reincorporate this stratification of human society when he argued for his Master Morality (that which exploits, injures, and gains preeminence over the weak) in his book, *Beyond Good and Evil.*[2]

The Christian worldview concerning slavery, however, is based on a biblical anthropology. Augustine of Hippo considered slavery an inevitable consequence of sin when he wrote, "The prime cause, then of slavery is sin, which brings man under the dominion of his fellow—that which does not happen save by the judgment of God."[3] Hence, the condition of slavery is non-optimal, and redemption of Christ should "set the captives free" in more ways than one.

Evidence of Christian opposition to slavery is found as early as the third century in the "Apostolic Constitutions." The Christian church was committed to setting the captives free, according to the wisdom passed down by tradition from the Apostles at Antioch, where this document originated. We read:

> "Therefore maintain and clothe those that are in want from the righteous labour of the faithful. And such sums of money as are collected from them in the manner aforesaid, appoint to be laid out in the redemption of the saints, the deliverance of slaves, and of captives, and of prisoners, and of those that have been abused, and of those that have been condemned by tyrants to single combat and death on account of the name of Christ. For the Scripture says: 'Deliver those that are led to death, and redeem those that are ready to be slain, do not spare.'"[4]

In a recently uncovered letter from St. Augustine written to his friend Alypius, Bishop of Thagaste, we find a true example of corporate manumission on the part of the church at Hippo. Augustine makes mention of slave traders who were kidnapping women and children in North Africa in order to sell them into slavery. Apparently, the church at Hippo intercepted one particular shipment to Galatia, and redeemed a boatload of slaves. Augustine explained,

> "I myself asked one girl of a crowd which had been freed by our Church from this miserable captivity, how she came to be sold to the slave traders. She told me she had been seized from her parents' house...
>
> "Some four months ago, there were people brought together from different places, but especially from Numidia, to be deported from the port of Hippo. This was done by Galatians, for it is only they who, out of greed, engage in such business.

"A member of our church became aware of it, and knowing our policy of helping with money in such circumstances, wished to tell us.

"I was not in Hippo at that time. But immediately our faithful liberated one hundred and twenty people, some from the ship on which they were already embarked, some from private prisons where they were hidden before being put aboard...I leave it to your imagination to estimate the enormous proportions which the deportation of miserable persons has assumed in other ports. Here in Hippo at least, by the mercy of God, the church is on its guard, so that unfortunate people are rescued from this type of captivity."[5]

In the letter, Augustine further pressed for a revision of law at the Imperial court. Then, he forcefully argued that every pastor is morally bound to address these social issues:

"For if we, that is, the bishops, do nothing, will there then be anyone, who has power on the shore, who will not sell these most cruel cargoes, rather than remove one of these unfortunate people from captivity, or stop someone from being put in chains, out of Christian or human compassion?"[6]

This is a beautiful example of how early Christians actually redeemed the slaves, while pagan tribes from Galatia perpetuated the slave trade. "He shall set the captives free" (Isa. 61:1, Luke. 4:18). Where Christianity has operated throughout the ages, it has always worked towards this end.

As the Christian church expanded throughout the Western world, the healthiest element of the faith demonstrated itself in the Scotch-Irish, Culdean church. Although the Roman church made an attempt to bring the Culdean churches under their organizational rubric at the Synod of Whitby in AD 664, this was not accomplished *en toto* until centuries later. The Culdean church was anything but hierarchical, as it relied mainly upon localized elder rule for its governance.[7] Between AD 430 and AD 1000, these Scotch-Irish Christians discipled large portions of Europe into the Christian faith and helped to form Western culture.

Meanwhile, the Eastern Church placed heavy emphasis upon hierarchy in its governance, and these cultures eventually produced the czars and communist dictatorships in Russia and Eastern Europe. Hierarchy came less naturally to the West, but by the fourteenth century the Roman pope had solidified control over most of the church, including France, England, Scotland, and Ireland.

No one person in the history of Christianity contributed more to the legacy of Western freedom than Patrick, the great missionary to Ireland. The Scotch-Irish church began with Patrick, and the faith of that church would be found in the veins of William Wallace, the Covenanters, and Patrick Henry (who carried the namesake of the great Christian missionary). Those who have enjoyed some measure of liberty in the Western world may thank Patrick of Ireland.

Fifth-century Ireland was isolated from the Roman Empire. It was the end of the known world. If civilization is defined as that which maintains an outward form of order and morality, Ireland had none of it. Ireland was the picture of what happens when the devil has free rein to molest an isolated people for multiple centuries on end. In the eyes of the civilized world, these peoples were beyond hope of a civilization. When called to war, they fought in the buff.[8] Witchcraft, human sacrifice, homosexuality, slavery, and gross poverty prevailed.

It is possible that Patrick's great appreciation for liberty developed out of early experiences in his youth. Kidnapped from his home on the western coast of Britain by a band of Irish marauders, he was sold into slavery in Ireland where he labored in that capacity for six years, before he was miraculously delivered. Although Patrick was raised in a Christian home (his father was a deacon in the village church), he later testified that his early life had been marked by gross sin. During his own journey to freedom from slavery, he experienced the powerful redemptive work of Jesus Christ saving him from the tyranny of sin.

Information concerning Patrick and his work is confined to several documents preserved over the centuries, "Patrick's Confessions" and his "Letter to the Soldiers of Coroticus." One thing that is clearly evident from his writings is his deep compassion for the women and men pressed into chattel slavery in Ireland. Truly, his "Letter to the Soldiers of Coroticus" remains one of the first testimonies of a Christian man who fought the slave trade. In his short epistle, the Apostle Paul had recommended that Philemon release his slave Onesimus. Neither of these men encouraged slave revolts, but they rather appealed to the hearts of slave owners to release their slaves from perpetual servitude. They also offered to pay the ransom to the slave masters, in order that they might set the captives free.

In Patrick's letter, he offered a severe rebuke, and more or less excommunicated Coroticus, the petty tyrant and his miserable band of slavers. "Let every God-fearing man mark well that to me they are outcasts: cast out also by Christ my God, whose ambassador I am," he wrote.[9] Patrick held nothing back. Apparently, this man Coroticus and his mercenaries had invaded Ireland, slaughtering the men and enslaving the women. Coroticus hailed from Britain and reputedly professed to be a Christian. Patrick, however, rejected this profession outright, pointing out the severe contrast between Coroticus' behavior and that of genuine Christians, writing,

> "Roman Christians in Gaul behave quite differently: it is their custom to send holy, capable men to the Franks and other nations with several thousand soldiers so as to redeem Christians who have been captured, yet you would rather kill or sell them on to a far-off tribe who know nothing of the true God."[10]

This comparison between Christian and infidel is not to be missed. Christians will ransom captives from slavery and only non-Christians will further the cause of slavery. Heightening the seriousness of his charges even more, Patrick requested that his letter be forwarded everywhere in the Christian world so that all Christians would know that Coroticus was no Christian at all. He wrote, "I most sincerely ask you, my fellow Christians, not to have anything to do with these men—don't eat and drink with them, don't even accept charity from them—until they beg and cry to God to forgive them. They must also free their Christian women and captives."[11]

Patrick also referred to his own slavery and his willingness to sacrifice his life for the deliverance of the Irish people from spiritual and physical slavery: "Can it be out of the kindness of my heart that I carry out such a labor of mercy on a people who once captured me when they wrecked my father's house and carried off his servants? For by descent I was a freeman, born of a Decurion father; yet I have sold this nobility of mine, I am not ashamed, nor do I regret that it might have meant some advantage to others. In short, I am a slave in Christ to this faraway people for the indescribable glory of 'everlasting life which is in Jesus Christ our Lord.'"[12]

Finally, Patrick closed his letter of roughly 2,500 words with another appeal for repentance: "May God inspire these men sometime to come to their senses in regard to God again, so that they may repent, however latter day, of their grave crimes, namely homicide against the brothers of the Lord, and that they free these baptized women whom they have taken, so that then they may deserve to live to God and be made whole once more, here, now and for eternity."[13]

There aren't many men who are willing to take on an economic institution like slavery, especially when it is generally accepted as an ethical norm by the rest of the world. In his "Confessions," Patrick spoke of many thousands of times his life was threatened, and his ministry opposed. His faith was secure in God, however, "Daily I expect murder, fraud, or captivity, or whatever it may be; but I fear none of these things because of the promises of heaven. I have cast myself into the hands of God Almighty, who rules everywhere, as the prophet says: Cast thy thought upon God, and He shall sustain thee."[14] It takes a free man with a vision for redemption to appreciate such faith and courage. Let us acknowledge the work of God in men like Patrick who introduced freedom to the Western world. Then, let us also mark out the tyrants and condemn them as Patrick did.

Although the form of slavery Patrick opposed was of a different variety than modern statist tyrannies, they do bear some similarities. For instance, petty localized tyrants in Patrick's day attempted to control every aspect of the slave's life, as does the modern despotic state. Oppressive feudal lords charged exorbitant rents for their lands, as modern tyrannies increase taxes to unbearable levels in exchange for "protection and security." Property taxation removes the right of a free man to own his property without payment to the state. Many of the serfs lost all opportunity to own property, and they were perpetually subservient to the lord of the manor. The worst form of slavery

therefore, is that which keeps a man and his posterity in the chattel
.condition with no hope for redemption generation after generation.
This was the business of the slave trade. If Jesus Christ is about the
business of redemption, slavery must be abolished everywhere it is
found. Only pagans and unbelievers will work towards perpetuating
the slave market. Only humanist philosophers like Aristotle will settle
for the "inevitability" of perpetual slavery.

Chapter 5

1215: FREEDOM CONCEIVED

Robert hurried out of the meeting with the nobles at the Runnymede convocation, and quickly mounted his horse. This time he would ride without armor so nothing could impede his speed on this critical expedition. Calling a small troop of his knights to him, they rode swiftly and silently towards London.

Robert FitzWalter had only one thing on his mind: he must assure the safety of the children at the Tower. Just a few days earlier, the tyrant had been forced to sign his name on a document that would forever change history. But it was not that document which was of first concern to Robert. One provision contained in the "Great Charter" or "Magna Carta" referenced the Welsh captives. It was the Welsh children who he had just learned were held captive at the Tower of London that mattered to Robert at the moment.

Mile after mile flew by as Robert urged his stallion forward. Layers of sweat formed on the horse's back. Today, Robert could not afford to lose a minute. Had King John worked his characteristic torture on these helpless young children from the Welsh royal family? This tyrant knew no limits for his acts of tyrannical violence upon the peoples he intended to subjugate. Three years earlier, Robert had sworn to Almighty God that he would never again raise a finger to aid this tyrant in his wicked machinations. He had witnessed firsthand the work King John did in the Welsh raid, and he would have no further part in it. At the risk of charges of treason, Robert renounced fealty, surrendered his lands, and fled to France.

As he approached the towering castle built by William the Conqueror over a century earlier, Robert gripped his sword and prepared for the worst. Evidence of a quick retreat met his eye. A few hours before Robert's arrival, the king must have evacuated the city. At this point, John would be well-nigh approaching one of his castles in the southern reaches of the realm. That was of little interest to Robert FitzWalter however, for his journey concerned the inmates in this castle. He dismounted and hurried towards the entrance of the tower. Immediately he was met by the remnants of the prison guard whom he dispensed with in short order. He examined the executioners' swords briefly.

Fresh blood. And this obviously was not his own. The executioners had not been afforded the opportunity to lift their swords against Robert and his men.

Robert's heart sank. He was too late. As he entered the tower, he could hear the screams. King John had taken advantage of his last hours in London to do his worst. Quickly, Robert climbed the stairs. The moaning and cries became more distinct. He ran to the dungeon. The door was locked, but a few swift blows with his claymore released the door. The sight that met his eyes was too much for him to bear— beautiful girls with their faces disfigured, noses and ears clipped off. Bloody marks stained the walls and floors. Robert approached one of the princesses. He caught her head in his hands; his locks of hair met her bloody face as he bowed and prayed to the God of heaven for her comfort and healing. Never again. Never again. Never again.

Meanwhile, FitzWalter's men had entered another cell, where at least ten young boys lay, castrated and bleeding. Robert commanded his men to remove the children from the cells and take them to the bed chambers at Buckingham where they could receive care until they were strong enough to return to Wales.

* * *

Perhaps my reader is surprised that I find both good and evil in history. Most modern historians are not so ready to delineate between the "good guys" and the "bad guys" in leadership over nations. Secularists are relativists, and they shudder to think there may be an absolute standard by which actions may be judged—ergo, the law of God. Their historical work therefore makes for bad story-telling, and really boring history. If there is no standard for good and evil, who cares what happens in history? If there is no standard, then all that remains is matter in motion, sheer meaninglessness.

However, the Bible does not shy from drawing thick lines between good and evil men. As you read Scripture, you will immediately get the idea that Ahab, Herod, Pharaoh, Zedekiah, Amon, Jehoash, and Ahaziah were wicked rulers who did "that which was evil in the sight of the Lord" (2 Kings 17:2, 21:2, 21:20, 23:37, etc.). Conversely, you will find that David, Asa, Amaziah, Hezekiah, Josiah, and others "did that which was right in the eyes of the Lord" (1 Kings 15:11, 2 Kings 12:2, 15:3, 18:3, 22:2). The Bible reveals that some leaders, though not perfect, are known for their humility and repentance. They set good trajectories. They promote greater freedom for the people and protection from evildoers. Others set bad trajectories for themselves and their nations, and thereby prove themselves to be evil leaders.

Historians in the City of Man are too easily enamored with power, and they will excuse the worst tyrants of everything, as long as these leaders are pragmatic men of action, power-mongers who seek more power and more empire for themselves. Therefore, they would support Adolf Hitler to begin with, and later oppose him, only because he lost his ill-gotten empire and his nation sank into ignominy. Then they embrace the Caesars or William the Conqueror despite their sordid lives and various atrocities.

ALFRED THE GREAT

> "Whosoever therefore shall break one of these least commandments, and shall teach men so, he shall be called the least in the kingdom of heaven: but whosoever shall do and teach them, the same shall be called great in the kingdom of heaven. For I say unto you, That except your righteousness shall exceed the righteousness of the scribes and Pharisees, ye shall in no case enter into the kingdom of heaven. Ye have heard that it was said by them of old time, Thou shalt not kill; and whosoever shall kill shall be in danger of the judgment:" (Matt. 5:19-21)

The English King, Alfred the Great (AD 849-899) successfully defended his country from the relentless attacks of the Vikings during the ninth century, and maintained remarkable peace throughout the country during his reign of twenty-eight years. To this day, his reputation is virtually untarnished. He improved the English legal system, incorporating a well thought-out combination of the Mosaic Law and the law of Christ. He was careful to include Matthew 5:19-21 in his law code, and proceeded to copy key Old Testament laws into the "dooms" (laws or judgments). By all accounts, Alfred was a devout Christian, known to have been both merciful and learned. He encouraged the education of his people, and generally improved their quality of life. Important for our purposes, he was born in Oxfordshire, England, and had a legitimate and direct right to the throne. Unlike many wicked kings throughout history, Alfred ascended without perfidy or bloody revolution. England's rule stabilized for 150 years, through the reign of Alfred's progeny until William the Conqueror appeared on the scene.

THE NORMAN CONQUEST

King Ethelred the Unready was the son of King Edgar, grandson of King Edmund, great grandson of King Edward the Elder, and great, great grandson of King Alfred the Great. As may be deduced from his name, Ethelred the Unready was a weak king. Unable to defend the nation from the Danes, he sought help from Normandy (and married into the family of William the Conqueror). William took full advantage of this weakness, and used it to wrest control of England out of the hands of Alfred's descendants.

William the Conqueror's life (1028-1087 AD) offers quite a different story in the history of English liberties. He was born illegitimate and spent most of his years securing his power base in Normandy (Northern France) and expanding his territories by offensive warfare. His nobles joined him in his imperialist quest, motivated by prospects of expanding their land holdings in England. This seizure of lands and property and violent imperialistic warfare defines tyrants. God-fearing leaders will eschew offensive warfare, and resist the assembling of standing armies (1 Sam. 8:19-21). This we do not see with William, who turned out to be the great progenitor of much oppression, tyranny, and anarchy in England. His eldest son Robert launched several insurrections against his own father, even wounding the elder man in the Battle of Vexin.

William's conquest of England meant a curtailing of liberty in that country. Previously, property owners held titles to their lands. Under the Normans however, the King claimed ownership of all lands, and effectively leased the land to the barons through what is called "feudal tenure" in exchange for military service.[1] This constituted a major power grab in the history of Western tyranny.

William withheld a great deal of property for his own use, such that his household owned more land than any other family in England by a significant margin. Further strengthening the tyranny in England, William organized his Domesday Book, which established records on every landholding in England. Although modern societies are well accustomed to governments keeping records on every piece of property owned and every dollar held in a bank account, this was not always the case. William's Domesday Book also established taxing authority in every county in England, and centralized more power in the state. William's tax on property was the only universal tax in all of Western Europe at the time. The power to tax is essential to the formation of powerful empires.

RESISTANCE

The idea that the English gladly accepted their new rulers from Normandy is a myth. From the time of the Norman invasion in 1066, the English attempted revolt against their captors during each administration without exception until the reigns of John, William I, William II, Henry I, Stephen, Henry II, and Richard. Most of these revolts assembled under the auspices of disgruntled royalty, brothers and sons of the kings. As early as 1100, Henry I published a charter to which he attached fourteen campaign promises and covenanted to "abolish all the evil customs by which the kingdom of England had been unjustly oppressed."[2] But alas, liberty did not run in the bloodlines of the Normans or the Plantagenets.

BAD SEED

The throne quickly slipped away from the House of Normandy and into the hands of the Plantagenets, largely because William's son Henry had nothing to provide his country but twenty-four illegitimate children. Not surprisingly, anarchy followed Henry's death. Soon after that, more tyranny suppressed the anarchy, and Henry II (grandson of Henry on his mother's side) took the throne. A ruthless leader, he gained control over Wales and eastern Ireland, as well as Brittany and Central France on the Continent. Henry did what tyrants do best. In his rabid quest to dominate Wales, he took the royal families of the nation, "cut off the noses and ears of the daughters, and blinded and castrated their brothers."[3] His son John carried on the same policies with the Welsh. Henry II was a tyrant and a terrorist, in the modern sense of the word. He used well-publicized acts of torture to inspire fear in those whom he wanted to dominate. Perhaps his worst act, for which he lost a great deal of popular support at the time, was the murder of Archbishop Thomas Becket. Although Henry did not perform the dirty deed himself, it would never have happened without his encouragement. Upon hearing that the Archbishop had removed some number of priests and prelates from their positions, he responded in uncontrolled rage, crying out: "What a pack of fools and cowards I have nourished in my house [speaking of his own men], that not one of them will avenge me of this turbulent priest!"[4] Four of his knights hurried off to Canterbury to do what fighting men do best. The Archbishop was assassinated on December 29, 1170.

The famous King Richard the Lionhearted and King John were the sons of Henry II. For some reason, the sons of powerful tyrants are often inclined to revolt against their fathers, in gross violation of the fifth commandment. Perfidy begets perfidy, and wickedness begets wickedness. Similar to William the Conqueror, Henry II faced deadly confrontations with his sons. First, his eldest two sons, Geoffrey and Henry, declared war on their father in an illegitimate struggle over power. After Geoffrey's death in battle, Richard ("the Lionhearted") joined the fray as well. The youngest son, John, did not see the political expedience in the revolution against his father, and held off joining until it was clear that the old man was failing politically and physically. When Henry heard that his youngest son had turned against him, he succumbed to an illness from which he could not recover. He was dead within days. "Henry died in despair, cursing the day he had been born."[5]

Sons and grandsons of tyrants generally make for more tyrants, and the Plantagenets created some of the most evil leaders the world has known. Some leaders maintain tyrannies, others construct them. That was the legacy of the family line of William the Conqueror.

The heritage of sexual sin continued, as Henry's son Richard fathered a child born out of wedlock and John produced at least seven. There is no historical record indicating that Richard's rule was anything less of a tyranny than that of the rest of the family. He taxed the church to fund his military exploits, and spent most of his career warring on foreign soil. Upon Richard's death in 1199, John ascended to the throne. More than all the others, it was John who perfected the art of duplicity and tyranny while he reigned as King of England. Tyranny is one thing, but duplicity is quite another. Duplicitous rulers are utterly intolerable, and they will always stir up dread, fear, anarchy, civil strife, and general misery among the populace.

KING JOHN

> "But whoso committeth adultery with a woman lacketh understanding: he that doeth it destroyeth his own soul. A wound and dishonour shall he get; and his reproach shall not be wiped away. For jealousy is the rage of a man: therefore he will not spare in the day of vengeance." (Prov. 6:32-34)

It is a great irony that such an evil man carried the namesake of the Apostle John. This is the nature of the great apostasy and attendant hypocrisies that sometimes characterize the Western world over the millennia. King John's sexual exploits were notorious even by modern standards. He divorced his first wife Isabel, and married another in 1200. He sold his former wife to Baron Geoffrey de Mandeville for 20,000 marks. Reports of John's having violated daughters and wives of other barons were common. He attempted to seduce Baron Eustace de Vesci's wife, and attempted a rape of Baron Robert FitzWalter's daughter. These two men became his most ardent enemies. It is one thing for a king to confiscate a man's property and material belongings, but should he go after the man's wife and daughter, he invites a war that will never end. When King John tried to take sexual advantage of FitzWalter's daughter the king went one step too far.[6] FitzWalter would champion the cause of the Magna Carta and lead the armies of the barons against the King. Perhaps Guallame de Jumage, an assistant to one of King John's commanders, said it best. In his extensive survey of the various dukes of Normandy, he described King John as "a very bad man, cruel and lecherous."[7]

King John was an apostate in the true sense of the word. Throughout his life, he repeatedly denied belief in the Christian religion. According to early biographer, Matthew Paris (d. 1259), King John attempted at one point to sell his people out to the Muslims.

> "King John sent secret messengers...to the emir of Morocco to tell him that he would voluntarily give up himself and his kingdom and also abandon the Christian faith, which is considered false [in the war with his nobles]."[8]

King John had inherited what may have been the largest and most wealthy empire in Europe. However, he didn't keep it—for his wickedness was only exceeded by his incompetence. If a man's success in governance is measured by the increase of his own net worth, John did well. He doubled the family's holdings between 1204 and 1215. By the time of the publication of the Magna Carta, John had obtained a total of fifty castles, palaces, houses, and hunting lodges. His extravagant lifestyle required hundreds of assistants, bakers, butlers, cooks, carters, chamber clerks, chambermaids, footmen, scullions, grooms, and knights. The whole entourage travelled with him as he moved from castle to castle.

To make matters even worse, this lecherous, greedy king maintained absolute sovereign rights over each family's inheritance of lands in all the realm. Upon a landholder's death, John would sell off both estates and wives for his own gain. And to further consolidate power, he would put an unreasonable "relief price" on the estate, and place the heir in his debt indefinitely. This kept the landholder in perpetual subservience to the King. "The rich ruleth over the poor, and the borrower is servant to the lender." (Prov. 22:7). One baron by the name of William de Briouze fell out of favor with the King. John called in the debt (requiring immediate payment), and William was unable to pay. He escaped the country to France, but his wife and children were arrested and most likely "starved to death in one of John's prisons."[9] Stories like this should highlight for us the evils of inheritance taxation, or what is sometimes referred to as "the death tax." Americans went to war over the Stamp Act, a fairly minimal death tax amounting to about 0.02 percent of the value of the estate. That is quite a contrast to the 50-75 percent tax rate imposed on the modern American by federal and state revenue services. However, the United States Government passed a death tax during the rise of the centralized state (in 1862). According to the Internal Revenue Service, the modern death tax has been in place since 1916.[10]

By 1205, the situation in England had reached a crisis point. Winston Churchill summed up the conditions: "By systematic abuse of his feudal prerogatives John drove the baronage to violent resistance."[11] King John had lost control of Normandy, and he was about to lose control of England by his greed and tyranny. After gaining control over every landowner in England, he had but one more competitor for power—the church. Therefore, he took to confiscating certain lands belonging to the Roman church, a tactic which brought the wrath of the Pope down upon him.

Pope Innocent III promptly excommunicated King John and placed the entire nation under interdict, after which John continued to line the state coffers with church income and property. In turn, the Pope combined forces with the King of France at which point John realized he had better back down. To further complicate the situation, John traded political control of England to the Pope for his favor, pitting the nobles and the Archbishop (as well as King Louis of France) against the Pope. He assembled all of his resources and attempted a battle against France on July 22, 1214, but his troops were completely routed. This was the beginning of the end for King John.

ROBERT FITZWALTER

The immediate preconditions for the Magna Carta materialized in the summer of 1212. Once again, King John dragged his English nobles into conflict with Wales (in which both he and his father tortured and executed the people over the years, including women and children). Several of the dukes, including Robert FitzWalter, rebelled. By this time, they had had enough of John's tyrannical ways. As legitimate lower magistrates, they laid out a plan for the execution of the wicked king and a revolt against his rule. Somehow, the plot was discovered, FitzWalter's sister and her husband were implicated, and their daughter Alice was taken as hostage by the king. Undoubtedly, the dreadful predicament facing his niece at the hands of a king known for rape and torture must have been a constant concern for Robert FitzWalter. Both FitzWalter and his friend Eustace de Vesci escaped to France, until both received a pardon from the Pope several years later.

FitzWalter serves as the prototype for Patrick Henry and William Wallace in several respects. First, he was a lower magistrate, a landholder, part of the gentry, and a freeman. Secondly, the man had the courage to initiate the struggle against the tyrant before any of his compatriots were willing to join the fight. This amazing foresight and courage is emblematic of the greatest heroes in the worthy contest for liberty. Undoubtedly, this man had the most to lose and the most to win. He recognized the injustice and acted before anybody else would act. He engaged when nobody else would, when the odds were the greatest against him.

By the end of 1214, John's political position had weakened, and FitzWalter's loyal opposition had developed substantially. Earlier in the year, the king had assigned the position of Justiciar (Director of the Treasury) to a foreigner named Peter de Roches, who promptly levied the heaviest scutage (tax levy) in the history of the English nation. This was to pay for King John's enormous war debts which had been incurred on the continent.

Tensions between King John and his barons had never been higher. Secret meetings proceeded and a coalition was developing against the King. In the fall of 1214, the nobles held a meeting in which they issued certain demands or what they called a "Charter of Privileges" of the King, and requested a second meeting for December or early January. The King had agreed to meet on his own home turf (in London), and the nobles showed up armed to the teeth on January 8, 1215. Liberty was foremost on their minds. Each of the men took an oath, committing to "stand fast together for the liberty of church and realm." This time they asked that John confirm the Charter of Privileges outlined by Henry II over a hundred years earlier, adding a few of their own demands. The Magna Carta was slowly taking shape. John requested a delay until Easter, though at this point no one trusted him on his word. Hence, the nobles requested three sureties from the King in the form of Stephen Langton (the Archbishop), William Marshal, and the Bishop of Ely. Both sides used the delays as opportunities to assemble their armies and fortify the respective positions. By Easter week, the opposition had assembled a respectable army consisting of 2000 knights, 40 barons, and 5 earls. They gathered at Stampton and marched towards Northampton, a royal dominion some ninety miles west. On May 5, 1215, the barons formally renounced their fealty to

King John, although they had secretly agreed to this on November 4, 1214 in a meeting with Archbishop Langton. They also chose Robert FitzWalter as their leader, and gave him the title, "Marshal of the Army of God and the Holy Church." The lone outlaw, the exile, the first resister, and the man who lost his estates (the King burned down his castles and woods two years earlier), was now head of the armies assembled by a confederacy of lower magistrates.

At first, Robert's army failed to take Northampton, but the ranks were growing. Bedford joined the resistance, and it wasn't long before Northampton and Lincoln fell. King John responded to the renouncement of fealty by ordering his sheriffs to seize the lands belonging to the nobles. His orders didn't get far, especially when it became clear that the King was losing on his own home turf. The City of London opened its gates to the resistance almost immediately for several reasons. First, the city was known as a place for free men. If a serf (one who had rented fields from the lords), could live in a town for a year and a day, he had earned his freedom. Also, years earlier, King John had taken the city for a lucrative tax base, and imposed duties on goods exchanged in the city. More taxes were collected in London than any other city at the time, and certainly the freemen of London were aware of this.[12] Perhaps the city still remembered what had happened to the last tax protestor, one William FitzOsbert in 1196. "After a rapid trial in the Tower of London, he and nine friends were tied to horses' tails, dragged to Tyburn and hanged."[13] The gibbet on which they were hanged became something of a sacred monument to those who had died for the sake of freedom.

In a last ditch attempt to salvage some support from Londoners, on May 17, King John granted them a new charter offering them elections of their own mayor and a guarantee of liberties. Evidently, their love for King John had grown cold, for the city rejected the charter. Just ten days later, they opened their gates to John's arch-nemesis and his armies. Somehow, in the confusion of it all, King John lost his treasury that had been kept in the city.

By the providence of our sovereign God, the worst of the Plantagenet tyrants had met his Waterloo. He had lost his holdings in

Normandy. He was drained of resources. His armies were virtually non-existent. He had forfeited his home base while the opposition kept growing stronger by the day. In total, John had lost the support of two-thirds of his baronage, including his own half-brother, William Longsword. John had made the mistake of attempting to rape Longsword's wife while William was languishing in a French prison.

On June 15, 1215, the parties assembled twenty miles to the east of London at a large meadow called Runnymede. This became the birthplace of Western liberties; the stopgap to the ever pressing demands of the tyrannical state. Never before had the world seen such a declaration of liberties, a written constitution that would bind the force of the tyrant. This was no mere peace treaty, for peace would not return for several years. Rather, this was a line in the sand, a written compact or covenant to which kings and rulers would be subject for centuries. The Magna Carta was a summary of the demands of Robert FitzWalter and the lords. It would place limitations on the prerogative of the state. However, John had no intention of taking the covenant seriously. The Pope, given his characteristic centrist and tyrannical inclinations, would soundly condemn the document as "not only shameful and base, but also illegal and unjust."[14] Nonetheless, FitzWalter and the nobles did take the covenant seriously, and pledged their lives to secure the freedoms contained therein. They had signed the document, and now they would live and die by it. Even the Archbishop was in full support of the document, and for his sacrificial commitment to liberty the Pope removed him from office. Even though the Pope eventually excommunicated each of the barons by name, it was too late to reverse the course of liberty.

Now, the Charter became something to defend. Between June 15, 1215 and October 19, 1216 (King John's death), Robert FitzWalter continued to fight so as to hold the monarchy to the Charter and the rights contained in it. By 1217, the Charter was as well-established in the realm as was the Constitution of the United States when it was ratified in 1789. Between 1215 and 1315, the charter would be amended and reissued thirty-eight times. Clearly, the document was fully accepted into English governance, and carefully adhered to by all parties concerned.

Besides FitzWalter and Stephan Langton, mention should be made of another important hero by the name of Elias of Durham. As an assistant to the Archbishop, he had opposed John from the beginning and thoroughly mistrusted him throughout the proceedings. Elias knew the King's administrative staff would refuse to distribute the Charter, so he secured four copies of it (on June 24), and another six copies (on July 22). Elias was fully aware that the information war is as important as that fought with sword and spear. Later, Elias publicly condemned the Pope's excommunications, declaring them "invalid, because the Pope had not been accurately informed of the true facts."[15] In 1217, he was exiled for the second time in his life, though by that time he had already done sufficient damage to the tyrant's cause.

That such a wicked tyrant and incompetent buffoon as King John should serve as the means through which Western liberties were birthed, can only be attributed to the work of Divine providence. These were dangerous times, no doubt. Without the willingness of men like FitzWalter and Langton to risk their lives, and forfeit properties and offices, there would have been no legacy of liberty passed on to England, Scotland, and America. This handful of men faced off the most powerful men in the world whether king or pope, but they accomplished a worthy cause for the benefit of billions of people in the centuries that followed.

THE GREAT CHARTER

The Magna Carta, or "The Great Charter," contained sixty-three provisions. Above all, the charter placed the king under the law. The document stopped short of referencing Scripture itself; that would come later in Samuel Rutherford's *Lex Rex*. Nonetheless, the principle remained the same—these men were subjecting the king to a Supreme law above the king himself. Winston Churchill emphasized this point in his *History of the English Speaking Peoples*: "The reaffirmation of a supreme law and its expression in a general charter is the great work of the Magna Carta; and this alone justifies the respect in which men have held it."[16]

- Provision 1 guaranteed the free election of church leaders (independent of pope and king). This was the first concrete step towards a reformation of church polity, and a decentralization of the power of Rome. "The English church shall be free, and shall have its rights undiminished and its liberties unimpaired."

- Provisions 2-8 established rights of inheritance for heirs and widows and limited related fees and taxes.

- Provisions 9-11 addressed debt. First, Provision 9 protected the debtor from land seizure or confiscation if the debt could be addressed by other means. Property is sacrosanct and the basis for liberty. While Christian countries were forbidden the use of usury, Jews were allowed an exception. Some controls were placed on Jewish lending in this provision.

- Provisions 12 and 15 concerned taxes imposed on the commoners and serfs, allowing for taxation only for certain emergencies (and providing limits for these emergency situations as well).

- Provision 13 granted liberties and secured historical freedoms for city dwellers (specifically for those who lived in London). The specific liberties were not delineated.

- Provision 14 provided for an informal Parliament consisting of all archbishops, bishops, earls, and barons who wished to appear, specifically to consider tax proposals for the land. No more would the country submit itself to taxation without representation.

- Provision 16 limited a knight's responsibilities to the contract based on what was known as a "Knight's Fee." Provision 29 also forbade arbitrary transfer of a knight's services with a fee.

- Provisions 17-22 provided legal rights in court proceedings. Provision 17 provided local courts in a fixed location for minor crimes. Provision 18 established circuit courts in which were seated two of the king's men and four knights from the area. Provision 20 was the rudimentary source of the 8th Amendment of the United States Bill of Rights. This provision forbade harsh punishment for minor crimes, and offered protection for a man's means of earning income. Provision 21 established the right to trial by peers.

- Provision 23 relieved the nobility of the responsibility of building new bridges.

- Provision 24 relieved local magistrates of trying the King's cases.

- Provision 25 limited taxes to what had been established historically.

- Provisions 26 and 27 provided for an honest, accountable method of distribution of inheritance and debt repayments upon a man's death.

- Provision 28 forbade government confiscation of harvest and livestock without just compensation at market value to the owner. Also, Provision 30 disallowed the confiscation of a man's carts and horses.

- Provision 31 disallowed the King's use of all forests not belonging to him.

- Provision 32 limited the King's access to lands owned by a man convicted of a felony. After a year and one day, the King must return the land to the heirs.

- Provision 33 disallowed the use of nets for catching fish in the nation's major waterways.

- Provision 34 provided another legal protection in that a man could not trade his lands for a right to trial in another district.

- Provision 35 required a standard weight and measure, in accordance with biblical law.

- Provision 36 disallowed fees for court trials.

- Provision 37 disallowed taxes or fees assessed across jurisdictional boundaries.

- Provisions 38-40 are effectively repeated in the 6th Amendment in the United States Bill of Rights. According to these provisions, no imprisonment and no exile may be enforced without a court proceeding "by the lawful judgment of his peers." Only "credible witnesses" may be used in the trial, or the accused must be exonerated. Provision 40 guaranteed a speedy trial.

- Provision 41 relieved merchants of tolls and fees, and guaranteed their safety while in England.

- Provision 42 guaranteed safe passage out of the kingdom, and back into the kingdom to any who wished to travel.

- Provision 43 prevented centralization of property under a single earl.

- Provision 44 protected the ownership of forests.

- Provision 45 guaranteed competent justices, sheriffs, and bailiffs.

- Provision 46 dealt with private abbeys owned by the nobles (not by the Roman Church).

- Provision 47 reversed possession of lands that had been seized by King John for forest land back to private ownership.

- Provision 48 required swift and thorough investigation of every case of bribery or severe, unusual punishment.

- Provision 49 provided for the release of English hostages.

- Provisions 50 and 51 required the removal of foreign mercenaries (brought to England by King John), and the forfeiture of their lands.

- Provisions 52 and 53 allowed for a court proceeding for those who had lost their lands under King Henry, King Richard, or King John.

- Provision 54 limited a woman's witnessing in a murder trial for anyone, other than witnessing against her husband in a murder trial. This clause appears extraneous to the document, and it remains a mystery how it was incorporated.

- Provision 55 provided for the return of monies unjustly confiscated from landowners, during the reign of the Plantagenets.

- Provisions 56 and 57 promised the restoration of lands, liberty, and unjust fines to the Welshmen who had been oppressed by the King. In addition, those Welsh princes and Scottish royalty held in hostage would be released immediately.

The remaining provisions established the House of Lords, the first representative government in England. Twenty-five men would be elected by the gentry, representatives who "shall be bound with all their might, to observe and hold, and cause to be observed, the peace and liberties we have granted and confirmed to them by this our present Charter."

This is the story of the birth of Western liberties, some eight hundred years ago. Over the centuries, these liberties have seeped into almost every country around the world in some form or another. With the exception of certain socialist and communist countries, banana republics, and Islamic jurisdictions, much of the world has been blessed with this vision of Christian liberty, laid out in sixty-three simple statements. Despite the evil proclivities of men, somehow the Carpenter from Galilee brings His blessings to the world, "far as the curse is found." The English had a defective monarchy. The Christian church had its obvious defects. Certainly, the resistance had its defects. However, a great document emerged which would bless the world for centuries to come and give birth to more liberty in England, Scotland, Wales, Netherlands, America, Canada, and elsewhere.

Chapter 6

FREEDOM ENGRAINED: THE SWISS HERITAGE OF FREEDOM AND HOW IT WAS WON

It was the year 1307 in the land of the Swiss. Landenberg, one of the bailiffs appointed by the King of Austria to subjugate the communities surrounding Lake Lucerne, had put out the eyes of an "upright man" of the Halden by the name of Henry. The old man had refused to identify the whereabouts of his son, who had refused to give up his best pair of oxen to one of the bailiff's minions.

In the distant horizon the frosty peaks of the high alps were visible beyond Lake Lucerne. The towering heights of the Mythen Mountains rose east of the little village of Schwytz. Evening was approaching as Konrad Baumgarten rushed up to the local docks where the fishermen were securing their boats in preparation for the coming storm on the lake.[1]

Looking up from his boat, Ruodi, a village fisherman, saw Baumgarten's approach and noted that he appeared to be on the run from something or someone. "Why all the haste, good man?" Ruodi asked.

"I need your boat," Konrad replied, then hurriedly added, "My life is at stake!"

"Who pursues you, my man?"

Quickly Konrad explained to Ruodi and the other fishermen on the dock that he had killed a man. "You know the imperial Seneschal who lived at Rossberg, the one appointed steward of the castle by the Austrian King?"

Fishermen Kuoni, Ruodi, and Werni were well familiar with the local tyrant who was sometimes called the Wolfshot. Though he was Swiss, he was a sycophant, a loutish man, and a traitor to Switzerland's liberties.

"What did you do to this man?" they inquired.

"What every free man in my position would have done!" Konrad cried. "I have only defended my wife's honor, according to my own household rights."

"Did he violate your wife's honor, then?"

"He would have, had it not been for God and for this my trusty axe." The fishermen noted that the ax was still red with blood.

"Tell us all that he did," Ruodi exclaimed.

"Well, when I was in the forest cutting timber my wife came running out in mortal fear. She said 'the Seneschal' was in the house. He had ordered her to get a bath ready for him, and then he tried to take advantage of her. I came quickly, and my axe has given his bath a bloody benediction."

The men nodded in approval. "The tyrant has his just reward," Kuoni noted.

"Quick now," Baumgarten continued, "Help me over the lake, for the troopers from the Castle are on my tail."

"Impossible," Ruodi told him. "A storm is on the horizon. It would be certain death for anybody to attempt to cross the sea now."

"But I cannot delay!" Baumgarten cried as he dropped to his

knees before the fishermen. "Take me across," he implored. "To delay would mean my certain death."

Unmoved, Ruodi shook his head. "If we go out into these winds and waves, we shall all die," he grimly replied.

As they spoke a young man from neighboring Uri, some twenty miles south of Schwytz, came walking up the dock. The villagers instantly recognized him as William Tell of Burglen. Known for his skills on the lake, the men explained the situation and asked his advice in the matter.

"A brave man will prefer others and think of himself last," Tell advised the men. "Put your trust in God and help this man in his need."

Ruodi still insisted, "This is pure madness, men!"

Tell turned to the fisherman. "Give me the boat, then," he said. "Better to fall into God's hands than into the hands of those troopers from Rossberg!"

The two men climbed into the boat and set off into the waves. The fishermen on the shore continued watching until they could hardly see the boat as it rose and fell on the mountainous waves.

"This Tell would take risks you wouldn't even touch," Kuoni told Ruodi.

"Far better men than I would never attempt the sea at this stage," Ruodi responded. "There is not a man alive within all these mountains who could match his courage and skill!"

Shortly after Tell's departure the King's horsemen rode up to the lakeshore and demanded the whereabouts of Baumgarten. Pointing into the churning sea, Werni replied, "He is in yonder boat. Ride hard and you may catch him."

The King did not take the spurning of his authority lightly. In retribution his troopers burned down several of the local cottages and slaughtered the herds belonging to many of the village farmers. God, however, showed Himself more merciful than the tyrants from Rossberg, and Baumgarten and Tell survived the sea.

THE STORY OF WILLIAM TELL

Nobody incarnated the free spirit of the Swiss people like the man from the forest state of Uri, William Tell. He was not at the meeting at the meadow of Rutli, where the thirty men swore to God they would defend the liberties of the free people of Switzerland.

Upon returning home after his daring adventure, his wife Hedwig chided him for risking his life in the storm on the lake: "It was a miracle you escaped, Wilhelm! Were you thinking of your wife and children?"

"Dear wife, I was indeed thinking of my family. But I also wanted to save another father for his family. Baumgarten surely would have lost his life if we had not escaped by boat through the storm! I was but trusting in God to save us!"

Unsatisfied with her husband's answer, Hedwig replied, "This was not trust in God. You were tempting Him to brave such a storm on the lake!"

"I trust not, dear wife," said William Tell. "Now I must be off to your father in Altdorf. The parliament held on the meadows of Rutli has issued a call for all able-bodied men to stand and defend our lands from tyranny."

"My dear husband, shouldn't you rather go hunting?" his wife pleaded. "If you should run into Gessler, he will not treat you kindly for delivering Baumgarten from his hand."

"I gave my promise that I should join the men of Uri," William replied. For a moment his eyes silently met his wife's frightened gaze. "Pray that God go with us," he added fervently.

As William prepared to depart his son Walter begged to be allowed to accompany him. Against his mother's wishes, the two set off together for Altdorf to join the confederacy.

Along the road to the city William explained to his son the tyranny experienced by those who submitted themselves to Austrian rule. "Our people are not free. Their fields belong to the King and the Bishop— very powerful men. They may not hunt freely in the woods, for all the animals belong to the King. Neighbors are fearful of each other and all are afraid of the King. Yet the people find security with the King, and they have no courage to protect themselves, my son."

"I should prefer breathing room than to live in such a land, Father," Walter enjoined.

"Yes, Walter. 'Tis better to have these glacier peaks behind one's back than evil-minded men such as the King of Austria, who would subjugate the people of the Swiss mountains."

As they entered the village the two happened upon a cap mounted on a stake.

"Whose cap is that?" Walter asked his father.

"Never mind, son! Just let us keep walking."

But it was too late. Almost immediately they were surrounded by horsemen. "Halt in the name of the Emperor! You are both under arrest!"

The agents told the father and son they had failed to render proper obeisance to "the cap," which (they soon learned) belonged to the Viceroy, a man named Hermann Gessler. A small crowd quickly gathered and it appeared that a riot would ensue until the Viceroy himself rode up on his horse.

The court adjourned immediately, if it could be called a court. When the crime was announced—that William Tell had refused to bow to the cap—the sentence was rendered.

"I hear," Gessler said slowly as he eyed the crossbow which hung across William Tell's back, "that you are a master with the bow. Perhaps you should like to ply your trade here."

Young Walter, fourteen years of age, interjected, "That is true, sir! He can shoot an apple at a full hundred yards."

Gessler turned to the boy, a spiteful look on his face. "Is that your boy, Tell?"

"Yes, he is my son."

"Then here is what we shall do," Gessler announced with a note of finality in his voice. "Take an apple off yonder tree and let us place it on the boy's head. And, Tell, you shall shoot an apple off the head of your son at one hundred yards. If you miss, my men shall take off your head."

A deathly silence hung in the air as Tell realized the sheer horror of the proposal. "It is a monstrous suggestion!" he cried. "What father would ever risk the life of his own son by such an act? I will not do it."

"Then I shall kill you both at once." Gessler ordered his men to bind the two men hand and foot and prepare for execution.

"Stop! Stop!" Tell protested, "Surely you are jesting with us!"

"Not at all," Gessler replied with a malicious glint in his eye. Plucking an apple from the nearby tree, he handed it to Tell. "Here is an apple. Will you do it or shall I be constrained to kill you both?" Silence greeted Gessler's question and he added quietly, "I will settle for eighty paces."

From the edge of the crowd a man stepped forth. His name was Rossellman, the local pastor. "There is a God in heaven to whom you will be held accountable for all your deeds," he warned the tyrant. But Gessler merely shrugged off the admonition. William Tell's father-in-law, Walter Furst, likewise attempted to intercede. Kneeling before Gessler, the old man pleaded for the life of his son and grandson.

Young Walter however, protested greatly. "Grandfather, do not kneel before this wicked man!" Then, turning to Gessler, he asked, "Where shall I stand, sir? Tell me where I should stand. I do not fear. My father will not miss… "

Gessler told the men to bind the boy to a tree, but Walter insisted, "I will not be bound. I will hold still as a stone. I will cease to breathe, and my father shall split the apple in the center!"

"At least bind the boy's eyes!" an onlooker cried.

But to this Walter also objected. "Do you think I fear an arrow from my father's hand?" he asked simply.

Taking his stand at 80 yards' distance, Walter turned to his father, "Father, show these men that you are an archer. Shoot the apple and spite the tyrant!"

Gessler, growing more impatient by the second, called out to William Tell, "Get on with it, archer! You proud peasants assume the right to carry these crossbows even though none should be armed but those who defend the castles! If it pleases you to carry crossbow and arrow, then I shall give you the chance to use it today. Take the shot, woodsman!"

Disregarding Gessler's command, Tell threw down his bow, ripped open his shirt, and cried out to the bailiff, "I cannot shoot at my boy. Command your men to shoot me instead, now!"

"No, no!" Gessler announced. "I do not want your life. You are the man who braves the storms to deliver a life. Now we shall see if you have the courage to deliver a shot to save the boy and your own skin!"

From where he stood in front of a tree Walter cried out, "Come Father, take the shot. I am not afraid!"

With that, William Tell retrieved his crossbow, fingered an arrow into the string, and leveled his aim upon the apple sitting on his son's head. A hush fell over the crowd as his fingers lingered on the bowstring. Then, with a gentle hiss, the arrow sped on its way. For a breathless second nobody in the crowd dared look at the boy.

"He's still standing there!" somebody finally shouted.

"The apple is gone from the boy's head!" cried another.

With a smile of triumph Walter ran to his father, "Here is the apple, clean snapped in half!" Father and son embraced as William Tell fell to his knees, too weak to speak. Grandfather Furst could only say, "My children, my children, God be praised!"

As the family rejoiced Gessler approached the archer and asked him, "What is the second arrow in your belt, Tell? What were you planning?"

"To be honest, sir," William replied, "I reserved a second arrow to split your skull should I have killed my boy. You can be sure I would not have missed with the second."

"That was what I suspected," Gessler snapped. "Guards, seize the archer and put him in my boat. We shall take him to rot in the dungeon of Kussnacht!"

As the guards dragged William Tell away, his son cried out to him, "Father, Father, where are they taking you?"

Tell's response was simply, "Your Father now is on high. Appeal to Him, my son. Appeal to Him. I thank God you are uninjured."

* * *

In the providence of God the ship heading across Lake Lucerne encountered a terrible storm. It was driven into Gotthardt's Gorge and "a hurricane swept down with such headlong force that every rower's heart within him sank."

Seeing their predicament, the men in the boat appealed to Gessler that he allow them to untie William Tell, for, as they said, "He knows how to steer with more than common skill, and this is our only hope for saving us now in the storm!"

In the desperation of the moment Gessler relented. When asked to assume control of the boat, William Tell replied, "With God's assistance I shall see what may be done, and may Heaven help us!"

As he steered the boat through the gorge, Tell took advantage of an opportune moment when the boat passed under an overhanging crag. With what he later called "one prayer to God for his assisting grace, and straining every muscle, I brought round the vessel's stern close to the rocky wall. Then snatching up my weapons with a bound I swung myself upon the flattened shelf, and with my feet thrust off, with all my mind, the puny bark into the hell of waters. There let it drift about, as heaven ordains."

In the ensuing confusion William Tell made his escape. It wasn't a week later, however, that he found a use for his second arrow. Knowing full well that the tyrant would kill his family, he circled the lake by foot to catch Gessler at Kussnacht.

Considering Gessler a lawless man, Tell justified his actions in that "self-preservation is our only judge. Either my innocent wife and child and fatherland must fall, or, bailiff Gessler, thou! Fall thou, therefore, and let liberty prevail!" With that he let the arrow fly—and Gessler fell, never to rise and tyrannize the Swiss people again.

A CHRISTIAN HERITAGE

"And Jesus came and spake unto them, saying, 'All power is given unto me in heaven and in earth. Go ye therefore, and teach all nations, baptizing them in the name of the Father, and of the Son, and of the Holy Ghost: Teaching them to observe all things whatsoever I have commanded you: and, lo, I am with you always, even unto the end of the world. Amen.'" (Matt. 28:18-20)

Switzerland would come to be one of the most free countries in the world—a country made up of decentralized powers, individual liberties, and great prosperity. It would become a seedbed for reformation faith, both in Zurich with Ulrich Zwingli and in Geneva with John Calvin and his fellow laborers in the Gospel. But how did this happen over the centuries? From where did the Swiss passion for freedom originate? The story must be told, for it makes up an important element of the chronicle of Christian freedoms which have developed over the centuries in the West.

The mountainous land making up much of Switzerland resists taming, and not many tyrants were successful at gaining control of it. If they did, their power hold was short-lived. Yet, the local tribalism was not strong enough to stave off tyranny through the centuries.

Christianity entered Switzerland as early as 200 AD when a missionary named Lucius (the son of a king) sowed the seeds of the Gospel in the eastern Rhetian Mountains. Around the time of the fall of Rome whole Christian communities moved into Thurgau on the German border. They built little churches and chapels and founded discipleship centers for schooling and prayer. In the early seventh century Irish missionaries Columban and Gall formed a discipleship center for young men on the shores of Lake Constance. Around AD 830 a missionary named Meinrad began evangelizing around Etzel Pass in central Switzerland. He was killed by robbers but was always remembered for his spirit of Christian hospitality.

The pastors of local churches were not celibate, which means they would marry and raise families themselves throughout the missionary era of the Swiss church. Discipleship centers like the Abbey of St. Gallen helped the people develop agriculture and technology. They taught the people how to weave wool and develop family economies, and introduced the ox and plough into Switzerland.

HOW SWITZERLAND BECAME FREE

"And there was a great outcry of the people and their wives against their Jewish brethren. For there were those who said, 'We, our sons, and our daughters are many; therefore let us get grain, that we may eat and live.' There were also some who said, 'We have mortgaged our lands and vineyards and houses, that we might buy grain because of the famine.' There were also those who said, 'We have borrowed money for the king's tax on our lands and vineyards. Yet now our flesh is as the flesh of our brethren, our children as their children; and indeed we are forcing our sons and our daughters to be slaves, and some of our daughters have been brought into slavery. It is not in our power to redeem them, for other men have our lands and vineyards.' And I became very angry when I heard their outcry and these words. After serious thought, I rebuked the nobles and rulers, and said to them, 'Each of you is exacting usury from his brother.' So I called a great assembly against them. And I said to them, 'According to our ability we have redeemed our Jewish brethren who were sold to the nations. Now indeed, will you even sell your brethren? Or should they be sold to us?' Then they were silenced and found nothing to say. Then I said, 'What you are doing is not good. Should you not walk in the fear of our God because of the reproach of the nations, our enemies?'" (Neh. 5:1-9 NKJV)

For hundreds of years the peoples of the far off districts behind the lakes were separated from the rest of the world. Nobody paid much attention to them. These people shared a single Christian church located in Muotathal. They formed their own government and elected their own leaders. Eventually the Schwyz, the Uri, and the Unterwalden separated into their own cantons (or counties) with their own governments and churches. A Christian discipleship center was established in Engelberg in AD 1083.

In the year 1113 a greedy abbot tried to take away pasture land from the shepherds of Schwyz. The Abbot appealed to the Holy Roman Emperor Henry V, and the Emperor took his side against the Schwyz. The Uri, the Unterwalden, and the Schwyz communities basically ignored the Emperor's edict. They argued that, "No Emperor can bestow what is our own: and if the Empire shall deny us justice, we can, within our mountains, right ourselves!" The powerful Bishop of Constance (located on the border of Germany and Switzerland) also took the side of the Abbot and excommunicated all the inhabitants of the three cantons (and would not allow them to receive the Lord's Supper).

The Bishop's excommunication did not appear to bother these Swiss mountain men, for they told their priests to ignore the Bishop and keep ministering to the flocks. The Bishop cursed the land, but the fields continued to yield good crops. As the Roman church centralized control and perverted power, the local churches and the local priests continued discipling the villages.

In AD 1273 a Duke named Rudolph from Aargau in Switzerland was elevated to the position of King of Germany. Rudolph I reigned until his death on July 15, 1291. The Schwyzers were friendly with Rudolph, who was a benevolent ruler during his reign. Determined to maintain self-rule, in August 1291 the three cantons formed a league. Formed between the men of the Dale of Uri, the community of Schwyz (from which is derived the name of the "Swiss"), and the men of the mountains of Unterwalden, the league was known as "the Bond."

THE BOND

"Be it known to every one, that the men of the Dale of Uri, the Community of Schwytz, as also the men of the mountains of Unterwalden, in consideration of the evil times, have full confidently bound themselves, and sworn to help each other with all their power and might, property and people, against all who shall do violence to them, or any of them. That is our Ancient Bond.

"Whoever hath a Seignior, let him obey according to the conditions of his service.

"We are agreed to receive into these dales no Judge, who is not a countryman and indweller, or who hath bought his place.

"Every controversy amongst the sworn confederates shall be determined by some of the sagest of their number, and if any one shall challenge their judgment, then shall he be constrained to obey it by the rest.

"Whoever intentionally or deceitfully kills another, shall be executed, and whoever shelters him shall be banished.

"Whoever burns the property of another shall no longer be regarded as a countryman, and whoever shelters him shall make good the damage done.

"Whoever injures another, or robs him, and hath property in our country, shall make satisfaction out of the same.

"No one shall distrain a debtor [or seize his property] without a judge, nor any one who is not his debtor, or the surety of such debtor.

"Every one in these dales shall submit to the judge, or we, the sworn confederates, all will take satisfaction for all the injury occasioned by his contumacy [rebellion against the judges]. And if in any internal division the one party will not accept justice, all the rest shall help the other party. These decrees shall, God willing, endure eternally for our general advantage."

The Bond of the three cantons was an early Bill of Rights, but written in the form of law. A more biblical approach to "rights" will always present God's law first. It is God's law that secures rights.

This statement defended the right to life and property for the citizens of Uri, Schwytz, and the Unterwalden. The first law is a reflection of Romans 13:4, Genesis 9:6, and Deuteronomy 19:

"But if any man hate his neighbour, and lie in wait for him, and rise up against him, and smite him mortally that he die, and fleeth into one of these cities: then the elders of his city shall send and fetch him thence, and deliver him into the hand of the avenger of blood, that he may die. Thine eye shall not pity him, but thou shalt put away the guilt of innocent blood from Israel, that it may go well with thee." (Deut. 19:11-13)

King Rudolph's eldest son Albert assumed the throne of Germany in 1298. He was a hard man, a tyrant who created great dissension within the empire during his short reign. Immediately after his ascension to the throne, Albert attempted to force the three independent Swiss Cantons to place themselves under the jurisdiction of Austria. The Cantons refused, preferring the self-governance they enjoyed in centuries past. This angered the King, and he sent bailiffs to subjugate the people of the Alps. Hermann Gessler of Brunegg and Knight Beringer of Landenberg moved in around 1301. They proceeded to tyrannize the locals, increasing taxes and imposing unjust fines and imprisonment for petty crimes.

Several men, including William Tell's father-in-law Walter Furst and Werner Stauffacher, organized a meeting of men representing the three Cantons at the Meadow of Rutli near Brunnen on November 17, 1307. There they protested King Albert's attempts to deprive them of their former freedoms granted under previous charters made with the Emperor. They insisted that "God had given to no king the right to commit injustice." At this point they had "no hope but in God and their own courage, and that death was much more desirable than so shameful a yoke." They raised their hands to heaven and "swore to God the Lord, before whom kings and peasants are equal, faithfully to live and to die for the rights of the innocent people." Some thirty men joined in this oath "to undertake and carry through every thing in unison and not separately; to permit no injustice, but also to commit no injustice; to respect the rights and property of the Counts of Habsburg, and to do no harm to the imperial bailiffs; but also to prevent the bailiffs from ruining the country." Together they swore, "We swear we will be free, as were our sires, and sooner die than live in slavery. We swear to put our trust in God Most High, and not to quail before the might of man!"

It wasn't long after the meeting in the Meadow at Rutli that William Tell was put to the severe test for refusing to bow to the cap. The first arrow split the apple on his son's head at 80 yards. But the second pierced the tyrant to the heart. Shortly thereafter a group of twenty men who had taken the oath entered the castle at Rossberg. In the night a young girl beloved of one of the men lowered a rope from her chambers inside the castle down into the moat below. The men handily overcame the steward and his men and took over the castle.

Meanwhile, down in the Unterwalden, twenty men overpowered the second tyrant bailiff, Landenberg. They sent him into the town of Lucerne on the condition that he would never return. Another band of men from Uri took Gessler's castle as well.

King Alfred was incensed by these actions. However, in the providence of God, he was killed by his own nephew on May 1, 1308.

Alfred's son Leopold gathered 4,000 men and on November 16, 1315, attacked 1,300 Swiss confederates on a small plain near Hasellmat. Fifty of the Schwyz volunteers positioned themselves on the cliffs of Siegler-Flue and pushed gigantic boulders down onto the mounted knights below. This placed the Austrian troops in disarray, and the shepherds from Uri and Unterwalden proceeded to attack with mace and halberd. Leopold barely escaped with his life.

After this the Swiss confederates renewed their ancient bond: "to die, all for each, each for all; to enter into no engagement with foreign powers except with consent of all; to respect foreign property and rights in the country." The Pact of Brunnen was signed on December 9, 1315.

FIRST BATTLES DEFENDING THE FREE STATES OF SWITZERLAND

Thus the confederacy was formed. For the following 75 years the God of Heaven blessed the Swiss cantons with a prosperity and freedom practically unmatched by any other land in Christendom. In 1385, Leopold III of Austria vowed that he would take vengeance upon the "insolent" confederates and assembled a great army of several thousand knights. Once again the Swiss gathered to protect their liberties, 400 from Lucerne, 900 from Waldstatten, and 100 from smaller villages. The knights attacked shoulder to shoulder, producing an iron wall of leveled lances. Beholding the overwhelming force of their enemies, the Swiss fell on their knees and prayed. Then, rising to their feet, they rushed into battle. Despite their bravery, the Swiss were no match for the armored knights, and their valiant charge was easily repulsed by the stationary row of lances. As the confederates staggered back after their initial assault, sixty of their countrymen lay bleeding on the ground.

For a moment indecision gripped the Swiss. Then suddenly the voice of Arnold Struthahn of Winkelried, an Unterwaldener, rang out, "I will open a path for freedom! Faithful and dear Confederates, take care of my wife and child!" With this injunction he ran into the enemy lances, grasping as many as he could, and buried them in his own chest. The confederates rushed over his dead body through the breach, encouraged by the stalwart courage of their fallen compatriot.

Once again the maces of the mighty shepherds cracked the helmets and breastplates of the armored men. Many lords and counts were killed in the fray. Leopold himself died on the field, as he watched the devastation of his armies. The knights attempted an escape. But, weighed down by their heavy armor, they were no match for the lean and powerful shepherds and huntsmen of the Swiss mountains. Hundreds more fell on their retreat. After the battle Austria negotiated a truce with the mountain peoples, and for generations afterwards the Swiss considered Austria to be the mortal enemy of liberty.

The battle for liberty is not easily won against the vehement thirst for power residing within the hearts of ungodly tyrants. In 1388 the Austrian monarch attempted another assault on the Swiss, this time with 6,000 men. The Swiss Captain Mathias am Buel assembled 500 men to meet the Austrian force. Retreating to Mount Ruti, the small Swiss force employed the rock-strewn mountain in their battle against the Austrian army. Again the Austrians could not stand up against the boulders rolled down on the cavalry. In the confusion, over 2,500 Austrians were killed.

A peace treaty was drawn up in which the Swiss retained possession of all their territory. By the grace of God, on June 10, 1393, the first free country with guaranteed liberties was established. On that day eight cantons of the confederacy met together in Zurich, swearing "to avoid useless feuds, but to unite all their efforts in case of necessary war; never to stop fighting even when wounded, until the decision of the affair; not to flee, but to remain masters of the field; not to pillage, except by permission of the general; to spare churches, convents, and defenseless wives and daughters." This was the law of the confederates, which was based on the biblical standards of warfare found in Deuteronomy 20.

The independent spirit of the Swiss provided a fertile spirit for the great reformation of the 16th century a little more than a century later. The resistance to centralized political control nourished in the hearts of the Swiss would enable resistance to a centralized ecclesiastical power (in the form of the Pope). Thus the confederacy paved the way for Zwingli, Farel, Viret, Calvin, and other reformers whom God would use to further establish the Christian faith in the coming centuries.

THE PACT OF BRUNNEN, 1315

"In the name of God, Amen! As nature is weak and fragile, it happens that what should be lasting and perpetual is soon easily forgotten; therefore it is useful and necessary that the things which are established for the peace, tranquility, advantage, and honor of men, be put in writing and made public by authentic acts.

"Thus, we of Uri, Schwyz, and Unterwald, let all those who read or hear these present letters know that foreseeing and apprehending untoward and difficult times, and in order to be better able to enjoy peace and rest, to defend and preserve our bodies and our property, we mutually promised each other in good faith and by oath, to assist each other with advice, help, body and property, and at our expense, against all those who will do or want to do insult or violence to us and ours, to our persons or our fortunes, so that if any damage is done to the person or property of any of us, we will support it, so that amicable or by justice, restitution or repair be made to him.

"Moreover, we promise by the same oath that none of the three countries and none of us will recognize anyone for his lord without the consent and will of others. Besides, each one of us, man or woman, must obey his lawful lord and the legitimate power in all that is just and fair, except to lords who will use violence against one of the countries, or who wish to dominate unjustly on us, because to such no obedience is due until they have agreed with the Countries. We also agree among ourselves that no country or Confederate shall take an oath and pay homage to any foreigner without the consent of other countries and Confederates; that no Confederate will enter into negotiations with any foreigner without the permission of the other Confederates, as long as the countries are without lord. That if any of our countries betrays their interests, violates or transgresses any of the articles contained in the present act, it will be declared treacherous and perjury, and its body and property will be confiscated for the benefit of the countries.

"In addition to this, we have also agreed to not receive and admit as judge any man who has bought his charge for money or otherwise, or who would not be our compatriot. If any dispute or war arises between the Confederates, the most honest and prudent men will assemble to pacify this dispute, or terminate this war either amicably or by justice; if one of the parties refuses to do so, the Confederates will assist the other so that, amicably or by justice, the dispute will be terminated at the expense of the person who has refused the means of conciliation.

"If one of the Confederates kills another, he will be punished with death, unless he can prove and the judges declare that he did so out of necessity, to defend his life. If the murderer runs away, anyone in our country will receive him, take him to his house and defend him, be exiled and not return to his homeland unless he is reminded of the consent of the Confederates.

"If one of the Confederates openly or secretly and intentionally sets fire to the house of another, he will be banished forever from our territory, and whoever receives him in his house, will give him asylum and protection, will be required to repair the damage caused by the incendiary.

"No one can take pledges except from his debtor or his guarantor, and he will not do so without the authority of the judge. Everyone will obey his judge and indicate the judge in our country before which he wants to appear.

"If anyone refuses to submit to the sentence, and his disobedience

damages one of the Confederates, the latter will compel him to in-
demnify him.

"And so that the above-mentioned assurances and conditions remain
stable and perpetual, we, named above, citizens and Confederates
of Uri, Schwyz and Unterwald, have affixed our seals to the present
act done at Brunnen, the year 1315 of the birth of our Lord Jesus
Christ, the first Tuesday after the day of St. Nicholas [December
9]."

Chapter 7

FREEDOM BIRTHED: THE BATTLE FOR SCOTLAND'S INDEPENDENCE

William Wallace, the young Scot, was 21 years of age when he entered the thriving town of Lanark, some 40 miles to the southeast of his family's estate in Elderslie. Cautiously he proceeded, for he was a wanted man ever since his arrest and the tortures that befell him in the gaol at Ayr. His altercation with English troops to the West had marked him for life, and he had barely escaped alive. William's father had refused to take the oath to King Edward, whom he considered to be a foreign king. To take the oath would mean to surrender Scotland's heritage of independence. For his steadfast resistance to the king, William's father was dead, killed by English sword. While his grandfather, on his mother's side, had sworn allegiance to the English, William could not bring himself to cast off his father's dying commitment to Scotland's independence. The die was cast, and Wallace was on the run.

It was market day in Lanark as William Wallace entered the city square. Almost immediately, he caught the eye of a beautiful young maiden, who couldn't have been older than eighteen years. What concerned him most was her expression of fear. She had a look of foreboding as if completely resigned to some inevitable evil force.

"Fair lass," he called out to her. "Why so cheerless on this fine day?"

Without answering him, the woman turned and hurried off in the opposite direction. Not to be discouraged, the young man hastened to catch up with her.

"Why dost thou fear? Who is it that thou dost fear?" he asked in lower tones.

"I am to be married, and I must not speak with you," she responded.

"Well that is fine and good," he replied. "But why art thou so cheerless and frightened if thou wilt be married? That is hardly the disposition of a betrothed woman, who is to marry the man she loves."

"I do not marry the man I love," she almost whispered.

"Then why dost thou marry, fair woman?"

"I must marry the son of the Sheriff."

"And this man is not a good man, I gather. Why must thou marry the brute?" he pursued.

"The Sheriff Heselrig has murdered my father and my brother, and now he would that I marry his son," the woman explained.

"Thou must not marry this man. For thou must marry me, and we shall fight for Scotland's independence!"

The young woman blushed. Before she could respond to the bold proposal, a small band of English soldiers approached the couple. "It's him!" she whispered. "Go! Leave."

"But, I do not know thy name," he cried out to her.

"Marian. Marian Bradfute. My father was Sir Hugh de Bradfute!"

Not two months later, in the Spring of 1296, William and Marian were married by the priest of Dunipace in a secret wedding ceremony without the knowledge of the Sheriff of Lanark. They both had their own reasons to support the struggle for Scotland's independence.

* * *

It was no ordinary marriage for William and Marian. For the following twelve months, Wallace gathered a small band of Scots who refused to submit to the English crown and prepared a resistance. It wasn't long before the Sheriff of Lanark and the English Captain Thorn were on Wallace's trail, and the young man could sense his danger. He spoke to his wife concerning the rising conflict.

"Thou must leave here now, my good wife. It is far too dangerous for thee to live in these environs, with the English pressing us sore," He told her.

"I cannot," the woman replied. "No, Hesilrig, red with my kindred slain! My friends are destroyed, and my brothers are slain. With you let me go. What though my tender nerves refuse to bend. The twanging yew [bow], and the fleet dart to send. I will stay in thy tent with thee. I shall wait impatient the decisive day when freedom on thy helm shall crested stand!"[1]

That evening, Wallace retreated to the Carlane Craigs to join his band of men.

The very next day, the sheriff and his men found Marian in the cottage several miles from the village of Lanark and there they murdered the woman in cold blood.

In the evening Wallace returned to the cottage, to find the bloody body of his beloved wife lying on the floor. Holding her limp frame close to his heart, he remembered her final words to him. The time had come to fight off the tyrants who would not stop short of killing women and children to gain their purposes. Now he must win Scotland's independence, or die trying.

In the dark of the night, Wallace's small band of men entered Lanark and proceeded to cut down every man in the English guard, including the Sheriff and the Captain of the English forces lodged in the town. It was a total rout. Not a single Scot was killed in the exchange. Thus began the eighteen year struggle for Scotland's independence.

THE INDEPENDENT CULDEAN CHURCH

The Scottish church had its roots in the Irish church of St. Patrick. This early Christian work in Scotland began at Iona somewhere around AD 550 with Columba, a missionary from Ireland. Iona is a rocky island located off the coast of southwest Scotland, consisting of not more than four square miles of land. For over a hundred years, this discipleship center on the island flourished as the base of operations for missionary work throughout Scotland, Northumbria, and eventually to the European mainland.

To the chagrin of the Roman see, this church operated independently under elder rule. The Venerable Bede of the Roman church records the proceedings of the Synod of Whitby in Northumbria in AD 664, in which the Roman Catholic leadership met with these Culdeans, in order to work out differences between them. As is the case with many church conflicts, the issues were relatively minor—the monk's hair cut (or tonsure), and the day on which the churches celebrated Easter (Christ's resurrection). The specific matters over which the two church traditions disagreed were of little consequence. Underlying the debates was the question of control and those incorrigible forces that would consolidate power in the Western church and enforce a uniform agenda. Despite Bede's commendations of the piety of the Iona church, his irritation with the church's independence is hard to miss in his historical survey of the English church. Nonetheless, the Culdean church remained independent of Rome through the succeeding centuries.

The ancient "Chair of Columban" was transferred to St. Andrews in Edinburgh sometime during the ninth century, and this became the seat of the Culdean (Scottish) church. In the sixth year of the reign of Constantine (AD 906), the Scottish church leaders gathered at a place called Mote Hill, known thereafter as "Hill of the Faith." They committed themselves by oath to reform the Church of Scotland, a clear reference to the independence of the church in the tenth century.[2] Later in the tenth century, an English princess by the name of Queen Margaret attempted to "reform" the Culdean Church according to Roman Catholic practices.

In the year AD 1144, King David I of Scotland officially removed the seat at St. Andrews and transferred it under the control of
Rome. In the new charter, David clearly addressed the Culdees who
refused to submit to Rome, allowing at least one more generation of
freedom from Roman control for the prior and canons (pastors and
elders). David ruled:

> "That they [the prior and canons] shall receive the *Keledei* of Kilri-
> mont into the canonry, with all their possessions, if they are willing
> to become canon-regular; but, if they refuse, those who are now
> alive are to retain their property during their lives; and, after their
> death, as many canons-regular are to be instituted in the church of
> St. Andrews as there are now *Keledei*, and all their possessions are to
> be appropriated to the use of the canons."[3]

As late as AD 1176, David's son William further urged the Culdean clergy to submit to Rome. A meeting was called in Northampton, and William encouraged subjection to the Archbishop of York.
A certain young man named Gilbert Murray rose up, challenging England's claim on Scotland:

> "It is true, English nation, thou mightest have been noble, and more
> noble than some other nations, if thou hadst not craftily turned the
> power of thy nobility, and the strength of thy fearful might, into the
> presumption of tyranny, and thy knowledge of liberal science into
> the shifting glosses of sophistry; but thou disposest not thy purposes
> as if thou wert led with reason, and being puffed up with thy strong
> armies, and trusting in thy great wealth, thou attemptest, in thy
> wretched ambition and lust of domineering, to bring under thy juris-
> diction thy neighbour provinces and nations, more noble, I will not
> say, in multitude or power, but in lineage and antiquity; unto whom,
> if thou wilt consider ancient records, thou shouldst rather have been
> humbly obedient, or at least, laying aside thy rancour, have reigned
> together in perpetual love: and now with all wickedness of pride that
> thou shewest, without any reason or law, but in thy ambitious power,
> thou seekest to oppress thy mother the Church of Scotland, which
> from the beginning hath been catholic and free... Therefore, thou
> Church of England, doest as becomes thee not; thou thinkest to car-
> ry what thou cravest, and to take what is not granted. Seek what is

just, if thou wilt have pleasure in what thou seekest. And to the end I do not weary others with my words, albeit I have no charge to speak for the liberty of the Church of Scotland, and albeit all the clergy of Scotland would think otherwise, yet I dissent from subjecting her, and I do appeal unto the Apostolical Lord, unto whom immediately she is subject; and if it were needful for me to die in the cause, here I am ready to lay down my neck unto the sword."[4]

Young Gilbert appears as the prototype champion for Scottish independence, well before the conflict with the English 120 years later.

SCOTLAND'S INDEPENDENCE

For almost 400 years, Scotland thrived as an independent nation, self-ruled under their own kings, all descendants of Kenneth I (AD 850). Through the centuries, the Scots fought occasional wars with the Vikings and the Danes, and survived border conflicts with England. But Scotland was free, and its church acted largely independent of the pope and his international politics. How would such a nation fare during the rise of the modern empires, and the centralizing, power-centered Church of Rome? The pressures towards centrism and the development of the totalitarian state had collected significant strength by the turn of the fourteenth century. William the Conqueror had laid the foundations for tyranny in AD 1066. Would Scotland survive as an independent state?

Intramural conflicts for the throne after the death of Malcolm III in AD 1093 resulted in three of his sons seeking exile in England. That is how his son David was raised in the English court of William II (the third son of William the Conqueror). Historians are fairly certain that William II was a key instigator in the civil wars that ensued in Scotland. Whatever the case, these political forces commenced an erosion of Scotch political independence. On his accession to the Scottish throne in AD 1124, David imported the Norman feudal system into Scotland, complete with state ownership of all the land. A trail of Norman lords immigrated from England into Scotland at this time, including significant players in the wars that followed such as Comyn and Baliol, Fitz-Allen and Bruce. Nonetheless, the Scottish monarchy was held by the house of Dunkeld without interruption from AD 1097 to AD 1286, the year of the death of Alexander III. Crown rights then fell to the last Dunkeld, Princess Margaret. However, Margaret was only a young child, and no woman had ever served as monarch of Scotland. Fearing civil war, the lords turned to King Edward I of England for help. It was a fatal decision. Over a period of a hundred years or more, Scotland had experienced great prosperity and peace with her neighbors—England, Norway, and Denmark. Under Edward I, Scotland was to enter the fight for her very life.

Edward quickly betrothed his five-year-old son to six-year-old Margaret, in hopes to consolidate the two kingdoms. Fearing just this consequence, the Scottish nobles organized a meeting with Edward at Birgham, and signed a treaty guaranteeing Scotland's independence and protection of historic liberties. The nobles agreed on unifying the crowns of England and Scotland, but specified "no taxation levied outside of what was needed for Scotland's defense, no outside interference on church matters, and no vassal of the Scottish crown was to do homage for his Scottish lands outside of the kingdom."[5] While Edward was signing the document, his troops were off invading the Isle of Man and seizing control of this strategic Scottish holding. Young Margaret died a month later, and Edward dropped all pretension of preserving Scotland's independence.

Meanwhile Edward's wife of 35 years died, and this tragic event seemed to drain all common grace from his life. From that point on, he turned into the tyrant of all tyrants. Historian Ronald McNair Scott writes of the change that came over the King of England at this time: "The savage streak, inherited from his Angevin ancestors, 'the Devil's breed', which had expressed itself in his youth by acts of wanton cruelty…was to break out in barbarous reprisals against those who thwarted his purpose."[6]

Back in Scotland, two potential candidates emerged as possessing the most royal blood, John Balliol and Robert the Competitor (the eighty-year-old grandfather of Robert the Bruce). To avoid civil war, the ruling earls of Scotland invited Edward to arbitrate. The King of England gladly obliged, and started the conversation with, "Can you produce any evidence to show that I am not the rightful suzerain [sovereign]?"[7] Nonetheless, the King chose John Balliol, partially because Balliol was a native of France, and married to the daughter of one of Edward's important military commanders. He was also willing to swear fealty to the King of England. Thus, Balliol became Edward's puppet in Scotland for a few years, until it became obvious to the Scots that he was more committed to the English power base than to Scotland's independence. The Scots attempted a revolt, and Edward responded with a swift and bloody blitzkrieg that stunned the nation. It began with the massacre of Berwick, in which even pregnant women in the process of giving birth were put to the sword. All told, thousands of citizens died in the unrestrained carnage. Such a bloody holocaust was a shock to the medieval world, and as a consequence, Edward had well secured his position as a tyrant in the eyes of all reasonable men. Following the massacre of Berwick, the Scots army was completely overcome at the battle of Lammermuirs on April 27, 1296. John Balliol abdicated with his tail between his legs, leaving Scotland entirely to the whims of an angry, tyrannical, foreign king. Edward assumed control of most of the major castles in the land, and appointed his own sheriffs and administrative staff to govern the nation. Historian McNair Scott sums up the state of Scotland at this point: "Scotsmen were no longer to be governed by Scotsmen, but by Englishmen with no lineal or landed ambitions in the area."[8]

Any of the property owners who refused to sign an oath of allegiance were hunted down, and their lands and goods were confiscated. Edward's administrative lead, Hugh de Cressingham, wasted no time collecting exorbitant taxes to line the coffers of the English government. All resistance was squelched. However, there were two men that Edward didn't calculate into his equation—William Wallace and Robert the Bruce.

After Balliol's abdication, the throne should have fallen to Robert the Bruce (after his grandfather, Robert the Competitor, had died in 1296). In fact, Edward had promised the throne to Robert, who refused to fight with Balliol during the early days of the revolt. However, as was his pattern, Edward reneged on his promise, choosing rather occupation and subjugation of Scotland. In 1292 and again in 1296, the Bruce clan took the oath of fealty to Edward I, and still considered themselves vassals of the King of England, until a legitimate king ascended to the throne of Scotland. However, when Edward called upon Robert the Bruce's father to seize the lands of a troublesome knight by the name of William Douglas, the test for the Bruce clan became the moment of truth. The elder Bruce sent his son Robert to do the business. In compliance with his father's request, the young twenty-two-year-old mustered the troops and began to lead them up the long valley towards the Douglas Castle. Something must have happened in the mind of that young man, as he traversed the valley. For Robert brought his horse to a sudden stop, and addressed his men: "No man," he shouted, "holds his flesh and blood in hatred and I am no exception. I must join my own people and the nation in which I was born. Choose then whether you go with me or return to your homes!"[9] From that point on, Robert the Bruce was forced to abandon his own lands, and join the Scottish resistance.

INITIAL RESISTANCE

When the bulk of the leadership of a nation has capitulated to tyranny, and the local magistrates are controlled almost entirely by foreign tyrants, there is little hope for any resistance. When both left and right, Republican and Democrat, are united in the cause of tyranny, freedom hardly has a chance. That any should oppose tyranny at these odds would amount to sheer lunacy in the eyes of the majority. It is under similarly difficult challenges that William Wallace and Robert the Bruce took up the cause of Scotland's independence.

William Wallace appeared on the scene for the first time in 1297. His family background rests in obscurity, in that he descended from the lesser nobility. He came out of nowhere as it were, and became a legend to the cause of liberty. In a day when fealty meant everything, Wallace felt no commitment to a nation and a king to which he swore no loyalty. Therefore, he considered the English-appointed sheriffs and the tax collectors as nothing but an occupational force at war with Scotland. There were others who had refused to submit, especially among the Scottish clergy. For example, the Bishop of Glasgow publicly supported Wallace in his initial resistance to England's illegitimate rule.

Under Edward, England had come to define tyranny in the true sense of the word. The English massacres were conducted, in the words of Blind Harry (the only ancient source of biographical information on William Wallace), "without remorse or any fear of God."[10] According to Harry's vivid description of the scene, Wallace was particularly enraged, "to see Saxon blood in Scotland reign, and governed by a most unrighteous king, who wrought great wrong in country and in town, wasted our lands, and broke our building down. Maids, wives, and widows' chastity they spill. Nor could the nun resist their lustful will. King Herod's part they acted in the land..."[11]

William's father was Sir Malcolm Wallace, Lord of Elderslie, and his mother's father was the hereditary Sheriff of Ayr. He spent his boyhood attending the parish church at Paisley, and it is here that "William Wallace contracted the livelong love for the Psalms which lasted until he died."[12] Almost to the end of his life, Wallace aired his desire "to serve God and the Kirk," probably as a pastor in the kirk.[13] William's father's brother was the "mighty parson" of the church at Dunipace, and historical records indicate William spent time under the tutelage of this "full kind man" in his later teenage years.[14] It is from this uncle that William learned the well-known Latin verse (translated below):

"My Son, I tell thee soothfastlie,
No gift is like to liberty;
Then never live in slaverie."

When Edward issued the general ordinance requiring "homage and fealty," there is no record that Sir Malcolm Wallace, William's father, appeared before the deputies at Ayr to take the oath. Consequently, Sir Malcolm was killed by an English deputy at Loudon Hill. He put up a worthy fight. Even after the stalwart knight's legs were sliced out from under him in the scuffle, he continued to battle on his knees until he died.[15]

All accounts indicate that Wallace was well-versed in the Scriptures, probably due to his connection with the church, and his two uncles who served as pastors in nearby parishes.[16] He claimed Christ as his Savior, according to Blind Harry.[17] He was known to pray twice a day, and carried a psalter with him.[18] At his execution, while he was tortured and disemboweled, William Wallace requested that a priest hold his psalter before his eyes so he could meditate on the words of God in his dying moments. Blind Harry includes one of William's prayers in his epic story. While his men were starving as they hid out in the forest, we read,

"He groaned and grieved sore.
Of all this want I am the cause
Yet since it is for Scotland's right and laws,
That thus we suffer by the divine will
Let none of us once grudge or take it ill.
For he that made us by his mighty power,
Can feed us by his providence, I'm sure...
Ah wretch, that ne'er could be content,
With all the wealth that God unto thee sent.
The lordships great, long since to thee assigned,
Could never please my fierce unstable mind.
They willful will to make thy nation free,
Though God's permission's brought this woe to thee;
For worthier by far, than ever I, with hunger now,
Are like to starve and die. O God, I pray,
Relieve them of their pain,
And let not this my prayer be in vain."[19]

We have a glimpse into the faith that motivated Wallace in the battle here. Earlier in the account we read Wallace's own view of just war as they approach the great Battle of Stirling Bridge:

"Who fight for just and righteous ends,
God unto them assistance always sends.
That though the enemy were ten thousand more,
Let's up and beat them as we've done before."[20]

Despite his reputation for intense and vicious attacks on his enemies, Wallace maintained a principled approach to warfare, carefully
excluding priests, women, and children from the slaughter. In Harry's
words:

> "Wouldst thou torment an honest sake's wife? Come forth to me,
> and we shall end the strife. It were great sin to kill the female Scot,
> Art thou a Christian? Tell me, yea or not. In all my victories, I have
> declared, priests, women, children always liberate were."[21]

FIRST FRUITS

Wallace's first major victory occurred at Lanark in May of 1297.
Presumably, the sheriff was there to prosecute the English tax in the
county. Wallace and most of the rest of the Scots did not take kindly
to this. Blind Harry includes the story of the sheriff's men killing Wallace's newly wedded bride, adding a vengeful element. Whatever the
case, this marked the beginning of a coordinated resistance against
the enemy.

Robert the Bruce and others of the nobles took the sideline in
these early days, choosing not to participate in the critical battle at
Stirling Bridge, where Wallace's ragged band of warriors met the Earl
of Surrey and his 5,400 fighting men on September 11, 1297. It was
here that Wallace proved himself to possess "military gifts of a high
order" (in Winston Churchill's words).[22] Just prior to the battle of
Stirling, several of the Scottish lords intervened and pleaded for a
truce in an effort to prevent "needless slaughter" in a battle bearing
such ridiculous odds. To this, Wallace gave his famous reply, "Tell
your commander that we are not here to make peace but to do battle
to defend ourselves and liberate our kingdom. Let them come and we
shall prove this in their very beards."[23] And this they did. Wallace and
his men held the English cavalry using a unique defensive method
called "Schiltrons" or wooden stakes driven into the ground along the
battle line. As the battle proceeded, the Scots cut the bridge down,
divided the army in half, and proceeded to decimate the entire English
army. The victory was a major psychological boost for Scotland.

Never had a small guerrilla force like this completely annihilated a professional army with these odds.

Edward responded like a psychopathic killer. His revenge against Wallace was without restraint. From this point on, "Scotland was to become the obsession of [Edward]'s remaining life, and even beyond the grave, for it is said he gave instructions that on his tomb should be inscribe the vengeful words, 'The hammer of the Scots.'"[24] A year later after Stirling Bridge, Edward executed his revenge against Wallace's army at Falkirk, and virtually wiped out the entire Scottish resistance. Wallace barely escaped alive, but the deed was done. A small force had given the tyrant a run for his money. By this time, Robert the Bruce was energized for the battle for Scotland's independence. He knighted Wallace, and proceeded to conduct his own military expeditions. Though the nation as a whole had lost its will for independence under the strong hand of Edward, a few more leaders began to catch a glimmer of hope for success.

After this, Wallace confined himself to minor raids, joining forces on occasion with a few Scottish nobles including Comyn, Fraser, and others. While a great deal of the nobility settled for peace with Edward at Stratford in 1304, Wallace steadfastly refused.

Not a single Scottish lord was willing to defend Wallace in his lifetime, however. They made no defense at his trial, and they offered no ransom. When it came to resisting the English, he was on his own. The king's pathological hatred for Wallace was palpable in the language of the treaty made with Comyn:

> "No words of peace are to be held out to William Wallace in any circumstances in our will…The Stewart, Sir John De Soulis and Sir Ingram De Umfraville are not to have safe conduct nor come within the King's power until Sir William Wallace is given up…"

Betrayed by his own people and arrested in Glasgow on August 3, 1305, William Wallace was sentenced to death, tortured, castrated, disemboweled while alive; his heart was ripped out, and his body was hacked into four pieces. Edward thought he had rid himself of the last freedom fighter, but instead he had turned Wallace into a national hero. The fires lit at Lanark and Stirling Bridge would never cool.

The rest of the nobles had barely kept their lands by their own acts of treachery and faked oaths of fealty to a treacherous king. But this landless obscure man of lesser nobility (whose first interest was the pastorate), had risked everything he possessed to accomplish more for Scottish independence than those who did nothing more than clutch at their lands and their titles.

ROBERT THE BRUCE

During the initial years of the resistance, both John Comyn and Robert the Bruce played political games, hoping to curry the king's favor in securing the throne of Scotland. However, soon after Wallace's capture and execution, Robert the Bruce was done with the endless train of treachery and perfidy. Late in the summer of 1305, Edward became ill, and some thought death was imminent. Robert the Bruce quickly arranged an agreement with John Comyn. He set forth an offer, "Help me to be king, and I will give you my estates. Or I will help you to be king, and you will give me yours."[25] Comyn chose the former, and documents to that effect were duly signed and sealed. In a final act of treachery though, Comyn sent a copy of the signed document to King Edward. By the providence of God, Robert the Bruce happened to intercept the messenger. Upon confronting Comyn, Robert the Bruce met violent resistance, ending in the death of John Comyn. There was no looking back now. Robert was fully invested in the war for Scotland's independence, and he was on the run.

King Edward chased down Robert's friends, and subjected most of them to a fate similar to that of William Wallace. Pursued to the very far reaches of Scotland, Robert the Bruce attempted to move his wife and sisters to safety, only to be betrayed by the Earl of Ross. Fearing the loss of lands, the earl handed the women off to Edward as an act of allegiance—who subjected them to gross humiliation and imprisonment for at least eight years in England.

By early January 1307, the man who would be King of Scotland was reduced to almost nothing. His friends were killed or captured. His lands were gone. His wife was in enemy hands. His brothers Thomas and Alexander had been hung, drawn, and quartered. The prospects were grim. However, as one historian describes Robert the Bruce, "[he] had a toughness and determination so strong that he was inspired to undertake one of the most colossal gambles in history."[26]

For a while, he hid out on an island with a renegade sea captain, Angus MacDonald of the Isles. He fought ground skirmishes through the highlands of western Scotland. He barely escaped with his own life many times. At one point, upon narrowly averting enemy hands, he found himself at the cottage of a poor widow. The exchange is especially poignant:

"He told her that he was a traveler passing through the country, to which she replied that all travelers were welcomed for the sake of one. He asked who that one might be.

'Our good King Robert the Bruce,' she answered, 'who is the rightful lord of this country.'

Then he said, 'I am that man.'

'But where are your men?' she asked.

'At the moment I have none.'

'This must not be,' she cried, 'for though I am a widow I have three stout sons each by a different husband, Murdoch, McKie, and MacLurg, and they shall become your sworn men.'"[27]

In April 1307, the Earl of Pembroke gathered 1500 knights and attempted a surprise attack on Robert's camp at Glen Trool at the foot of Mount Merrick. By God's providence, a woman revealed the earl's plans to Robert the Bruce, and his 300 men overwhelmed the English troops. He defeated a second army of 3,000 a month later at Loudoun Hill, and soon thereafter the tables began to turn.

A few months later, on July 11, 1307, Edward I died. In his last moments, he requested that his flesh be peeled away from his bones, and the English armies carry his bones into battle with the Scots. The king's maniacal obsession with subduing this freedom-loving people under English tyrannical rule did not abate until the very end. His son, Edward II, ignored the request, and it was years before England attempted any serious conflict with Scotland. This allowed Robert the Bruce plenty of time to assemble his armies, solidify his rule, and root out the English influence in his country, castle by castle.

The tyrant was dead. As in the case of Robert FitzWalter's conflict with King John, one of the best strategies to overcome tyrants is to outlive them. This strategy has been proven repeatedly throughout history. Good overcomes evil, as it persists and endures to the end. The principle derived from Psalm 37 and elsewhere in Scripture remains constant—the wicked flourish for a while, but they soon wither as the green herb (Ps. 37:2).

In sharp contrast with Edward's vindictive and cruel policies, Robert the Bruce was generous with his enemies almost to a fault. The Bruce readily forgave the man who turned his own wife over to the English. Despite the Earl of Ross' lack of integrity, Robert allowed him to hold on to his lands so long as he asked pardon for his trespasses. He also treated Dugald MacDowall, the man responsible for the deaths of his brothers, with magnanimity (although the man betrayed him later on). Though Robert felt he may have crossed over the line in his quarrel with Comyn, he carefully sought forgiveness from family members and from God on several occasions for his part in the fatal exchange.

Ranked among the three most accomplished knights in all of Europe, Robert the Bruce was a formidable warrior against the enemy. In multiple instances, he would dispense with four or five attackers simultaneously. At the battle of Inverurie, he dragged himself from a sick bed onto a horse, and proceeded to lead his men to an important victory. "As the Lord wills," he told his men, "I shall either destroy them or they me."[28]

On March 17, 1309, the Scottish parliament officially crowned Robert the Bruce King of Scotland. The same assembly issued a Declaration of Independence. Not surprisingly, Pope Clement V, in sympathy with the centralizing efforts of Edward II, pronounced excommunication upon Robert the Bruce, "for damnably persevering in iniquity."[29] The Scottish clergy immediately called a convocation, and issued a statement to all the faithful, declaring Robert the Bruce "chosen before God and man as the rightful King of Scotland, that he might reform what is deformed, correct that which needs correction and straighten that which has gone awry."[30] Not surprisingly, this independent country became a hotbed of the Protestant Reformation, a mere 250 years later.

JUNE 1314 - BANNOCKBURN

Seven years after his father died, upon hearing of Robert's coronation, Edward II had had enough of it. He wasn't about to let Scotland slip from his grasp, although that is exactly what had happened since his father's passing. Edward assembled an army of 20,000, including 2,500 seasoned cavalry. England's confidence in their war machine had never been greater, especially in view of their opposition. Robert the Bruce's army was only 5,000 strong, and hardly a professional army, something scraped together over seven hard years of guerrilla warfare.

The troops assembled in a valley called Bannockburn. On the morning of June 23, 1314, the Scottish troops held a prayer service and heard the preaching of the Word. They observed a fast, and their King offered to each division the Deuteronomy 20 exemption (allowing any who feared the confrontation to leave). On the morning of June 24, Robert addressed his troops with words that draw an important distinction between wicked and righteous rule, sinful and righteous warfare:

> "Sirs, we have every reason to be confident of success for we have right on our side. Our enemies are moved only by desire for dominion, but we are fighting for our lives, our wives, and the freedom of our country. And so I ask and pray that with all your strength, without cowardice or alarm, you meet the foes whom you will first encounter so boldly that those behind them will tremble...You could have lived quietly as slaves, but because you longed to be free you are with me here, and to gain that end you must be valiant, strong and undismayed..."[31]

The pastors preached again, this time from Isaiah 40, and the men prepared for the battle of their lives—the battle that would direct the future of nations over centuries of human existence. Robert rallied the men to advance, but then something unexpected happened. We have the account from the English side:

"When Edward II saw the Scots coming forward on foot over open ground he cried in amazement, 'What, will yonder Scots fight?'

"To which Sir Ingram de Umfraville replied, 'Surely sir: but indeed this is the strangest sight I ever saw for Scotsmen to take on the whole might of England by giving battle on hard ground.' And even as he spoke the Scots, who were not some hundred yards away, knelt down and made a short prayer to God to help them in the fight, at which the English King exclaimed triumphantly, 'They kneel for mercy!'

"Sir Ingram replied, 'For mercy, yes, *but not from you*: from God for their sins. These men will win all or die.'" [32]

Fateful words. God's mercy turned out to be of higher importance in the battle than the mercy of a human king, as important though Edward may have felt himself to be. The English could not break the hedgerow of spears that the Scots presented to them. With all of the force of cavalry the English could muster, they could not break that line. The spirit of the English quailed, and the Scots kept their steamroller of twelve-foot pikes moving. The English king quickly abandoned the field as the Scots drew closer. At the key moment, Robert the Bruce gave the signal, and several thousand untrained camp followers, cooks, and roadies rushed down the hill carrying banners on poles, hollering at the top of their lungs, "Upon them! Upon them!" This was more than the weary English army could bear. Thinking it was a second army coming upon them, the English men abandoned the field, and the victory was secured for the Bruce and his men.

THE AFTERMATH

Seventeen years after William Wallace and his ragged band descended on Lanark, Scotland's war for independence from England was finally over. Until the horrible reign of the Stuarts 300 years later, Scotland continued to enjoy independence.

Several years after Bannockburn, Robert the Bruce offered assistance to Ireland if they should like to seek independence from England as well. His interest was to "permanently strengthen and maintain inviolate that special friendship between us and you, so that with

God's will your nation may be able to recover her ancient liberty."[33]

Despite England's refusal to acknowledge Scotland's independence and settle for peace, Robert the Bruce continued requesting this of Edward II. In this letter penned in 1319, Robert wrote:

> "We in our humility have judged it right to entreat of your Highness most earnestly that, having before your eyes the righteousness you owe to God and to the people, you desist from persecuting us and disturbing the people of our realm, so that there may be an end of slaughter and shedding Christian blood."

Finally, on April 6, 1320, the Scottish Parliament of Lords, produced the "Declaration of Arbroath", which is generally recognized as the first declaration of independence. The document is essentially an apologetic arranged as a letter to the pope. Portions of it are included below.

First, the assembly offered a brief history of the Christian church in Scotland:

> "The high qualities and merits of these people, were they not otherwise manifest, shine forth clearly enough from this: that the King of kings and Lord of lords, our Lord Jesus Christ, after His Passion and Resurrection, called them, even though settled in the uttermost parts of the earth, almost the first to His most holy faith. Nor did He wish them to be confirmed in that faith by merely anyone but by the first of His Apostles—by calling, though second or third in rank—the most gentle Saint Andrew, the Blessed Peter's brother, and desired him to keep them under his protection as their patron forever."

Then, the assembly reviewed the tyranny of English rule:

> "Thus our people under their protection did indeed live in freedom and peace up to the time when that mighty prince the King of the English, Edward, the father of the one who reigns today, when our kingdom had no head and our people harboured no malice or treachery and were then unused to wars or invasions, came in a guise of a friend and ally to harass them as an enemy. The deeds of cruelty, massacre, violence, pillage, arson, imprisoning prelates, burning down monasteries, robbing and killing monks and nuns and yet other outrages without number which he committed against our people,

sparing neither age nor sex, religion nor rank, no one could describe nor fully imagine unless he had seen them with his own eyes."

Following this, the assembly underscored the freedoms obtained by Robert the Bruce:

"But from these countless evils we have been set free, by the help of Him who though He afflicts yet heals and restores, by our most tireless prince, King and lord, the lord Robert. He, that his people and his heritage might be delivered out of the hands of our enemies, bore cheerfully toil and fatigue, hunger and peril, like another Maccabaeus or Joshua. Him, too, divine providence, the succession to his right according to our laws and customs which we shall maintain to the death, and the due consent and assent of us all have made our prince and king. To him, as to the man by whom salvation has been wrought unto our people, we are bound both by his right and by his merits that our freedom may be still maintained, and by him, come what may, we mean to stand."

Finally, the men pledged every ounce of blood in the nation to ensure the maintenance of that independence:

"Yet if he should give up what he has begun, seeking to make us or our kingdom subject to the King of England or the English, we should exert ourselves at once to drive him out as our enemy and a subverter of his own right and ours, and make some other man who was well able to defend us our King; for, as long as a hundred of us remain alive, never will we on any conditions be subjected to the lordship of the English. It is in truth not for glory, nor riches, nor honours that we are fighting, but for freedom alone, which no honest man gives up but with life itself."[34]

CONCLUSION

Scotland's great struggle for independence is a vital part of the story of freedom in the Western world. Each story presents a check for tyrannical governments, especially here in the West. These are the reasons that the most free nations in the world to this day are America, England, Scotland, Netherlands, Canada, and so on. At present, tyranny is on the rise worldwide. Should the Lord tarry, the heritage of liberty in the Western world must be passed on to another place and another time in human history. This legacy must be preserved at the highest costs. Freedom is a rarity, and it is not easily maintained or won.

While documents like the Magna Carta and the "Declaration of Arbroath" laid down the foundations for freedom, the Kings and Queens of England contributed little to the cause. They were too busy building their power base. It was the Scottish struggle that did the most to build up this heritage. The Reformation in Scotland was more effective than that in England under the Tudors, thanks largely to the independence of the church. Towards the end of the American War for Independence, some in the English parliament referred to the war as the Scottish Presbyterian Conflict. For it was the Scotch-Irish Presbyterians in South Carolina that turned the battle, and we shall tell the story later on in this account of the history of Western liberties. The United States Declaration of Independence also finds its prototype in the "Declaration of Arbroath." It is a legacy never to be forgotten.

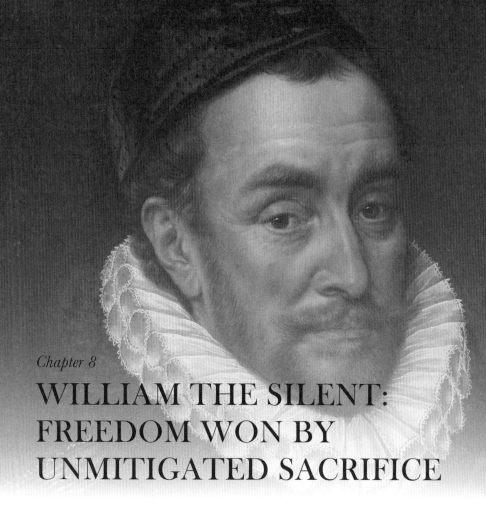

Chapter 8

WILLIAM THE SILENT: FREEDOM WON BY UNMITIGATED SACRIFICE

The noble William, Prince of Orange, rode with his troops into Rijsel of Flanders in the early fall of 1558. It was obvious at first glance that this was a man of wealth, privilege, and position. Since he was just a young lad the prince had been specially favored by the great emperor Charles. In his early adult years, William had proven himself a capable military leader. He seldom lost a battle with the enemies of the empire, and he was immensely popular in the court. Now, at 25 years of age, the young man exuded confidence, strength, winsomeness, and political position. Dashing, daring, and well received by just about everybody at the capitol of Brussels, William was at the height of his political career. Little did he know that his life's direction would shift dramatically in the space of a single year.

"What is the smoke that rises over yonder street?" he asked a priest who was hurrying along the road at the edge of the town.

"It is the Inquisition," the man of the cloth replied. "Titelmann has caught another wretch and his two sons, and they shall burn."

"What is the crime, my man? What possible evil have these miserable souls committed to warrant such a dreadful end?" William further inquired.

"They have admitted to falling on their knees and praying that God would enlighten their minds and pardon their sins," he said, quickly adding in a hushed tone, "They do this in secret. They pray for their magistrates, that God would preserve them. These are their words they testified to the judge in the trial."

"Harsh punishment for such a confession," William offered.

"No, no." The priest insisted. "Titelmann has shown his leniency. These men absent themselves from mass. But the inquisitor has graciously released the younger boy and consigned the father and eldest son to the fire."

Sending his men ahead, William proceeded by himself to the place of execution. There he heard the voice of a youth who could not have been older than 16 years, crying out at the stake: "O God, Eternal Father, accept the sacrifice of our lives in the name of thy beloved Son!"[1]

A monk sharply corrected the lad, "Thou liest, scoundrel! God is not your father, ye are the devil's children."[2]

As the flames rose, William heard the boy speak to his father, "Look my father, all heaven is opening, and I see ten hundred thousand angels rejoicing over us. Let us be glad, for we are dying of the truth."[3]

"Thou liest, thou liest!" The monk screamed in a maniacal voice.

The men in the fire paid no attention to the monk. William continued hearing the father and son speaking to each other in low tones, even as the flames burned at their hottest and consumed the flesh off the bones of these martyrs until they expired.

William stood by his horse transfixed, staring quietly into the flames for several minutes. Several stories of these tortures and killings had already met his ears, particularly since Philip's ascension to the Spanish throne. As he contemplated the meaning of such injustices, he could not help but question...well, everything...the powers that legitimized such miserable, devilish work—the cardinals...the bishops...the pope...the emperor. Surely, the fault did not lie merely with a third-rate petty tyrant like this Peter Titelmann. Was there something quite corrupt and evil lying at the root of the empire itself?

* * *

It was early December of the same year as William approached the town of Antwerp. He was on official business to raise monies to prosecute the war with France, and Antwerp was the financial capital of the Lower Countries. Not a mile from the entrance to the city, somewhere near to the road he heard a raised voice—the unmistakable tone of preaching. "What is this religious service out here in the fields?" He asked his colleague, a man who did business regularly in the town.

"It is the Dutch Reformed Protestants." The man replied. "They have taken to preaching in the open air."

"Haven't they seen the placards?" William enjoined. "Philip swore to his father he would prosecute the Inquisition at his ascendance to the throne."

"Aye. But these Protestants feel they have no choice. If they continue with their secret conventicles, they are subjected to popular mistrust, slander, and false accusations from the Inquisition. Many have been unjustly accused as witches and Cathari and worse—and public opinion turns hard against them. Also, their numbers are growing and they cannot very well meet in secret and avoid detection by the authorities."

William could see the size of the crowd from his vantage point. There had to have been as many as 3,000 congregants in the field listening to the preacher.

Just then, the two men heard the sounds of hooves beating hard on the road. They witnessed a large Spaniard corps led by the sheriff from Antwerp approach, and veer off towards the field where the people were gathered.

His companion explained, "The leader is a Calvinist preacher by the name of Van Haemstede. Last time I had heard, the Inquisition had a price of 300 gulden on his head."

"What will happen to these people?" William asked.

"No doubt they will capture the leaders and their families. They will apply quite exquisite tortures to their mortal bodies, and then consign them to the flames. That is the typical treatment."

Just then, a man rushed out to the road with what appeared to be his wife and two daughters close behind him. It was clear that these were avoiding capture at the hands of the Spaniards. As the man approached William, it seemed that he recognized the fact that he was in the presence of a man of position.

"Sir William of Orange?" He asked.

William nodded.

The man bowed, and said, "I plead for clemency at the hands of your honor. Have mercy on my wife and my daughters!"

"And who do I have the pleasure of addressing?" William asked.

"I am Anton Verdickt, and these are my wife and children."

"What can I do for you?"

"These Spaniards intend to submit myself and my family to the powers of the inquisitors, and this will be the end of us." The man replied, sweat running down his face. "I cannot bear to see my daughters tortured and drowned."

"But why should they come after you?" William further inquired.

"I am a teaching elder of the Protestant church in Antwerp. I have preached from the Scripture, in opposition to the king's placards," the man replied.

William looked at the tender children standing beside their father, neither of whom could have been older than 10 years of age. He could not imagine what it would be like if his own children were subject to the torture of severed limbs, burning, or drowning. But what could he do? His position as Councillor of State, appointed by King Philip himself, made it nigh impossible to oppose the Spanish king's agenda in Antwerp. After all, he had come to advance it by raising funds for the armies of the empire. Yet, his heart burned within him. These were innocent children; helpless citizens persecuted by the state.

"There is not much I can do for you, do you understand? I hear the courts of Antwerp offer more mercy to the Protestants than those in Flanders," William said weakly. Within seconds, the Spanish troop of twenty soldiers had surrounded the family and taken them into custody.

Several weeks later, news reached William's ears that seven Calvinists had been executed in Antwerp—four men, one woman, and two young girls.

THE INQUISITION

Although roots of the Inquisition date back into the 1200s and 1300s when the Pope joined forces with the state to exterminate the Cathari and the Waldensians, the Spanish Inquisition began in earnest in 1478. Both Charles V and his son Philip II bear most of the responsibility for the deaths of those killed in Spain. This Inquisition sent the first Protestants to the stake in Spain in 1540, and by 1559, 87 percent of the victims were Protestant.[4] After his father left the throne, Philip II affirmed his commitment to the repulsive business when he told a victim appealing for his mercy, "I myself would bring the faggots to burn my own son, were he as perverse as you."[5]

In the case of the Netherlands, Charles incorporated something called the "Placard" as early as 1531, in order to criminalize all expressions of Protestantism as a capital offense.[6] He called the Reformed faith "treason against God," and distinguished it as an "exceptional crime," not subject to normal legal procedures and privileges in the Netherlands. Upon Charles' abdication in 1556, the proceedings conducted in Brussels included the publishing of a political agenda that would govern the empire in the ensuing years. The dreaded placards were particularly emphasized in his agenda (using the following language):

> "Above all to observe the placards or edicts regarding religion which Charles had published..."[7]

The key phrase "above all" rendered a chilling effect upon the reforming people of the Low Countries. In the succeeding years, Philip II did not disappoint his father. Effectively, he took up the Rehoboam policy recorded in 1 Kings 12:11: "And now whereas my father did lade you with a heavy yoke, I will add to your yoke: my father hath chastised you with whips, but I will chastise you with scorpions." The persecutions heated up when Philip II sent one Fernando Álvarez de Toledo, or the Duke of Alva into the Netherlands, to prosecute the Dutch Inquisition in 1567.

To this day, Christians and non-Christians alike condemn the tyrannical Roman Catholic inquisitions. These make for some of the blackest marks on the face of religion and human civil government in all of history. When tyranny or despotism is mentioned, the Inquisition comes to mind immediately. True, the humanist, apostate leaders like Hitler and Stalin killed their millions in the twentieth century. However, the tyrants overseeing the inquisitions killed equally large percentages of the overall population. The inquisitions majored in spurious accusations, and the Cathari and Waldensians were usually subjected to false accusations of witchcraft, probably the easiest to prosecute. In one canton in Switzerland where an inquisition was prosecuted, archives indicate some 3,371 victims were executed.[8] The Spanish Inquisition at first was more concerned with Jews than with Protestants, and claimed anywhere between 30,000 and 300,000 victims.[9] The Dutch Inquisition pursued by the Habsburgs in the Netherlands claimed the lives of 18,000 men, women, and children (and that only accounts for what the Duke of Alva admitted to killing). This amounts to approximately one percent of the population. If this were applied to modern day America, the elimination of one percent of the population would account for 3,000,000 men, women, and children.

Almost no other historical travesty compares to the horrors of the Inquisition. Many gross violations of biblical law surface in these kangaroo courts and religious persecutions (reference Deut. 19:15-19, 2 Cor. 13:1). Some malevolent spiritual force must have infected the highest echelons of power during the later medieval period. Certainly, it was an unholy coalition between the powerful Pope and the powerful kings of Europe.

The all-powerful humanist state will always attempt to control the beliefs and thoughts of every citizen dwelling within its purview. Extremely rigid rules for private speech, the press, and assembly usually develop. If Old Testament law at any point required uniformity of thought and belief within Israel, then the Parable of the Wheat and the Tares clearly modifies this point (Matt. 13:29). Both wheat and tares grow together in the world (the field), and they may not be separated until the end by Divine dictate. Moreover, foreigners could freely operate in Old Testament Israel without being forced into participation with the religious rites such as circumcision and Passover. Sometimes Deuteronomy 13 is used to legitimize all forms of thought crime and religious persecution, however this applies the text wrongly. Jesus Christ clarified this in Matthew 13:29. Nonetheless, Deuteronomy 13 references false teachers or apostates who are demonic miracle workers (verses 1-2). Elsewhere, the law informs us that serving false gods involves human sacrifice (Lev. 18:21, Deut. 18:10). Still to this day, there are limits to which most governments will allow such religious practices. Human and animal sacrifices to false gods are ordinarily prohibited by Christian governments, and for good reason.

ENTER WILLIAM OF ORANGE

There aren't many great heroes for liberty in history who gave it all. Political leaders don't usually give much at all, especially those of the Gentile ilk. In the war for liberty, the foot soldiers are called to give it all, and they seldom receive the earthly honor due them. Yet there was one outstanding visionary leader in this epochal war for liberty who is worthy of this honor. He sacrificed everything he had to give: his own freedom, his reputation, his honor, his earthly possessions, his brothers, his son, and ultimately his life for the cause of liberty. Comparably few books have been written on this man's life and contribution to the great cause of freedom. No scholarly work is presently in print at the time of this publication, and only a few children's books on the life of William of Orange are available via obscure publishers.

Nonetheless, honest historians would certainly place this man in the "History's Heroes Hall of Fame." William the Silent belongs in the lineage of the greatest leaders who fought the battle for religious and political liberty. His name is well-known in history; it is just that nobody knows very much about him. In a world dominated by tyrants, no wonder the heroes of liberty get lost in the shuffle. Few people outside of Holland know anything specific about what this great leader did to advance the cause of liberty in our world. Generally the populace prefers to hear about the magnificent tyrannies. When it comes to worldly history-telling, William the Silent has three strikes plus one against him. First, he was successful in gaining some margin of liberty for his people. Second, he was a true reforming Christian. Third, he sacrificed everything for the people he loved. Fourth, he was murdered at the behest of "more important" powerful men who ruled the world (or thought they did). William the Silent was the ultimate underdog, and his story is one of the very best stories ever told. For the rest of time, this man will be the hero for every other underdog who ever had a vision for freedom under severe tyranny.

William was born into the Holy Roman Empire on April 23, 1533. This misbegotten empire arrived at the zenith of its power under Charles V, who reigned between 1519 and 1556. For centuries, the empire had struggled to centralize power over Germany, Netherlands, Switzerland, Hungary, Austria, and Italy. Under Charles V, this empire extended westward into Spain, southward into Naples, Italy, and northward into Poland. His major adversary and contender for power in Europe was France. Arguably, Charles V was the most powerful king since the days of the Roman Caesars. The German Reformation had weakened Charles' hold on certain German provinces, and he was determined to prevent any such thing from happening in the Netherlands.

To fully understand the horrors of the Inquisition is to know something of William's passion for liberty and his desire to protect the Dutch people from the Spanish tyrants. This is nicely expressed in his own words in what he called his Apology written four years before he died.

> "I was bred up a Catholic and a worldling, but the horrible persecution that I witnessed by fire, sword, and water, and the plot to introduce a worse than Spanish Inquisition which I learned from the King of France, made me resolve in my soul to rest not till I had chased from the land these locusts of Spain. I confess that I sought

to ally my friends and nobles of the land to resist these horrors, and I glory in that deed. And of the resistance to the tyranny of Spain in all its stages I take the responsibility, for I view with indignation the bloodthirsty cruelties, worse than those of any tyrant of antiquity, which they have inflicted upon the poor people of this land."[10]

Who would ever disagree with his sentiment and his life mission? Who would not cheer at this cry for liberty and repudiation of tyranny? These are words that reflect the heart and the life of a true leader and hero for the cause of liberty. We shall validate the truthfulness of these words and the character of this man's life by revisiting the historical facts in the remainder of the chapter.

From all historical reports, young William lived a happy life with his parents at the Castle in Dillenburg, where his father was known as the Count of Nassau. During his eleventh year, his cousin René of Chalons died in battle leaving no progeny as heir to the principality of Orange, a territory far off to the Southwest in France. The office then fell to young William. However, this introduced a conundrum to Charles V, the emperor who ruled over the lands in which William and his family lived. He was certainly aware that both of William's parents had received the Reformation faith, thanks to the influence of Martin Luther. There was nothing that perturbed the powerful "holy Roman" emperor as much as the Protestant influence in Europe, perhaps even more so than the Muslim incursions from the south. Therefore the king required one condition for William's title—that he be raised in Brussels, the city of birth and residence for Charles V and his family. Consequently, William was assigned to the household of Queen Marie, Regent of the Netherlands and Sister to Charles V. According to one historian: "The Emperor was persuaded to fulfil the solemn promises he had made to Prince René [William's cousin], but he remained inexorable in regard to the exclusion of the father from the slightest jurisdiction over his son's person or his property."[11] William's story is very similar to that of Moses, who though raised in Pharaoh's household, pursued a very different course later on in his life.

During his young adult years, William faithfully fought the empire's wars for King Charles V and King Philip II (after Charles' abdication in 1556). William was silent concerning his disagreements with the empire during these years. After the war ended with France, William joined Philip in Paris for the peace negotiations in 1559. In part, to reward William for his faithful military service in the war against France, Philip appointed him Governor (or Stadtholder) of the Netherlands. This was a decision the King would live to regret.

While in Paris, two seemingly innocuous events occurred that would define William as a true opponent of tyrannical government and a defender of liberty. While he was on a hunt with members of the French nobility, some miscreant lowered a hook through the iron grating of a window above William's room, and lifted his silverware. Several hours or days later, somebody informed him that the culprit had been captured, and was about to hang for his crime. Immediately, William took his horse at full gallop for the gallows, and held off the execution until he had approval from the King of France for the dismissal of the case. "[The thief] was dismissed after a little gratuitous sermon from his deliverer as to the evil of his ways and the need of radical reform."[12] According to biblical law, no man is to be hung for the crime of theft (reference Ex. 22:1-3). Wherever inappropriately severe punishments like this are meted out, they are examples of tyranny—men asserting power over men apart from God's laws.

The second providential event which would set the course of his life and the rest of history took place in the forests of Vincennes. There are these singularly significant moments in the life of a person that shift the direction of the flow of all of human history. This was one of those instances. As a consequence of these events, William of Orange would be known for the rest of history as William the Silent.

The young prince was on another hunting excursion around the same timeframe that he was robbed, but this time he was with the King of France. They found themselves alone together in the forest. The King quite unexpectedly began to speak of a conversation he had with Philip II during the negotiations. (This is the meeting that William mentions in his Apology written 21 years later.)

> "When I was in France, I heard out of King Henry's own mouth
> that the Duke of Alva had discussed with him the annihilation of

all suspected of the religion in France, in the Netherlands, and in all Christendom. The king thought, since I was one of the plenipotentiaries in the peace negotiations, that I was informed of this important circumstance and that I belonged to the same party. So he revealed to me the secret schemes of the King of Spain and the Duke of Alva."[13]

Maintaining his characteristic rock-hard self-control and keenly wise judgment for which history will always remember him, William only listened in complete silence. But under that iron-clad exterior, his passions burned white-hot towards these heinous plans. He testified further concerning the resolution that formed in his heart then and there, "I confess that from that moment I determined in earnest to chase the Spanish vermin from the land and I never repented my resolution."[14] If the King of France had seen through the impassive exterior, would the Empire have rid itself of that resistance boiling within the heart of William the Silent?

Philip was true to the commitment he had made to Henry of France. Inquisitors were appointed throughout the provinces, and a certain Peter Titelmann proved himself the most indefatigable of them. He left meticulous historical records of every grotesque detail concerning the arrests, the tortures, and the executions conducted under his watch. The following summarizes the horrible deeds committed by this tyrant.

"He executed his infamous functions throughout Flanders, Douay, and Tournay, the most thriving and populous portions of the Netherlands, with a swiftness, precision, and even with a jocularity which hardly seemed human. There was a kind of grim humor about the man. The woman who, according to Lear's fool, was wont to thrust her live eels into the hot paste, 'rapping them o' the coxcombs with a stick and crying reproachfully, Wantons, lie down!' had the spirit of a true inquisitor. Even so dealt Titelmann with his heretics writhing on the rack or in the flames. Contemporary chronicles give a picture of him as of some grotesque yet terrible goblin, careering through the country by night or day, alone, on horseback, smiting the trembling peasants on the head with a great club, spreading dismay far and wide, dragging suspected persons from their firesides or their beds, and thrusting them into dungeons, arresting, torturing, strangling, burning, with hardly the shadow of warrant, information, or process.

"The secular sheriff, familiarly called Red-Rod, from the color of his wand of office, meeting this inquisitor Titelmann one day upon the high road, thus wonderingly addressed him—'How can you venture to go about alone, or at most with an attendant or two, arresting people on every side, while I dare not attempt to execute my office, except at the head of a strong force, armed in proof; and then only at the peril of my life?' 'Ah! Red-Rod,' answered Peter, jocosely, 'you deal with bad people. I have nothing to fear, for I seize only the innocent and virtuous, who make no resistance, and let themselves be taken like lambs.'"[15]

Philip could hardly hold back his enthusiasm when commending the inquisition work, claiming it to be "much more pitiless than that of Spain."[16] It was truly a reign of terror, a hell on earth hardly ever seen before.

"Men and women were broken on the wheel, racked, dragged at horses tails, their sight was extinguished, their tongues torn out by the roots, their hands and feet burned and twisted off between red hot irons. They were starved, drowned, hanged, burned, killed in every slow and agonizing way that the malicious inventiveness of priests could devise. Sometimes they were suspended by the feet and lingered in misery for days. Sometimes racked, torn tongueless, their arms and legs were fastened together behind their backs and each was hooked by the middle of the body to an iron chain; and then made to swing to and fro over a slow fire until entirely roasted."[17]

On January 24, 1566, William the Silent finally intervened with an official appeal. Although his position as Stadtholder was only that of an advisor to Margaret, Philip's Regent in Brussels, this marked his first public statement opposing the king's agenda in the Netherlands. Excerpts of his appeal follow:

"The opposition excited by the establishment of the new bishoprics was wholly caused by the fear lest under this guise some form of the inquisition might be introduced; moreover your Highness must remember that his imperial Majesty and Queen Mary repeatedly assured the inhabitants of the Netherlands, by word of mouth and in proclamations, that the said inquisition should never be introduced, and that these provinces should be maintained as of old...As to the third point by which his Majesty orders all the placards issued by the emperor and the king to be literally carried out in all rigor; Madame, this seems to me very hard, as the placards are numerous and diverse, and have never been enforced, even when there was not such widespread misery as at present...and now their execution would be unbearable, and hence inexpedient."[18]

Finally, William threatened his resignation over the enforcement of the tyrannical edicts: "I would prefer to resign rather than incur the blemish which would stain me and mine if misfortune came to the lands under my charge."[19] The queen refused his resignation. Henceforth, he proceeded to organize a formal petition signed by the nobles of the Netherlands, addressed to the Regent and to Philip II. On March 29, 1566, William appeared at the official Council meeting in Brussels, and addressed the matter plainly, "To see a man burn for his opinions, does harm to the people; the judges will not execute the placards, and the rigorous decrees do nothing to maintain religion." His advice to the council: "Draw up a draft of moderation." Margaret responded by refusing to rescind the placards, but agreed to recommend "gentleness and discretion" in the enforcement of them.[20]

William well perceived the tremendous instability to the entire social order brought about by the violent, lawless inquisition. Lawless tyranny typically produces lawless anarchy from the dregs of society, resulting in a truly dreadful state of affairs for a country. Given that the Queen Regent still leaned heavily upon William to maintain civil order in the state, his position became increasingly untenable. In one report for the Regent concerning the state of affairs in Antwerp, he told her that "the city was divided against itself. The magistrates distrusted the citizens; the citizens, the court and magistrates; the Protestants, the court, magistrates, and other citizens; and finally the Protestants were themselves divided, on one side Calvinists, Lutherans on the other, with the Anabaptists antagonistic to both." Despite great political opposition to public sermons, William fought hard to retain rights for each party to preach their sermons, as long as they were given "quietly and peaceably." Several weeks later, on August 25th, Margaret agreed to the policy of moderation, signing articles stipulating "that public preaching should be accorded to the dissenters in all places where sermons had already taken place."[21] She furthered declared the Inquisition to be put in abeyance.

In early 1567, William once again offered his resignation to the Regent, in response to the King's requirement of an oath that would have bound him to participate in killing his own citizenry. Again, the Regent refused to accept his offer to resign. On April 10, he issued his letter of recusal to the King and fled the country. Now considered a traitor by both Margaret and Philip, William was to be a wanted man for the rest of his life. As one historian put it, "Surely, never did a traitor—and from the Spanish point of view, such was Orange undoubtedly—leave the land which he had resolved to free from a tyrant's hand, with a deliberation equal to that of William of Nassau."[22] His decision to resign would become his death sentence. As it was, he surrendered his properties in the Netherlands, his position of authority, and his reputation throughout the empire. Williams' career in the echelons of power amongst the ruling elite of Europe was over.

During the next few difficult years, William was also beset by a bad marriage to an adulterous and unfaithful woman, Anna of Saxony. Although ostensibly a Protestant, she was highly unsupportive of William's principled stand and resignation. She undercut him at every point, her main concern being retention of her possessions and status in the Netherlands.

William wrote a letter to Anna's uncle who served as her ward, in which his concerns focused mainly on the spiritual. "We have indeed noticed for some time in your niece, not without deep anxiety, an uncertainty in religious matters, and that she cares little for religious things or teachers, and occasionally even talks shamefully of God's word. Also I must consider that your ward might, on this very account, be turned from the true knowledge of Christ (although formerly she had such a warm inclination for religion) to popish horrors, or other errors painful to you, and of a kind to make my life wretched, and prove a bad example to many."[23]

When she and her paramour were finally caught, William refused the death penalty for the two (as would have been the custom of the period).[24] Anna died a dissipated and insane woman shortly after the divorce.

Meanwhile, Philip was wasting no time in restoring the Inquisition with even greater force, sending the dreaded Duke of Alva into the Netherlands. Alva created the Council of Troubles, its authority superseding all other courts in the land. "Its function was to dispose summarily of every case having to do with treason towards the king or dissension from the Church. This court violated in the most flagrant manner all the cherished privileges of the provinces. The conviction of any offence was punished by death, and so swift and sanguinary was the so-called course of justice on the slightest web of evidence, that the Netherlanders, epigrammatic even in their darkest hours, dubbed the tribunal the 'Blood Council.'"[25]

Effectively, Alva was made a dictator in the tradition of Idi Amin, Fidel Castro, Pol Pot, Vladimir Lenin, Robespierre, and Adolf Hitler. He proceeded to murder two key leaders in the government of the Netherlands, Egmont and Horn, both of whom had been devout Catholics and unrelentingly loyal to the king. Their only crime was their acquaintance with William of Orange. A warrant for William's arrest was issued, charging him with every manner of treason, as well as promoting heresy and schism in the realm. William's eldest son Phillip was kidnapped and exiled to Spain for the succeeding twenty years.

In answer to the pleas coming from the nobles, governors, and cities of the Netherlands, William went to work assembling an army to rescue the people out from under the iron grip of Alva. Armies cost money, and this one especially was no exception to that rule. It was hard for William to find anyone willing to fight except for foreign mercenaries from Germany, France, and Italy. Of his own funds, he provided 50,000 florins for the cause, which constituted the proceeds from sale of his personal belongings (tapestries, jewels, etc.). Others contributed 25,000 florins or less. William's brothers also offered their own possessions and lives into the conflict.

In a key battle near Groningen that fell in favor of the Nassau brothers, brother Adolph was killed. The war turned against them quickly as early as 1568. Initially, William faced lackluster involvement from the Dutch themselves. Their leaders were fearful (after all, they were all subjected to a reign of terror). Hence, there was no appreciable internal organization. To make matters worse, the bitter and blind sectarianism among the Protestant factions prevented unity among the not-so-loyal opposition. William fought in a number of important battles, but his more significant role involved raising funds for his armies. Meanwhile, Alva found a convenient way to raise funds for his military force—by levying taxes against the Dutch, a one percent, one-time property tax, a five percent tax on every transfer of property, and a ten percent tax on sales. Although these taxes amount to only a fraction of what modern citizens are used to paying to federal and state governments, at that time they were received as draconian and highly unreasonable measures. The nobles refused to pay the five and ten percent tax outright.

For several years, the whole contest amounted to one-on-one conflict between William and the European tyranny. By 1571, he was virtually bankrupt. He encouraged the faithful by writing letters, and providing wise counsel to the fledgling resistance within Holland. But then the tide turned, quite unexpectedly.

On April 1, 1572, in the providence of God, a convoy of twenty-four ships, carrying a fledgling band of disorganized freedom fighters made port at Brill in North Holland. The shipmen known as "the Beggars" were starving, having been denied admittance from English ports by Elizabeth. They were hoping for a little food; however, they found the town deserted—the magistrates afraid that the city was come under attack. So the Beggars proceeded to claim the town "in the name of William of Orange, as legitimate stadtholder." Shortly thereafter, the town burghers returned and agreed to take the oath of allegiance to William of Orange as well. This diminutive resistance held off a counterattack from Alva's troops, and it wasn't long before other towns joined the movement and took the oath to William. These included Flushing, Zealand, Friesland, Guelderland, and Utrecht. From this time forwards, "the people raised the prince's standard and he became the personification of resistance to the tenth penny [ten percent tax] and all tyranny."[26]

Though thousands of Protestant martyrs submitted themselves to the fires of the inquisitions, the Roman Catholics make something of the eighteen Catholic men who were killed after a siege on a town called Gorkum. William the Silent, however, intervened here as well, reminding all those in authority that they were to leave all "religious men" unmolested. "Do everything to win the hearts of the Catholics as well as of the reformers; above all, protect both religions." Later in 1574, he arrested Captain de la Mark for his ill-treatment of the Catholics during military service. William's magnanimity towards all on the basis of liberty of conscience was unprecedented for that era and prepared the way for greater religious freedom in England and America. Regrettably, the Spanish and French Inquisitions were not formally discontinued until the nineteenth century.

On July 15, Prince William summoned the nobles of Holland to gather for a meeting, where "he was formally recognized as lawful stadtholder over Holland, Zealand, Friesland, and Utrecht…He pledged himself to take no action without consulting the states, while they promised to urge the other provinces to agree to his appointment as protector of the whole land. His principle of toleration was likewise accepted, and public exercise of religion was to be permitted to all alike. Duke De la Mark read the commission he had received from Orange, which was duly ratified."[27]

This was not the end of it, however, for the Protestants in Western Europe. A month later, Charles of France instigated the St. Bartholomew's Day Massacre, in which at least 40,000 French Huguenots were executed. This dragon was not dead yet. Around the same time, William attempted to save his brother Louis at the siege of Mons; however, his troops were taken by complete surprise during the night. Had it not been for his trusty little dog awakening him in his tent, William would have been killed. It wasn't long before William was out of troops and money again, yet the towns of Northern Holland held out for dear life against the siege attempts of Alva and his Spanish armies. A truce was attempted with Philip II…William's terms were simple, "Liberty of conscience and of worship—restoration of ancient privileges, and expulsion of the Spanish garrisons."[28]

The war continued on, and the town of Haarlem fell to the Spanish in mid-1573. It must not be forgotten that this diminutive Dutch resistance was up against the most powerful country on earth at the time—the burgeoning Spanish empire. To cries of surrender on the part of the Dutch resistance, William responded, "Before I took the cause of defending the Christians and the other oppressed people of these lands, I made a sure alliance with the highest Prince of princes, and I am confident that all who trust in Him will be delivered by His powerful hand in spite of His and our enemies.[29] His motto was "Je maintiendrai—"I will persevere."

Shortly thereafter, William lost two more brothers, Louis at age thirty-four and Henry at twenty-four during the battle of Mook on April 14, 1574. If anything, this battle served as a short delay in the Spanish siege on Leyden. From that point on, William put every sinew of his being into the salvaging of Leyden. He wrote letters to the defenders, encouraging them to hold the city, despite the starvation and disease that ravaged. He suggested the piercing of the dikes, which would draw the 200 ships from the resistance closer to the Spanish forces, and threaten the Spanish with flooding. After piercing the dikes, almost a month passed before the winds and tides brought the water to the rescuing of the town. The next several years brought more setbacks, at which point William even suggested finding a new land for the Protestant Dutch "across the great sea." God's providence directed another way—the Spanish soldiers mutinied against their king in 1576, and all of Holland reverted to William's control.

Philip II made several attempts to drive a wedge between William and the nobles of the Netherlands, but to no avail. Promises were issued, offering the return of vast wealth and lands which had been lost to his family's dynasty over the preceding 20 years, along with the return of his son from Spain. For William, however, the sacrifices he had made for the liberty of his oppressed people had been well worth it, and he was not about to recant now. Besides, what was there to trust in Spain? His response: "Neither for money or goods, nor for the sake of my own life, nor for my wife or children will I mix one drop of this traitorous poison in my cup! These my people and I have begun this perilous struggle together—and together, with the strength God will give, we will persevere."[30] In a final act of blind, desperate rage, Philip issued a contract on William's life offering a reward of 25,000 gold crowns ($3,000,000 in current monetary value), as follows:

> "We declare him [William the Silent] an enemy of the human race ...and in order the sooner to remove our people from his tyranny and oppression, we promise on the word of a king and as God's servant, that if one of our subjects be found so generous of heart and so desirous of doing us service and the public, good, who has any means of executing this ordinance and ridding us of this said pest, either by delivering him to us quick or dead, or by depriving him at once of life, any way, we will give him or his heirs, landed estates or cash at his desire, to the amount of 25,000 golden crowns."[31]

HOLLAND'S DECLARATION OF INDEPENDENCE

None of these threats deterred William's efforts towards Holland's independence. On July 26, 1581, the nobles signed the first modern Declaration of Independence. It is a clarion endorsement of freedom from tyrants. The preamble to the document begins:

> "As it is apparent to all that a prince is constituted by God to be ruler of a people, to defend them from oppression and violence as the shepherd his sheep; and whereas God did not create the people slaves to their prince, to obey his commands, whether right or wrong, but rather the prince for the sake of the subjects (without which he could be no prince), to govern them according to equity, to love and support them as a father his children or a shepherd his flock, and even at the hazard of life to defend and preserve them. And when he does not behave thus, but, on the contrary, oppresses them, seeking opportunities to infringe their ancient customs and privileges, exacting from them slavish compliance, then he is no longer a prince, but a tyrant, and the subjects are to consider him in no other view.

And particularly when this is done deliberately, unauthorized by the states, they may not only disallow his authority, but legally proceed to the choice of another prince for their defense. This is the only method left for subjects whose humble petitions and remonstrances could never soften their prince or dissuade him from his tyrannical proceedings; and this is what the law of nature dictates for the defense of liberty, which we ought to transmit to posterity, even at the hazard of our lives. And this we have seen done frequently in several countries upon the like occasion, whereof there are notorious instances, and more justifiable in our land, which has been always governed according to their ancient privileges, which are expressed in the oath taken by the prince at his admission to the government; for most of the Provinces receive their prince upon certain conditions, which he swears to maintain, which, if the prince violates, he is no longer sovereign."

Blame for the tyrannical proceedings is put solidly on the head of Philip II:

"Now thus it was that the king of Spain after the demise of the emperor, his father, Charles the Fifth, of the glorious memory (of whom he received all these provinces), forgetting the services done by the subjects of these countries, both to his father and himself, by whose valor he got so glorious and memorable victories over his enemies that his name and power became famous and dreaded over all the world, forgetting also the advice of his said imperial majesty, made to him before to the contrary, did rather hearken to the counsel of those Spaniards about him, who had conceived a secret hatred to this land and to its liberty, because they could not enjoy posts of honor and high employments here under the states as in Naples, Sicily, Milan and the Indies, and other countries under the king's dominion."

Mention is made of the religious persecutions as well:

"And, especially, seeing that he did not only seek to tyrannize over their persons and estates, but also over their consciences, for which they believed themselves accountable to God only. Upon this occasion the chief of the nobility in compassion to the poor people [speaking of William the Silent], in the year 1566, exhibited a certain remonstrance in form of a petition, humbly praying, in order to appease them and prevent public disturbances, that it would please his majesty (by showing that clemency due from a good prince to his people) to soften the said points, and especially with regard to the rigorous Inquisition, and capital punishments for matters of religion. And to inform the king of this affair in a more solemn manner, and to represent to him how necessary it was for the peace and prosperity of the public to remove the aforesaid innovations, and moderate the severity of his declarations published concerning divine worship, the Marquis de Berghen, and the aforesaid Baron of Montigny had been sent, at the request of the said lady regent, council of state, and of the states-general as ambassadors to Spain, where the king, instead of giving them audience, and redress the grievances they had complained of (which for want of a timely remedy did always appear in their evil consequences among the common people), did, by the advice of Spanish council, declare all those who were concerned in preparing the said remonstrance to be rebels, and guilty of high treason, and to be punished with death, and confiscation of their estates; and, what is more (thinking himself well assured of reducing these countries under absolute tyranny by the army of the Duke of Alva), did soon after imprison and put to death the said lords the ambassadors, and confiscated their estates, contrary to the law of nations, which has been always religiously observed even among the most tyrannic and barbarous princes."

In the conclusion to this historical document, the under-magistrates of Holland formally declare their independence from the King of Spain:

"So, having no hope of reconciliation, and finding no other remedy, we have, agreeable to the law of nature in our own defense, and for maintaining the rights, privileges, and liberties of our countrymen, wives, and children, and latest posterity from being enslaved by the Spaniards, been constrained to renounce allegiance to the King of Spain, and pursue such methods as appear to us most likely to secure our ancient liberties and privileges. Know all men by these presents that being reduced to the last extremity, as above mentioned, we have unanimously and deliberately declared, and do by these presents declare, that the King of Spain has forfeited, ipso jure, all hereditary right to the sovereignty of those countries, and are determined from henceforward not to acknowledge his sovereignty or jurisdiction, nor any act of his relating to the domains of the Low Countries, nor make use of his name as prince, nor suffer others to do it. In consequence whereof we also declare all officers, judges, lords, gentlemen, vassals, and all other the inhabitants of this country of what condition or quality soever, to be henceforth discharged from all oaths and obligations whatsoever made to the King of Spain as sovereign of those countries."[32]

THE ASSASSINATION OF WILLIAM THE SILENT

The first attempt on William's life occurred on March 18, 1582, as he sat at dinner following a Sunday worship service. A certain Juan Jaureguy pulled a pistol and shot him in the neck. As his bodyguards swarmed the shooter, William was heard mumbling the words, "I forgive him my death!"[33] The Prince barely survived the attack. However, two years later, on July 10, 1584, another assassin completed the task commissioned by Philip II. As William lay at the bottom of the staircase where he had been fatally shot, his sister asked him the simple question, "Do you die reconciled with your Saviour, Jesus Christ?" His lips formed the word…"Yes."[34]

* * *

That is the story of how the great William of Orange gave everything he had for the cause of freedom—his son, his brothers, his own freedom, his earthly possessions, his honor, his safety, his comforts, and his life. Four of his mother's sons had died in the noble conflict. In a letter William wrote to his brothers John and Louis of Nassau, we catch a glimpse into the heart of the man. Why did he give everything he had for freedom?

"My Dear Good Brothers, Counts John and Louis of Nassau, etc. I have received your letter and learned what the situation is from it as well as from the report of the person you sent to me. I cannot thank you too much for your many good offices on my behalf and the trouble and labors which you undertake. To answer the points that you raise, you know quite well that it was never and is not now my intention to seek the slightest advantage for myself. I have only aspired and claimed to seek the country's freedom in the matters of religious conscience and government, in which the foreigners tried to oppress it. I therefore see nothing else to propose but that it be permitted to practice the Reformed religion according to the word of God, and that this whole country and state return to its ancient privileges and liberty. To achieve this the foreigners in the government and the army, especially the Spaniards, must be driven out."

To which we say, Amen.

William the Silent takes his place among a line of outstanding leaders who fought hard for the cause of liberty over the centuries. Without a free Holland, there would have been no place for the Pilgrims to flee in 1606, a mere twenty years after William's death. There would have been no Glorious Revolution in England and no accession for William and Mary in 1689. The Stuart tyrannies most certainly would have continued, and religious freedom would have been delayed until another era.

Incredibly, the Netherlands was radically transformed in the space of only forty years (between 1566 and 1606). The worst hell hole on the planet had become the best place—a haven for freedom for the Pilgrims who fled persecution from England in 1606. The most dangerous place became the safest. And, the city of Leyden, where the battle line was held against the Spanish, was the port of protection for the Pilgrims from 1606 until 1620. No individual person may take more credit for this stunning accomplishment than William the Silent, the Prince of Orange.

Yet, tyranny also retains a legacy as well. The King Philips of the sixteenth century turned into the Adolf Hitlers and the Josef Stalins of the twentieth century. For rulers like Philip, religion was only a ruse to turn the state into a tyranny. By the twentieth century, Hitler and Stalin outwardly admitted that religion was of little use unless it would aggrandize the state. Absolute control over the religious conscience in the sixteenth century turned into absolute control under the socialists and the communists of the twentieth and twenty-first centuries. From all indications, Philip II and Charles V were not Christians. They were big government advocates who endeavored to turn the state (and by implication, themselves) into god on earth. Human religion works hard to elevate man into god. In contrast, the Christian faith presents God who comes down to man, incarnated in human flesh in order that man may have fellowship with God forever. These are quite different faiths.

APOLOGY OF WILLIAM THE SILENT

Upon learning that Philip II of Spain, son of Charles V, had placed a contract on his life, William issued his famous *Apology*. This powerful piece will remain one of the most dramatic, passionate, courageous, plain-spoken attacks on tyranny ever penned. He defends himself, but he also defends liberty. He defines the tyrant, and pledges his life to God for the cause of liberty. The document was written two years before the first assassination attempt on his life and four years before the second assassin consummated the deed.

"The Prince of Orange, Count of Nassau and so forth, etc., etc., Lieutenant-General in the Low Countries and Governor of Brabant, Holland, Zeeland, Utrecht, and Friesland, and Admiral thereof, to the States-General Greeting:—

"I take it as a signal honor that I am the mark of the cruel and barbarous proscription hurled at me by the Spaniard for undertaking your cause and that of freedom and independence; and for this I am called traitor, heretic, hypocrite, foreigner, rebel, enemy of the human race, and I am to be killed like a wild beast, with a price offered to my assassins. I am no foreigner here, no rebel, no traitor. My princedom, which I hold in absolute sovereignty, and all my baronies, fiefs, and inheritances in Burgundy, and in the Netherlands, are mine by ancient and indisputable right, and have the sanction of my good friend the late Emperor and the public law of Europe. My ancestors were powerful Lords in the Low Countries, long before the House of Austria set foot therein, and, if need be, I will rehearse the ancient history of the House of Nassau to whom Dukes of Burgundy and the Emperors have owed so much for generations past. So far back as the year 1039 my ancestors were reigning Counts and Dukes in Guelderland for centuries, whilst the ancestors of the King were mere Counts of Hapsburg in Switzerland. King he may be in Spain or Naples, or of the Indies, but we know no King here: we know only Duke or Count—and even our Duke is limited by our ancient privileges, to maintain which Philip has pledged his oath on his accession, though he professes to have been absolved from it by the Pope.

"Traitor, he calls me, against my lawful sovereign—he himself deriving his crown through Henry, the bastard, that traitor and rebel against Pedro, his liege lord, his own father's son, whom he killed with his own hand. If Don Pedro were a tyrant, what is Philip? What was Philip's own ancestor, then a Count of Hapsburg, when he turned his sword against my ancestor, his liege lord Adolphus, the Emperor? Adulterer, he calls me, who am united in holy matrimony by the ordinances of God's Church to my lawful wife—Philip who married his own niece, who murdered his wife, murdered his own son, and many more, who is notorious for his mistresses and amours, if he did not instigate Cardinal Granvelle to poison the late Emperor Maximilian!

"The mischief has all arisen from the cruelty and arrogance of the Spaniard, who thinks he can make slaves of us, as if we were Indians or Italians; of us who have never been a conquered people, but have accepted a ruler under definite conditions. This is the cancer that we have sought to cauterise. I was bred up a Catholic and a worldling, but the horrible persecution that I witnessed by fire, sword, and water, and the plot to introduce a worse than Spanish Inquisition which I learned from the King of France, made me resolve in my soul to rest not till I had chased from the land these locusts of Spain. I confess that I sought to ally my friends and nobles of the land to resist these horrors, and I glory in that deed. And of the resistance to the tyranny of Spain in all its stages I take the responsibility, for I view with indignation the bloodthirsty cruelties, worse than those of any tyrant of antiquity, which they have inflicted upon the poor people of this land. Has not the King seized my son, a lad at college, and immured him in a cruel prison? Does he not delight in autos-de-fe? Did he not order me to kill worthy persons suspected of religion? Never! I say. By fire and sword no cause can be gained. Did he not send here the monster Alva, who swore eternal hatred to this people, and boasted that he had put to death 18,000 persons innocent of everything but differing from him in religion, a man whose tyranny and cruelty surpass anything recorded in ancient or modern history?

"He accuses me of being a demagogue, a flatterer of the people. I confess that I am, and whilst life remains, shall ever be on the popular side, in the sense that I shall maintain your freedom and your privileges. And all the offers that have been made to me, the release of my poor son, the restoration of all my estates and honours, and the discharge of all my debts—I have treated these with scorn, for I will never separate my cause from yours. And equally I spurn his setting a price on my head. Does he think he will frighten me by this, when I know how for years I have been surrounded by his hired assassins and poisoners? Does he think he can ennoble my assassin; when, if this be the road to nobility in Castile, there is no gentleman in the world, amongst nations who know what is true nobility, who would hold converse with so cowardly a miscreant?

"As for myself—would to God that my exile or death could deliver you from the oppression of the Spaniard! How eagerly would I welcome either! For what think you have I sacrificed my whole property, my brothers who were dearer to me than life, my son who was kidnapped from his father; for what do I hold my life in my hand day and night, if it be not that I may buy your freedom with my blood? If you think that my absence or my death can serve you, I am willing. Here is my head, of which no prince or monarch can dispose, but which is yours to devote to the safety of your Republic. If you think that my poor experience and such industry as I have can serve you yet, let us all go forward with one heart and will to complete the defense of this poor people, with the grace of God, which has upheld me so often in dire perplexity and straits, and let us save your wives and your children, and all that you hold dear and sacred.

"JE LE MAINTIENDRAI" (I will persevere)

Written: December 13, 1580. Translation: Frederic Harrison, 1897.

Chapter 9

FREEDOM SOUGHT: THE COURAGE OF THE PILGRIMS

O n May 29, 1593, three Christian men dropped from the scaffolds on St. Thomas-a-Watering in Central London, just south of the river Thames. The dreaded Star Chamber had sentenced John Penry, Henry Barrow, and John Greenwood to death by hanging. Their crime—authoring books dealing with the local church's obligation to provide good spiritual discipline for its members. The rising influence of Puritans and Separatists in England had become an irritant to the state-regulated church.

From a biblical point of view, it should be obvious that authoring books which espouse right or wrong views of church government should never merit the death penalty. When tyrants confuse major issues with minor issues, it is never long before they are executing citizens on trivial charges. Queen Elizabeth I and her appointed prelates illustrated the problem for us in the latter half of the sixteenth century. In some respects, the Star Chamber was one of the first regulatory bureaucracies of the modern state. Archbishop Whitgift had formed the tyrannical tribunal, eerily representative of the Spanish Inquisition. This kangaroo court would apprehend a person without a charge and without an accuser. If he could not answer the questions directed to him, he would be remanded to the jailhouse until he was willing to do so. Between 1583 and 1593, twenty-five pastors were confined to the jails in London, many of whom were cruelly beaten. At least three died while in prison.

The Protestant Reformation had promised some respite from persecution at the hands of the Roman Catholics. However, the state-controlled church under the auspices of the Tudors (Henry VIII, Bloody Mary, and Elizabeth) wasn't much of an improvement, and this new tyranny proved to be a bitter pill for many Protestants. Elizabeth's sister Mary had murdered at least 300 pastors and believers between 1554 and 1558.

To this point England had not faced anything close to what had happened under the dreaded Spanish Inquisition. However, these early English Puritans and Separatists were concerned. Was it time to leave England to seek protection for their families and their churches elsewhere? It was a valid question. Only recently, several of the early Pilgrim pastors, namely Thomas Helwisse and John Robinson, had written extensive treatises on the biblical basis for flight. They addressed the question: Is it good and wise for persecuted Christians to flee their persecutors in search of freedom? In his lengthy treatment of the subject, Robinson referred to biblical examples such as Jacob (fleeing from Esau), Moses (fleeing from Pharaoh), David (fleeing from Saul), Jeremiah and Elijah (fleeing from evil kings), and Jesus Christ (avoiding confrontations on several occasions during His ministry). The Pilgrim pastor carefully exposited 1 Corinthians 7:21ff, and concluded that flight is preferred if Christians may "better give themselves to the Lord," and if they "might enjoy their mutual fellowship and ministers [as a church], and bring up their children and families in the information of the Lord and His truth." Robinson concluded that this cannot possibly be done in England any longer "as all men know."[1] This classic treatment entitled "Of Flight and Persecution" is still an important document for all Christians who appreciate the heritage of freedom in the West, and for those who still face rising tyrannies in nations around the world today. As long as evil tyrants endure on the earth, we will want to avail ourselves of the wisdom and strategies developed by this first Pilgrim movement to Holland and to America.[2]

After experiencing numerous arrests and intolerable harassment at the hands of the British authorities, the first group of Pilgrims chose to flee England. Led by Captain John Smythe, the little group arrived in Holland in 1606. It was the land of William the Silent, a haven of liberty won in a titanic struggle several decades earlier.

John Robinson's group experienced a great deal more difficulty leaving England. They made three separate attempts, finally arriving on the free shores of Holland in 1608. It was only a temporary refuge, however. Over the next ten years, it became increasingly clear that these Pilgrims could not assimilate into the Dutch culture and economy. For more economic opportunity and the freedom to advance "the gospel of the kingdom of Christ in [the] remote parts of the world,"[3] the little group decided they would venture on to the new world as a covenanted body.[4]

Their ventures would not be without risk and severe hardship, and they knew liberty would not be easily won. William Bradford, their governor, challenged his people to endure much hardship in this journey of faith, reminding them, "For, though many desired to enjoy the ordinances of God in their purity, and the liberty of the gospel, yet, alas, they preferred to submit to bondage, with danger to their conscience, rather than endure these privations."[5] Despite the fact that many had coveted the liberties the Pilgrims sought, few had the courage to apply themselves to the venture.

On September 6, 1620, a merchant ship called the *Mayflower* sailed for America, bearing the precious cargo of 101 Pilgrims bound for Virginia. Although their initial charter gave them access to Virginia, the ocean currents drove them into Massachusetts Bay in November of the same year. Pastor Robinson was unable to join the first voyage, but we find the motives for the Pilgrim's courageous vision clearly recorded in his writings:

> "Now as the people of God in old time were called out of Babylon civil, the place of their bodily bondage, and were to come to Jerusalem, and there to build the Lord's temple...so are the people of God now to go out of Babylon spiritual to Jerusalem."[6]

Note that Robinson's concern was "bodily bondage" or temporal slavery to the tyrants in England. Similarly, Elder William Brewster who served the Pilgrim Church in Plymouth Plantation for the first few years, testified of a sincere desire for liberty:

> "They shook off this yoke of antichristian bondage, and as ye Lord's free people, joined themselves by a covenant of the Lord into a church estate, in ye fellowship of ye Gospell, to walk in all His ways, made known or to be made known unto them, according to their best endeavors, whatsoever it should cost them, the Lord assisting them."[7]

The motive that drove these Pilgrims to submit themselves to loss of life and threats to life and limb was this love for freedom and a commitment to build the kingdom of Christ.

It was a brutal first winter for the little settlement. After 47 of the initial 101 Pilgrims died during the first harsh winter (mostly women), not one family elected to join the *Mayflower's* return voyage to England. They had bought a one-way ticket. It was do or die. Their task was to build a Christian community where they would enjoy freedom to worship, and they were committed to it to the death. Upon hearing that so many had died in the first year, their pastor encouraged them onwards in a letter dated June 30, 1621. Robinson wrote,

> "In a battle it is not looked for but that divers should die; it is thought well for one to die if it get the victory, though with the loss of divers, if not too many, or too great. God, I hope, hath given you the victory, after many difficulties, for yourselves and others."[8]

This was the first ship to arrive in New England filled with passengers seeking the liberty to worship God. Millions of others would come in subsequent years, many of whom sought that same freedom from "bodily bondage." According to the testimony contained in these early documents, it is clear that the Pilgrims came to America for religious freedom and to establish another bulwark for the kingdom of Jesus Christ. The laws of this kingdom are not always obvious to everyone. Religious persecution dies hard. Some of England's religious regulations filtered into the colonies via Massachusetts Bay and Virginia. In 1660, three Quakers were executed at the gallows in Boston for what was taken as contumacious and generally obnoxious behavior. Certain factions of the Puritans did succumb to regulative law (well beyond the just limits set out by God's laws), and this served as something of a precursor for the modern regulative state. However, the Pilgrims were generous to others desiring similar liberty. In 1638, the colony allowed liberty for a Baptist pastor despite theological differences. Varying perspectives on denominational liberty were to be found in the various colonies for the first several generations—the colonies of Connecticut, New York, and Pennsylvania allowing for more cross-denominational ecumenicity. Liberty began to dawn in the new world, and it wasn't long before Puritan Congregationalists like Cotton Mather were attending ordination services for Baptists in Boston.[9]

In retrospect, was this bold venture a wise move for the Pilgrims, or did they overreact to the political situation in England? Should they have stayed through the Stuart monarchy? Obviously, those Americans who preferred freedom from a state-controlled church have benefited greatly by the Pilgrim's courage, and would still enthusiastically support the venture. The later record of the Stuart monarchy was rough, to say the least. In some respects the Stuarts of the seventeenth century represented a worst record of tyranny than Elizabeth I in the sixteenth century. The consolidated United Kingdom (now including Scotland, England, and Ireland), meant more centralized power in the monarchy, more bloody wars, and of course more tyranny. Ireland had surrendered its independence to Henry VIII in 1542. Scotland had enjoyed independence and only surrendered it after the ascension of James I to the throne in 1603. Charles I appointed the autocratic Charles Laud as Archbishop of Canterbury in 1633 who came to be infamous for his generous use of the Star Chamber for the Puritans with whom he disagreed. For example, one pastor was held in solitary confinement for fifteen weeks until his hair fell out, and his skin peeled off. He was tied to a stake and received thirty-six stripes with a heavy cord on his naked back, and was placed in the pillory for two hours in November's frost and snow; he was branded in the face, had his nose slit and his ears cut off, and was condemned to imprisonment for life.[10]

After the reinstatement of Charles II, between 1660 and 1688, thousands of Protestant pastors in England were imprisoned or exiled. Thousands of Scottish Covenanters were hunted down and executed in the most cruel manner during the same timeframe. These stories describe some of the most heart-wrenching martyrdoms in the history of the church. Both women and children were tortured and killed by these cruel tyrants. Dr. W. H. Carslaw summarizes the historical research he conducted on the Killing Time in Scotland in these words:

> "While during the twenty-eight miserable years between the Restoration and the Revolution, apart from untold hardships and sufferings, the slain on the scaffold and in the fields cannot have fallen much short of two thousand, including 360 executed after some form of examination had been perfunctorily and summarily hurried though. Moreover, it is impossible to count the men and women and children who succumbed to rain and frost and fatigue and hunger in their wanderings across mosses and mountains."[11]

A conservative estimate would suggest about 0.2 percent of the Scottish population was martyred inside of those 28 years. Given the present population of America at 300,000,000, a similar purge of 0.2 percent would amount to at least 600,000 martyrs.

Until the Glorious Revolution began in 1688, it is hard to say that life had improved much for devoted Christians in England. Many of Britain's most committed Christians—Separatists, Puritans, and Presbyterians escaped to America during the "Killing Time." Thus, America became the great depository for some of the most devoted Christians the world had ever seen. The commitment to the Kingdom of Christ is evident from the beginning, especially in the words of the famous compact penned and signed as the *Mayflower* sailed into Plymouth Harbor.

THE MAYFLOWER COMPACT

"In the name of God, Amen. We whose names are underwritten, the loyal subjects of our dread Sovereign Lord King James, by the Grace of God of Great Britain, France, and Ireland King, Defender of the Faith, etc.

"Having undertaken for the Glory of God and advancement of the Christian Faith and Honour of our King and Country, a Voyage to plant the First Colony in the Northern Parts of Virginia, do by these presents solemnly and mutually in the presence of God and one of another, Covenant and Combine ourselves together in a Civil Body Politic, for our better ordering and preservation and further-ance of the ends aforesaid; and by virtue hereof to enact, constitute and frame such just and equal Laws, Ordinances, Acts, Constitu-tions and Offices from time to time, as shall be thought most meet and convenient for the general good of the Colony, unto which we promise all due submission and obedience. In witness whereof we have hereunder subscribed our names at Cape Cod, the 11th of No-vember, in the year of the reign of our Sovereign Lord King James, of England, France and Ireland the eighteenth, and of Scotland the fifty-fourth. Anno Domini 1620."

Chapter 10

OLIVER CROMWELL: THE GREAT WAR AGAINST TYRANNY AND A LEGACY FOR LIBERTY

Oliver Cromwell is a complex and controversial figure in the history of Western liberty. He inherited a tyranny in that he joined the English Parliament during a period of statist expansion. The power transfer from pope to prince had already taken place a century earlier under Henry VIII. England had assumed control of Scotland and Ireland, and the "re-conquest" of Ireland had come about in 1603 under Queen Elizabeth I. Cromwell's involvement in quelling the Irish rebellions continues to generate passionate debate (especially between Roman Catholics and Protestants).

The historical record is not always clear or easily interpreted, partially because all historians bring their own biases to it and those biases are often formed by a wrong worldview. Also, every good leader must deal with a bad situation—bad conditions in a fallen world, that which he inherits and the remnants of a sinful nature within himself. Worldviews matter. Those who do not like Protestants and Puritans especially, usually do not favor Oliver Cromwell. If that is their pre-disposition, they will fail to realize the problem of the Irish rebellion, in which anywhere between 12,000 and 200,000 Protestants were massacred, depending on which side is reporting the numbers.

There appeared to be no stopping the tyrannical development of the English monarchy in the first half of the seventeenth century. Charles I revived the Rehoboam domestic policy, as many other tyrants have done in history: "My father hath chastised you with whips, but I will chastise you with scorpions." (1 Kings 12:11). When Parliament refused to collect taxes for the King in March 1629, Charles dissolved the Parliament. Then he proceeded to imprison a number of Parliamentarians, and in a rather undemocratic spirit, prevented the legislature from convening for eleven years. One of the members of Parliament, Sir John Eliot, would eventually die in prison. Charles also imprisoned and fined merchants who refused to pay his illegal tax that Parliament refused to adopt. Would this be the beginning of a long era of absolutism in England? The threat was real in the minds of the middle class Puritans. Historian D'Aubigne summarizes the conditions at this time as it affected the church:

> "Two thousand ministers were driven from their benefices; the churches were oppressed; the noblest hearts of the country were forced to seek a refuge in distant lands; vast colonies in America were peopled by them; and England would have become like Spain, and worse than Spain, and no William III would have resumed the task so energetically begun by Cromwell."[1]

During the first years of Charles' reign, Archbishop Laud took full advantage of the dreaded Star Chamber, condemning ministers like Alexander Leighton to prison and torture. For their religious convictions, three other men (Prynne, Bastwick, and Burton) were sentenced to lose their ears, each fined 5,000 pounds, and sentenced to life in prison. These accumulated tyrannical activities stirred up a concerted number of freedom loving Englishmen, God-fearing Puritans that formed into a cadre of middle-class, well-educated, principled leaders. At this point, they had had enough of this tyrant, enough of his cruelties and perfidy, and they understood the legitimate role of lower magistrates to declare the illegality of absolute power, and oppose it to the point of arms if necessary. This was the legacy of the Magna Carta signed, sealed, and delivered four hundred years earlier. As one historian put it, "If the feudal aristocracy took part in the development of nations, it was by struggling against royal tyranny, by exercising the rights of resistance, and by maintaining the maxims of liberty."[2] Parliament declared war on the King, and the Parliamentarian War began in earnest on October 23, 1642 with the Battle of Edgehill. Oliver Cromwell had rounded up some one hundred volunteers and there he fought his first successful battle.

Six months later, Cromwell showed up at the Battle of Belton with a force of two thousand men. Again, his band of merry warriors completely dominated the conflict, with a kill ratio of 50 to 1. He reported back to his superiors, "God hath given us, this evening, a glorious victory over our enemies." In January 1644, Prince Rupert led the King's Cavalier army into the Puritan town of Bolton and massacred men, women, and children. He pursued the Puritan armies to Marston Moor, where he was met by Cromwell's cavalry and Rupert's forces were decimated. In historian Otto Scott's words, "Marston Moor became the largest burial ground in the nation, and Cromwell became the military hero of the revolution."[3]

Cromwell's army had no equal in its discipline and immediate success, perhaps in all of history. In his leisure hours, Cromwell would be seen singing psalms with his officers, and attending the preaching of the Word."[4] He was convinced that any "profaneness and impiety and the absence of all religion, the drinking and gaming, and all manner of license and laziness," was unacceptable behavior for his "New Model Army." Robert Southey summarizes Cromwell's military philosophy: "Till the whole army was new modeled and governed under a stricter discipline, they must not expect any notable success in anything they were about."[5]

This new discipline paid off at Naseby, the final decisive battle in the war. Cromwell's cavalry defeated the King's troops while Rupert's less disciplined cavalry were off plundering the Parliamentary baggage (things left at the camp) two miles away.

As history books tell the story, Charles I was tried by 135 commissioners, convicted of treason, and executed. Oliver Cromwell was given the title of Lord Protector of England and the monarchy was suspended for six years until his death.

AN ARDENT SUPPORTER OF LIBERTY

From the outset, as chief in the government of England, Oliver Cromwell's major agenda was liberty. In a letter he wrote on September 12, 1654, Cromwell laid out his vision of a Statement of Rights which he called, in his words, "fundamental, somewhat like the Magna Charta, which should be standing, be unalterable."[6] There is no question that this great leader wanted to make a mark for liberty in the history of the Western world. He delineated three basic rights which he felt to be most essential:

1. "That Parliament should not make themselves perpetual is a fundamental."

2. "Liberty of conscience in religion (equally removed from profaneness and persecution) is a fundamental."

3. "Another Fundamental is that the power of the Militia should be shared between the Protector and the Parliament."[7]

The second liberty would later be guaranteed to Americans in the First Amendment of the United States Constitution.[8] The third fundamental liberty is a balance of powers that is carefully reflected in the United States Constitution as well. Although the U.S. President is designated Commander in Chief of the Armed Forces, Congress still approves budgets and declares war.[9]

Cromwell supported a parliament that was limited to assembly for five months, without possibility of dissolution by himself or any other. One of the means the King had used to control Parliament was his right to dissolution at his whim. Charles I had dissolved three parliaments in the first year of his reign, actions that created the tension between the throne and the representatives of the people, which eventually led to his beheading.

RELIGIOUS LIBERTY

After nearly three centuries of persecutions, tortures, inquisitions, bloody purges, and senseless wars, it was now clear to Oliver Cromwell that something had to be done about the source of all of these troubles—the unbiblical interaction of church and state. A sensible political leader understands the jurisdictional role of the state in restraining murder, thievery, and rape. But why should William Tyndale burn at the stake, and John Robinson be jailed over church polity questions? There has to be something ungodly, something insidious and wicked going on when somebody is burned at the stake for subscribing to the wrong form of church government or translating the Bible into English. This heavy regulation of church organization is nothing less than statism or state worship. The English government had violated God's law when it sentenced godly men to hanging or prison for failing to wear the right vestures in ministerial service. This misguided view of church and state, this big-government impulse, had produced untold sorrow and mayhem in almost every major country in Europe including Germany, Italy, Switzerland, France, Spain, Portugal, Belgium, and Holland. Even Cromwell's recent experiences in Ireland testified to the insane consequences of this thinking. Not many political leaders dared oppose the cause of religious tyranny in Europe in the year 1650. However, over the subsequent 200 years most Western nations opened the doors to religious freedom, and Cromwell served as a pioneer for the cause.

Weary of the persecution and bloodshed he had witnessed firsthand in Ireland, England, and Scotland, Cromwell committed himself to the fight for religious liberty. This was his "governing passion," according to historian D'Aubigne. The matter appeared front and center in his first speeches which he presented to the Parliament as Lord Protector:

"Liberty of conscience is a natural right; and he that would have it, ought to give it. Indeed that hath been one of the vanities of our contest. Every sect saith: 'O, give me liberty!' But give it him and to his power—he will not yield it to anybody else! Where is our ingenuousness? Liberty of conscience is a thing that ought to be very reciprocal. All the money of this nation would not have tempted men to fight upon such an account as they have here been engaged in, if they had not had hopes of liberty of conscience better than Episcopacy granted them, or than would have been afforded by a Scots Presbytery—or an English either, if it had made such steps, and had been so sharp and rigid, as it threatened when first set up. This, I say, is a Fundamental. It ought to be so. It is for us and the generations to come."[10]

Oliver Cromwell could not have been more direct, or more emphatic. The entire speech is a remarkable defense of religious liberty. I challenge my reader to find another example in history of such language from a civil magistrate prior to 1650. Cromwell addressed the Parliament again in his fifth speech on September 17, 1656 in a similar vein:

"I will tell you the truth. Our practice since the last Parliament hath been to let all this Nation see that whatever pretensions to Religion would continue quiet, peaceable, they should enjoy conscience and liberty to themselves and not to make religion a pretense for arms and blood. Truly we have suffered them and that cheerfully so to enjoy their own liberties. Whatsoever is contrary and not peaceable let the pretense be never so specious if it tend to combination to interests and factions we shall not care by the grace of God whom we meet withal though never so specious if they be not quiet. And truly I am against all liberty of conscience repugnant to this. If men will profess be they those under Baptism—be they those of the Independent judgment simply, or of the Presbyterian judgment—in the name of God encourage them, countenance them, so long as they do plainly continue to be thankful to God and to make use of the liberty given them to enjoy their own consciences. For as it was said today, undoubtedly this is the peculiar Interest all this while contended for. An excellent Interest very indispensable in a state of genuine Protestantism which latter has itself for some time been indispensable enough."[11]

Cromwell rightly interpreted the religious ruse for the tyranni-cal use of government, when he spoke of "the pretense for arms and blood." He suggested toleration for the most eccentric cults, as long as they were not out to foment violent revolutions and wars as a means of advancing their cause. Cromwell here specifically enumerated Bap-tists, Independents, and Presbyterians in his call for religious liberty. What a refreshing shift in policy is seen here as Christian magistrates came to realize that no degree of political power could stop the explo-sion of sectarianism, ecclesiastical disunity, cults, and demagoguery of every sort! By God's providence, the breakdown of truth is usually accompanied with confusion and disunity in the organized church. Regrettably, disorganization and heterodoxy became the rule of the day for the Christian church in the Western world. Nonetheless, au-thentic faith could not be defined and enforced by the state. God did not design the state for this purpose. At the very least, the state should refrain from persecuting the true church, wherever it would manifest itself over the succeeding centuries.

Of the various denominations that formed at this time, the Quak-ers, or "The Children of the Inner Light," was probably considered the most eccentric by the vast majority of Catholics and Protestants. Although not nearly as many Quakers were martyred at the hands of power-driven governments as French Huguenots, Scottish Cove-nanters, and Dutch Reformers, a concerted number lost property and suffered imprisonment between the 1650s and the 1690s.

Oliver Cromwell's five separate meetings with Quaker leader George Fox in 1556, 1557, and 1558 marked an important move to-wards religious liberty. Fox later reported, "I had much fearless dis-course with him...and he would often interrupt me by saying: 'That is very good—That is true!' And he carried himself with much mod-eration towards me. As people were coming in, he caught me by the hand, and with tears in his eyes, said: 'Come again to my house, for if thou and I were but an hour a-day together, we should be nearer one to another, adding, that he wished me no more ill than he did to his own soul."[12] We also find records of a letter from Cromwell to Parlia-ment interceding for one James Naylor, a rogue Quaker (whom even

George Fox had rejected), who had been prosecuted for impersonating Jesus Christ.

As it turned out, Parliament was not as interested in supporting religious liberty as was Cromwell. In their first assembly, "the House voted to suppress not only the Deists, Socinians, and Roman Catholics, but the Arians, Antinomians, Quakers, and others as well."[13] Cromwell took this as a direct assault on his position on religious liberty. In response, he chided Parliament by letter:

> "Is there not upon the spirits of men a strange itching? Nothing will satisfy them unless they can press their finger upon their brethren's consciences, to pinch them there. To do this was no part of the contest we had with the common adversary. And wherein consisted this more than in obtaining that liberty from the tyranny of the bishops to all species of Protestants to worship God according to their own light and consciences? For want of which many of our brethren forsook their native countries to seek their bread from strangers and to live in the howling wilderness; and for which also many that remained here were imprisoned, and otherwise abused and made the scorn of the nation...What greater hypocrisy than for those who were oppressed by the bishops to become the greatest oppressors themselves, so soon as their yoke was removed?"[14]

It is worth noting that Cromwell did not recommend persecution of Roman Catholics, although he did allow for civil prosecutions for "profane persons, blasphemers such as preach sedition; the contentious railers..."[15] Such language was an attempt to end the endless tit-for-tat persecutions with which the Roman Catholics had maltreated Protestants, and vice-versa.

Although Oliver Cromwell's vision for English liberties came to an abrupt halt with his death in 1658, the Protector had planted the first seeds in Britain that advocated religious liberty in any meaningful way. Powerful men seldom take advantage of their time in office to send the nation in a good direction. Given that Cromwell served only five short years as head of state, he accomplished more for liberty than had one hundred years of Tudors and Stuarts. Following Oliver Cromwell's death, England would have to wait for the great-grandson of William the Silent before religious freedom would be finally won.

OLIVER CROMWELL'S FAITH

Every political figure will bear criticism from those who would have handled a situation like the Irish revolts and Scottish wars differently. Anarchy and civil wars are hopelessly convoluted and difficult affairs. Political independence for Scotland and Ireland would have been preferred. Nonetheless, no one questions Cromwell's magnanimity with George Fox, let alone George Fox himself, the founder of the Quakers. No one questions his passionate speeches and letters in favor of religious liberty, when few other leaders of state were willing to extend themselves on the issue. No one questions his top-notch military prowess and discipline. It would be hard to find another political leader in history given some measure of power who was so intensely committed to liberty.

Oliver Cromwell's personal letters (and there are hundreds to review) are, almost without exception, filled with Scriptural admonitions, evangelistic zeal, personal testimony of God's grace in his life, and transparent references to his own spiritual struggles. With perhaps the exception of men like Samuel Rutherford, John Bunyan, or Thomas A'Kempis, you'll rarely encounter such a strong devotional flavor anywhere else. Is there any other political leader in the history of the world with such an outspoken love for Christ and His Word, as Oliver Cromwell? Any president can fake a Christian testimony in exchange for the evangelical vote, but would they lace every single letter and speech with that personal testimony? Either Oliver Cromwell is the greatest fraud who ever lived, or he is the real deal. There is hardly any middle ground when it comes to one's perspective of Cromwell— especially if one has spent more than an hour studying his life. History provides a great test of true faith. We define our heroes and villains according to the worldview framework by which we interpret their actions, for better or for worse, for good or for evil.

Cromwell provided his personal testimony in a letter written to a cousin on October 13, 1638.

"The Lord forsaketh me not. Though He do prolong, yet He will, I trust, bring me to His tabernacle, to His resting-place. My soul is with the congregation of the First-born, my body rests in hope; and if here I may honor my God either by doing or suffering, I shall be most glad. Truly no poor creature hath more cause to put himself forth in the case of his God than I. I have had plentiful wages beforehand; and I am sure I shall never earn the least mite. The Lord accept me in His Son, and give me to walk in the right—and give us to walk in the light, as He is in the light...Oh, I lived in and loved darkness, and hated light; I was a chief, the chief of sinners. This is true; I hated godliness, yet God had mercy on me. O the riches of His mercy! Praise Him for me; pray for me, that He who hath begun a good work would perfect it in the day of Christ..."[16]

The famous poet John Milton was well acquainted with Cromwell in his early years, and wrote, "[Oliver] had grown up in peace and privacy at home, silently cherishing in his heart a confidence in God, and a magnanimity well adapted for the solemn times that were approaching. Although of ripe years, he had not yet stepped forward into public life, and nothing so much distinguished him from all around as the cultivation of a pure religion and the integrity of his life."

While serving in the army, Cromwell wrote a letter to a Colonel who had lost a son in battle, mentioning that he had experienced a similar tragedy. His words: "Sir, you know my trials this way; but the Lord supported me in this. The Lord took him into the happiness we all pant for and live for...God give you his comfort...You may do all things by the strength of Christ. Seek that and you shall easily bear your trial. Let this public mercy to the Church of God make you to forget your private sorrow. The Lord be your strength; so prays, your true faithful and loving brother, Oliver Cromwell."[17]

On his first successes in battle, he wrote to the Speaker of the Parliament, "This is none other than the work of God. He must be a very Atheist that doth not acknowledge it. It may be thought that some praises are due to those gallant men, of whose valor so much mention is made—their humble suit to you and all that have an interest in this blessing, is 'That in the remembrance of God's praises they be forgotten. It's their joy that they are instruments of God's glory and their nation's good.'"

When was the last time a military general of this order scoffed off the praises of men in favor of the praises of God like this?

Upon his daughter's marriage, his counsel was: "Who ever tasted that the Lord is gracious, without some sense of self, vanity, and badness? Who ever tasted that graciousness of His, and could go less in desire—less pressing after full enjoyment? Dear Heart, press on; let not thy Husband, let not anything cool thy affections after Christ. I hope he will be an occasion to inflame them. That which is best worth of love in thy Husband is that of the image of Christ he bears… "[18] Not many a Christian pastor writes letters of this sort today. Cromwell's faith oozed out of every pore of his being, such that it becomes the most obvious fact about him to his biographers.

CONCLUSION

Good men can make a difference in the annals of history. To ignore the contributions made by Jesus Christ and His followers upon history, is to do Him and His rule a disservice. Truly, much of the good that is done happens in small corners, little churches, charitable hospitals, and orphanages around the world. Nonetheless, there are godly men who have done great things in politics, war, business, art, and culture as well. Let us then recognize the contribution of Jesus Christ to human culture over the last two thousand years, especially when He really does set the captives free.

Chapter 11

FREEDOM ESPOUSED: THE PASSION OF PATRICK HENRY

Through the centuries that England fell prey to empire building fever and tyrants came to power, good men continued the
fight for liberty in Ireland, Scotland, and the mother country.
Every chapter in this great saga is worth telling, and contributes to the
sum total of freedom still extant in the world. By the latter half of the
eighteenth century, America had become the great repository of the
heritage of freedom. The respective governments of each of the thirteen colonies were duly appointed or elected magistracies. They had
been self-governing from the beginning according to charters provided
by the monarch. In fact, the first legislative assembly in the New World
convened in Jamestown in 1619. Virginia governed its own national
affairs for over 150 years before America's bid for independence.

Threats to American self-rule dated back to the 1690s, when Increase Mather crossed the ocean in hopes of securing a new and better charter for Massachusetts Bay from King William.[1] The struggle for domination accompanies the formation of empires. The obligatory wars in this power struggle are costly in lives and money, and they must be financed by more taxes. The European wars (between the English and the French) were no exception to this rule. As the struggle for power intensified, the American colonies were reluctantly dragged into the European conflicts, and subjected to taxation without representation. The English parliament also chose to enact legislation that would further restrict the colonies' economic and political well-being. The colonies viewed the actions as a exercise of tyranny and a violation of charter. As duly organized lower magistrates, the colonial governments felt bound to act in order to protect the liberties of their people.

Virginia was the most populated and most prosperous of all of the American colonies—all eyes turned to Virginia. The battle for liberty shaped up in May of 1765 when a young lawyer from Hanover County rode into Williamsburg to serve his first term in the Virginia House of Burgesses. The young patriot had already made a name for himself at the Hanover County courthouse two years earlier, when he had successfully argued against the Parson's Cause. There in an obscure rural courthouse, he had set himself against the ruling of the powerful King of England, and won the case. The matter concerned an onerous tax on tobacco which would have enriched the Virginia clergy at the expense of impoverishing the farmers in a bad crop year.

Just months earlier, the British parliament had passed the Stamp Act, creating an additional tax on all official government documents in the colonies. It was the principle of taxation without representation that concerned the young lawyer, Patrick Henry. The noose of tyranny was tightening, and this young freedom loving patriot of Scotch-Irish heritage did not like the feel of it. For much of his youth, he had heard the clear and fiery preaching of the famed Presbyterian preacher, Samuel Davies. A passion for truth, liberty, and justice (as defined by God, not man), coursed through his veins. Young Henry waited until the end of the session, and moved his resolutions—forever re-membered as "The Stamp Act Resolutions."

Henry proceeded, in his characteristic manner, to defend the res-olutions before the Virginia House with an impassioned zeal and fiery rhetoric virtually unparalleled by any other great leader in this na-tion's history. He never kept notes of his speeches, and the only his-torical record are those fragments found in the memory of those who were present at the memorable moment. He ended with the words: "Caesar had his Brutus. Charles the First his Cromwell, and George the Third... may profit by their example." Shouts of "treason!" were heard resonating through the chambers. To which Henry cried out, "If this be treason, let us make the most of it!"

It was a moment that shifted the direction of human history—a true David and Goliath moment. One young man inquiring as to the right of this "uncircumcised Philistine" to defy the God-given liberties of a free people. Patrick Henry was challenging an empire, as he had done with the Parson's Cause. But this time it was in the presence of the most influential leaders in the country. Despite measurable op-position in the assembly against his resolution, it was his passionate rhetoric that committed the hearts of the majority in the room to lib-erty. Judge Paul Carrington described Henry's eloquence "as beyond my powers of description."[2] Senator John Randolph, considered by some the best orator in America, said of Patrick Henry, "He was the greatest orator who ever lived."[3] And George Mason wrote, "He is by far the most powerful speaker I ever heard."[4]

In the end, Patrick Henry's persuasive rhetoric won the day. Five of the resolutions passed the House, a great way to celebrate his 29th birthday. The next day, he mounted his horse and returned to his family and his fields. Historian Cabell Rives summarized the historical moment in these words:

> "By his ever memorable resolutions in opposition to the Stamp Act, and the lofty eloquence with which he sustained them, he struck a timely blow which resounded throughout America and the whole world, and roused a spirit that never slumbered till its great work was accomplished. *The moment was opportune and critical, and he seized it with*

a bold and felicitous energy that belonged to his ardent and impassioned nature (italics added)."[5]

No one else possessed the courage or the foresight to submit these resolutions and argue for them with such passion. All of the colonies and the world were watching Virginia, but men like George Washington and Richard Henry Lee were undecided and generally uncommitted to independence in 1765. Over the course of the subsequent months however, the other colonial governments followed suit, producing similar resolutions. Patrick Henry played a key role when he toppled the first major domino in a sequence of events that led to America's independence. God used one man at one moment in time to shift the very course of history.

But that was not the end of Patrick Henry's historical contributions. The second pivotal event on Virginia's (and America's) road to independence occurred in 1775. The Second Virginia Convention assembled at St. John's Church in Richmond so as to avoid the notice of the royal governor in Williamsburg. Of immediate concern to the delegates was the governor's confiscation of the colonial munitions from the Williamsburg armory. Tensions were high. Representatives from each of Virginia's counties were crowded into the church (the largest building in Richmond at that time). The question before the assembly was whether or not to create a militia. Once again, it was Patrick Henry who moved the resolution, seconded by Richard Henry Lee. After Chairman Peyton Randolph entertained several arguments contrary to the motion from certain commissioners, Patrick Henry took the stand and delivered his famous speech in defense of his resolution. The motion barely passed, but the course of history was set. A committee was organized, with Patrick Henry assigned the responsibility of convener. America's War for Independence was now in motion, and Virginia was committed to the fight.

Patrick Henry's "Give Me Liberty" speech on the floor of the Virginia Convention was momentous. It was the speech of the millennium. No further speech was offered or solicited on the floor. Its force carried the vote, but it also inspired a nation. Words can carry more force than bullets, and these were the words that ignited the souls of men to engage the War for Independence more than any others.

If there were two critical moments in Virginia's history which paved the way for the American War for Independence, they were the Stamp Act Resolutions of 1765 and the Second Virginia Convention in 1775. Without question, Patrick Henry was the major player at both events. But why this man? How does Patrick Henry differ from the humanist revolutionaries like Robespierre, Lenin, or Mao? Why did America gain more genuine and enduring liberty than the Soviet Union, China, and France? What made the difference? I would offer several distinctive qualities of a true advocate for liberty in a world of tyranny.

1. Patrick Henry loved liberty, and he utterly repudiated human tyranny. From all indications, tyranny was on the rise, and the American colonies were on the verge of becoming a police state. It would be nigh impossible to find a founding father who was as excited about liberty and defended it with as much ardor as this man. He would have rather died than live enslaved by the unnecessary servitude of men. He knew that civil governments were necessary, but he also believed that which governs least governs best. He considered this the opportune moment to strike a blow for liberty. History doesn't present many opportunities like this. In most eras of human history, the population is overwhelmed by tyranny, and wicked men (who have not the slightest interest in protecting liberty) maintain full control of the political stations.

Some have questioned whether these were legitimate conditions under which Americans could obtain more political freedom and "use it rather" (1 Cor. 7:21). Was the American war with Britain a lawful defense of liberty? Much has been written on the matter, but I would point out several strong arguments in favor of the moral legitimacy of this war. First, the colonies were self-governing magistrates. They understood the biblical doctrine of interposition defended by John Calvin and Samuel Rutherford in which lower magistrates are responsible for defending the liberties of the people when these liberties are threatened by a higher magistrate. Second, Patrick Henry perceived that support from the other colonial legislatures was at least achievable. In the words of Christ, a king must count the cost before taking on an invading force (Luke 14:31). Henry believed that here was a true opportunity to win a war for freedom given the three million "armed in the holy cause of liberty." Third, the British government was guilty of ratcheting up the tyranny and violating the constitutional rights of British citizens as guaranteed by the charters and the Magna Carta. Political expedience often forces the abridgment of liberties, but the resultant tyranny also gives just cause for resistance for the lower magistrates where those liberties are abridged.

True Christians will never abandon this struggle for freedom. When and where shall freedom return to the earth? Although the prospects worldwide appear more hopeless now than ever, Christians must never forfeit the battle. The true freedom fighter will identify every opportunity and take full advantage of it. There is no eschatological view of the future in which Christians are exempted from this battle. Paul addresses personal liberties where he states, "Stand fast therefore in the liberty wherewith Christ hath made us free" (Gal. 5:1). Whether it be church or state that attempts the curtailment of liberty, the lawful struggle to retain that liberty is legitimate as long as we define "lawful" by God's law.

Nonetheless, wisdom is essential in this great spiritual and physical struggle. We cannot water every plant with our blood. We must choose our battles wisely. Our battle fronts may not seem as significant as they were for Patrick Henry, as we are reduced to a side skirmish here and there. We may be pressed to fight for islands of freedom, but as the man said, "We must fight!"

2. Revolutionaries who promise the people more liberty usually wind up delivering more tyranny at the end, because they give way to the power principle. This is the pattern that appears with the French Revolution and the Communist revolutions in the East. However, Patrick Henry successfully resisted the lure of power throughout his life, serving as Governor of Virginia for only three terms (between 1776 and 1778). Patrick Henry's real interest was his farm at Red Hill. Though he would have to dedicate a week here and there in Williamsburg to the business of "changing the world," he would disappear

quickly from the public eye. He returned home to care for his invalid wife, homeschool his children, read the Bible, and plow his fields. This was his life. Unlike other American leaders such as John Adams and Thomas Jefferson, Patrick Henry would not allow politics to interrupt his household affairs. He truly lived out his profession, and on a number of occasions, he turned down powerful political positions.

During his fierce debates at the Virginia Constitutional Convention, his major fear was that America would give in to the "empire impulse." He preferred that the United States Constitution begin with "We the States" vs. "We the People." He could see that America would turn into a democratic tyranny in the years to come, and prophesied to this effect on the floor of the convention. He argued strongly against "converting this country into a powerful and mighty empire."[6] Thomas Jefferson, on the other hand, began using the term "empire of liberty" for this country during his presidency.[7]

Thus develops a clear distinction between the tyrant and the courageous advocate of liberty. The tyrant is willing to sacrifice the liberties of others to collect power and reputation for himself. The advocate of liberty is willing to risk his everything for the liberties of others, and cares little for power or reputation. Most Americans know little or nothing about Patrick Henry. There are no monuments in his honor except for one tiny bust in the Virginia State Capitol in Richmond. The Washington Mall contains nothing for him. Patrick Henry leaves the notoriety for George Washington, Thomas Jefferson, Abraham Lincoln, and Franklin Delano Roosevelt, some of whom consolidated power and influence in the Federal Government by their political endeavors.

3. Patrick Henry was willing to place the first finger on the trigger in the battle for American liberty. He was the first to raise his voice against the tyrants and the first to pledge his own life. It is extremely difficult to break the silence when nobody else will. It takes tremendous faith to be the first one to step out against Goliath and ask the question, "Who is this uncircumcised Philistine that should defy the armies of the living God!?" It takes an extraordinary combination of wisdom and courage to lead in this way. Patrick Henry

spoke passionately, plainly, resolutely, and loudly of that which others feared to whisper. Eventually, men like Benjamin Harrison, George Washington, and Thomas Jefferson did join him in support of liberty. Nonetheless, someone had to strike the first blow for freedom, and this was the unique privilege of one of the most courageous men in all of history.

4. Patrick Henry fought hard to include the Bill of Rights in the United States Constitution. This document marked another significant foothold for liberty in the Western world. The convention had already rejected a "Bill of Rights" on September 12, 1787. Returning to Richmond in 1788 after having retired from politics, Patrick Henry once again acted as the most dominant and influential member of the assembly during the ratification debates.[8] In the debate on the floor, Henry spoke more than any other delegate. His speeches could fill an entire book. What follows is a portion of Patrick Henry's plea for the first Ten Amendments:

"Mr. Chairman, the necessity of a bill of rights appears to me to be greater in this government than ever it was in any government before…Let us consider the sentiments which have been entertained by the people of America on this subject. At the revolution, it must be admitted that it was their sense to set down those great rights which ought, in all countries, to be held inviolable and sacred. Virginia did so, we all remember. She made a compact to reserve, expressly, certain rights.

"When fortified with full, adequate, and abundant representation, was she satisfied with that representation? No. She most cautiously and guardedly reserved and secured those invaluable, inestimable rights and privileges, which no people, inspired with the least glow of patriotic liberty, ever did, or ever can, abandon. She is called upon now to abandon them, and dissolve that compact which secured them to her. She is called upon to accede to another compact, which most infallibly supersedes and annihilates her present one. Will she do it? This is the question. If you intend to reserve your unalienable rights, you must have the most express stipulation; for, if implication be allowed, you are ousted of those rights. If the people do not think it necessary to reserve them, they will be supposed to be given up. How were the congressional rights defined when the people of America united by a confederacy to defend their liberties and rights against the tyrannical attempts of Great Britain? The states were not then contented with implied reservation. No, Mr. Chairman. It was expressly declared in our Confederation that every right was retained by the states, respectively, which was not given up to the government of the United States. But there is no such thing here. You, therefore, by a natural and unavoidable implication, give up your rights to the general government..."[9]

Against James Madison's protests, George Mason, the author of Virginia's Bill of Rights, also spoke in favor of including a statement of basic political rights in the Constitution.[10] Patrick Henry's substitute motion on the floor, requiring amendments and a Bill of Rights prior to ratification in the Virginia Assembly, lost by a vote of 80-88. Another delegate, Edmund Randolph, attempted a slightly modified motion which was approved. Randolph employed softer language but still pressed the need for stated rights. Subsequently, the Convention formed a committee to suggest a list of amendments of rights to the Congress. Just prior to the vote, Patrick Henry had drafted up his own list, most of which the committee incorporated into its final proposal.

In its first assembly, the United States Congress complied with the request from Virginia's delegates for a Statement of Rights. A similar request came from Massachusetts via motions from two men just as dedicated to liberty, Samuel Adams and John Hancock.

Had the ratification of the Constitution been left to the others, it is doubtful there would have been a Bill of Rights. Most of the Constitution has not proved as useful in binding the ever expanding role of the Federal Government. Nonetheless, that one page document containing our Bill of Rights remains critical to American freedoms to this day. It has provided a restraint to many a tyrant who would have rather liked to persecute innocent citizens and create a police state in this country.

During the constitutional debates, Henry was concerned that the citizens of the United States would be "transformed from respectable, independent citizens, to abject dependent subjects or slaves."[11]

He forewarned that any federal power to tax would create conditions where "rich, snug, fine, fat Federal officers—the collectors of taxes and excises—will outnumber anything from the States."[12]

Patrick Henry would have been horrified by the rise of the modern socialist state and the massive increase in the size of the federal government in the United States. He would have found the federal income tax, public schools, the 100,000 pages of the Federal Register, compulsory school attendance laws, child protective services, gun registration requirements, the regular exercise of eminent domain, zoning laws, wetlands regulations and enforcement, the 50 percent of the GNI consumed in government spending—all of it as a massive incursion on the liberties of a free nation. Perhaps that is why so few people in our day appreciate the man responsible for spearheading this nation's independence. Walter Williams, professor of Economics for George Mason University, points out that,

"In 1787, federal spending was about $3 million a year, or about $1 per citizen. By 1910, the Fed spent a little more than $600 million, about $6.75 per person. By 1929, the Fed spent $3 billion per year, $29 per person. Today, the Federal Government spends over $4 billion per day [or $8 billion per day at this time]! That comes to more than $6000 per year per person, or controlling for inflation, a 9,000 percent increase in federal spending between 1929 and today. The Colonists, who were paying about 67 cents a year in taxes, went to war with Great Britain."[13]

5. To the end, Patrick Henry maintained a strong faith in God, and operated from a true Christian worldview. He clearly recognized the sovereign hand of God over nations of men. During this period of the rise of deism and humanism, it is truly remarkable that the most influential leaders in this country retained such a commitment to God's providential direction over all things. In Henry's famous speech, he reminded the delegates in St. John's Church that, "There is a just God who presides over the destinies of nations and He shall fight our battles for us!"

Patrick Henry considered his cause righteous and just, not on the basis of some humanist manifesto or by the standards of Jean-Jacques

Rousseau. A just cause, as defined by Henry, could only be judged by a just God—not according to the will of the people. This is significant. Henry was willing to position himself and his nation at the feet of the Judge of Nations, and plead for His mercy. This sentiment would be supported whole-heartedly by the Continental Congress, as we will demonstrate in the next chapter.

There may be a little debate over the faith of some of America's founding fathers, but there is none concerning this man's Christian belief. He was unabashed in his profession of faith in Christ. In a letter to his sister, he writes, "O may we meet in heaven, to which the merits of Jesus will carry those who love and serve him."[14] While the trajectory of many living in the eighteenth century shifted from Christianity to Deism (even to Agnosticism), Patrick Henry remained solidly in the faith. In the final portion of his will, he included these memorable words: "I have now disposed of all my property to my family. There is one thing more I wish I could give them, and that is the Christian religion." His dying words included a testimony of his faith in Christ in the ears of the deist Dr. Cabell. As an eyewitness reported, "[Patrick Henry] prayed in clear words, a simple childlike prayer for his family, for his country, and for his own soul in the presence of death... speaking great words of love to his family, he told them that he was thankful for the goodness of God...Finally, fixing his eyes with much tenderness on his dear friend, Dr. Cabell, with whom he had formerly held many arguments respecting the Christian religion, he asked the doctor to observe how great a reality and benefit that religion was to a man about to die...after which they who were looking upon him, saw that his life had departed."[15]

CONCLUSION

Patrick Henry is hardly appreciated by this nation for his love of liberty. Most of the populace in our day do not resonate to his moving words because they do not appreciate freedom. They do not want a free country, but would prefer slavery to sin and tyrants over liberty. Election after election, they vote for tyrants to rule over them. But, there is still a faint heart beat for freedom that resonates in a small minority of Americans today. There are still some who make the pilgrimage into the Virginia House in old Williamsburg to recite the words of the famous speech again. They work their way up into the old homestead in Scotchtown and Red Hill, to visit the gravestone of an old freedom fighter, and to register their commitment to the age-old, noble cause of liberty once more.

The embers of liberty have died down, but they are not completely extinguished. There is still hope for freedom here or somewhere in the world, as long as there remain men of courage who follow the One who died to set us all free.

Chapter 12

FREEDOM SECURED: THE BLESSING OF GOD'S PROVIDENCE

Far out on the American frontier in Northeastern, Tennessee, music and shouting could be heard for a mile down the Holston River. A horseback rider approached the scene, bustling with neighbors gathered for some kind of celebration. The festivities were in high gear. Horse racing, barbecue, and dancing filled the farm yard.

"Hello Joseph! What's all the commotion?" The man on horseback addressed a young man who stepped out of the crowd to secure the rider's mount.

"Hullo Colonel Shelby! It's a celebration for Father and his new wife. He has remarried. Mother died eight months ago, you know."

"I had heard that. Who is the woman?"

"Catherine Sherill. My father saved her life four years ago during the Cherokee attack at Watauga. She failed to make the fort before the gate closed, but Father managed to lean over the fort wall and pull her to safety in the nick of time. I guess she figured she owed him her life, and she might as well give him the rest of her life."

"Bonnie Kate of Tennessee. I know of the woman." The visitor offered.

"She's a nice lady."

"I guess she'll have her hands full with ten children, and more to come no doubt."

"What's the business, Colonel? From the looks of your horse, you've come a·fair distance at an ambitious clip...bearing news no doubt."

"Yes, I must see your father immediately. We should not delay with this business."

Several years earlier Joseph's father, John Sevier, had received the rank of Lieutenant-Colonel, appointed to head the Washington County militia in the State of Tennessee. A seasoned Indian fighter, he had defended the settlers from many an attack on the frontier.

Standing in the veranda of the rough-hewn but sprawling farmhouse, Colonel Isaac Shelby quickly briefed Sevier concerning the purpose of his visit.

"The problem is Ferguson. He approaches with an army of thousands. You heard of the Waxhaws massacre at the hands of Commander Tarleton, and surely you know by now of Cornwallis' victory at Camden. He has decimated the American troops on the southern front, fairly well sealing the British foothold in the Carolinas. The only resistance left is whatever remains of the militias in the respective states, and that's not much. My 200 men have barely stayed a day ahead of Ferguson for weeks now. Tories everywhere are signing up by the thousands. They think nothing of American liberties, and they will kill their fellow countrymen on sight. As far as they are concerned, the war is as good as won. Ferguson sent a message carried by a certain prisoner—Samuel Phillips—to our camps most recently. He is marching his troops over these mountains, and he promises to kill every leader of the resistance and destroy every home and farm in this country."

John Sevier thought for a moment. "So it has come to this?" He said. "Either we fight or we will die and our families shall starve to death."

"Yes. I realize you may be out of harm's way for now, but rest assured, Ferguson's armies may very well make the Holston River in five days," Colonel Shelby said quietly.

"Then we shall fight. What do we have thus far in troops?"

"Whatever we can muster from the county militias. We cannot expect anything from General Washington, and Gate's army was destroyed at Camden. *We* are the extent of the resistance now, my friend."

"What can you provide from Sullivan County?" Sevier asked.

"About 240 seasoned frontier fighters—all good men."

"I can provide something similar from Washington County. May God's merciful providence attend our every move."

For the next three days, the two men, known to Major Patrick Ferguson as the leaders of "The Over Mountain Men," met and strategized a military defense of hearth and home. Messengers were sent to John Adair, tax collector for Sullivan County for emergency expenses, and both Sevier and Shelby offered their personal guarantee to return the funds should the State of North Carolina require it.

Meanwhile, Catherine Sevier's honeymoon was cut short, and she busied herself preparing new uniforms for her husband, and her new stepsons, Joseph, James, and John Jr.

* * *

It was agreed that the troops would muster in Sycamore Shoals, forty miles to the northeast of John Sevier's homestead, on September 25, 1780. And muster they did. Entire families from surrounding counties gathered, both men and boys with well-worn rifles in hand ready for battle. Women, children, and sweethearts were present to say farewell to their men. Never were men more determined to defend hearth and home. By this time, Ferguson's threats had made a deep impression upon the mind of every Over Mountain Man and his family. These men were eager to engage the battle. Everyone had heard the stories of the recent massacre of women and children at one of the frontier forts at the hands of a British captain with Indians in tow. There was the Redcoat captain who also had shot a small boy in cold blood, the son of a patriot in western South Carolina. Coupled with Ferguson's menace, the hangings at Camden, and the senseless brutality at Waxhaws, these Over Mountain Men had a clear understanding of what they must do. Colonel Arthur Sullivan and Colonel William Campbell together added 400 troops from Virginia, completing the makeshift army of a strictly volunteer militia.

Later that evening, the six militia leaders met for a consultation. Plans were made to march over the mountains south to Gilbert Town, North Carolina. Then, John Sevier addressed his fellow captains:

"Men, we shall not overcome our enemy except by the gracious providence of almighty God. I am the son of a Huguenot from France, and my ancestors have themselves witnessed the bloodshed, the massacres of innocent people at the hands of tyrants. Today, we find our opponent to be another great and formidable empire of man. Better men have lost battles to such forces. Hence, I have asked that a certain Reverend Samuel Doak, a Presbyterian minister, preach to our men on the biblical story of Gideon tomorrow morning at 7AM, before the march. I trust this is acceptable with my compatriots."

The captains agreed on the plan, and the next morning, the troops gathered in their respective companies with their families to hear this man of God preach a powerful message, and intercede before almighty God for their deliverance from the hand of the foe.

Rev. Doak's final words rang forcefully through the cool mountain air. Men were stirred. Hearts were ennobled to the great conflict, as the parson cried out to God above in prayer, "Oh God of battle! Arise in Thy might! Avenge the slaughter of Thy people. Confound those who plot for our destruction! Crown this mighty effort with victory. And smite those who exalt themselves against liberty and justice and truth. Help us as good soldiers, to wield the sword of the Lord and of Gideon!"[1]

Upon hearing these words, the troops marched out of the camp at Sycamore Shoals, and up Gap Creek, repeating that great battle cry from Scripture, "The Sword of the Lord and of Gideon!"

* * *

Rain poured down from the heavens, as sixteen-year-old, John Jr., seventeen year old James, and nineteen year old Joseph together entered their father's tent at the camp in Cowpens.

"Father, when will we see battle with Ferguson and his troops?" James asked.

"Tomorrow, we shall march on Kings Mountain. The British Major claims that he is king of that mountain, and that God Almighty cannot remove him from it. That is the word of Joseph Kerr, who has given us the whereabouts of the enemy. This Ferguson is a proud man, and I believe God will bring him down."

"How far is this mountain, Father?" his oldest son inquired.

"It is about twenty-six miles, and we shall march at the first break of dawn," his father replied.

"Then we will fight?"

"Yes. I will fight, and you will fight the British. Remember sons, we fight for our home and our liberty."

"How do we win this battle, Father?"

"You remember the words Reverend Doak told us. The Almighty will attend you, he said. He did not say that the Almighty may attend you, but that He will attend you. We must believe this, my sons." He paused for a moment. "But you know that we have the advantage?"

"If the British are at the top of the mountain, how do we have the advantage?" James piped in.

"We fight for our homes, and the British fight for an empire. This is a difference. I want you to remember that you were raised in these hills, my sons. You were born with rifles in your hands, and I believe every one of you can shoot straighter than a military man who picks up a gun every year or so. We shall fight like Indians. We shall move from tree to tree, and from boulder to boulder. Do not allow the enemy to see your face for more than two seconds—that's two counts. I know that you can aim and take a shot inside of a second and a half. Sons, I am very happy that you are here. Tomorrow you will prove yourselves men, who are able and willing to defend their homes. To-morrow will mark a glorious day for liberty!"

With that, the men retired to bed.

* * *

At 3PM on the following day, 800 men marched silently towards the decisive battle in the American War for Independence. The men were hungry, wet, and tired. For two weeks, they had pursued Ferguson and his men through the mountain country of the Carolinas. Besides a little parched corn and some raw turnips, they had had little to eat in several days. But, the moment had finally arrived. Everything was at stake in this battle—their homes, their wives and children. Liberty, the Carolinas…America was at stake. Truly, the outcome of this conflict would be either death or victory. This day they would fight for liberty all the way to the death. This was their commitment to a man, includ-ing the sixteen and seventeen-year-old men in the battle like John Jr. and James Sevier, James Collins, and Robert Henry from South Fork.

At the signal, John Jr., James, and Joseph joined the center col-umns on the eastern face of Kings Mountain. Instantly, a mighty volley of shot was heard from the enemy. John Jr. took cover, firing in the direction of the Tories above. The charge was a difficult one; the rock-strewn hill was very steep. Trees provided adequate coverage. He let go shot after shot, until he could see the Loyalists advancing on the American troops. Through the thick haze of gun smoke, John Jr. made out the movement of a Tory's bayonet sliding up his gun barrel. Before he could react, the sharp end had pierced his hand. He tripped on something in the commotion as he heard a rifle shot and saw his antagonist fall. His brother Joseph yanked him to his feet and they joined the retreat of the American troops. Taking refuge behind cover of trees near the base of the mountain, the American troops again returned volley for volley. Quickly wrapping his hand in a piece of cloth torn from his legging, John Jr. reloaded his rifle, and set the piece for another shot. He found that he could rest the gun barrel between his left arm and knee, while he took aim and pulled the trigger. Four more shots, and the Americans were advancing on the mountain again. Having gained half the distance up the mountain, again the British pressed down with bayonets, forcing a second retreat. It was clear by now that this battle would be a question of willpower. The Over Mountain Men had marched 140 miles over two weeks to defend their homes and their liberty, and they would not be easily resisted now.

On each of the three Loyalist attacks, John Jr. found himself returning to the same position under the fallen log near the bottom of the mountain. Each time, he fired off another 3-4 shots into the Tory column. "Two seconds...one and...aim and squeeze." Then, he would whip back under his refuge behind the fallen tree. He couldn't help but think to himself, "Nobody told these Tories about the two second rule." Young John was thankful for his father's instructions. At least three times, he witnessed enemy soldiers fall to his rifle shots.

Each time that the enemy retreated to its position up the mountain, John Jr. advanced, climbing over boulders and the bodies of wounded and dead men all the way. He could not help but notice that mostly redcoats were scattered on the field. "We must be winning," he thought. But this was no time to rest. He thought of his brothers, his sister, neighbors and friends. He thought of liberty for this new nation. Every inch of ground, every bullet fired mattered now. And so, the sixteen-year-old Over Mountain Man from the hills of Tennessee fought valiantly up the steep incline in the Battle of Kings Mountain.

On the fourth advance, it was clear that the enemy was distracted and confounded by the other two advancing columns towards the south and west approach to the mountain summit. The pressure placed on the eastern field had provided the opportunity for an advancement on the other side. As John Jr. approached the summit, he saw the figure of Maj. Patrick Ferguson attempting to abandon the field on horseback. The young man took aim and fired. At least seven other guns fired in unison, and the British captain fell to the ground. His two lieutenants fell beside him, sharing the same fate. It was at this moment that John Jr. saw his father leading his troops over the summit, firing hard as they advanced. Colonel Shelby and his men followed close behind. Minutes later, the white flag was visible from all sides of the mountain. Ferguson was dead. Of the 1,100 enemy troops, 375 were dead and the rest were taken prisoner. The Americans sustained a loss of only twenty-eight men.

* * *

On the following Tuesday morning, John Sevier and Isaac Shelby met with Colonel Campbell on the matter of the prisoners taken at Kings Mountain. Their militiamen from the Carolinas had recognized some of the men taken as culprits in recent acts of terror imposed on the citizenry of these states.

"Colonel," Sevier enjoined, "we would recommend that at least thirty-two of these men be taken to trial for atrocious crimes committed against the people of the Carolinas."

Campbell quickly agreed, "Yes. By court martial, we shall strike fear in the hearts of any that might be tempted to perpetuate these crimes in the future. It shall be done."

A proper court was held, and nine men were executed including Walter Gilkey, who had shot the young boy without provocation. And, Colonel Mills was executed for his raids on American settlements (killing women and children).

* * *

Four years earlier, thirteen colonies joined forces to face off against the most powerful empire on earth. The British Empire was flush with an almost unbroken record of military wins, consolidated political power, and unparalleled economic strength. This tremendous expansion came at the price of the ungodly slave trade, mercantilist policies, and taxation without representation. Seldom in the history of mankind has any people ever successfully resisted the imperialism of a rising empire and survived. Yet, that did not dissuade these young self-governing colonies from going to war against Britain, which had come to the zenith of its power.

During the initial meetings of the Continental Congress in the first year of the war, Benjamin Rush asked John Adams if they could win this contest. John Adam's reply is memorable and will resound in the hearts of free men until the end of history: "If we fear God and repent of our sins."[2] Such private testimonies like these are not political speeches given for effect. And they certainly cannot be taken as rash statements considering the circumstances. Here were men who feared God more than human empires. Why else would free men pledge their lives, their fortunes, and their sacred honor to a cause they would likely lose?

These were colonies without trained armies facing the most powerful empire of the day. Of course, there was a rising interest in deism. But the prevalent faith was anything but deism. These colonial leaders clearly believed that the winning and losing of wars was in the hands of God. Repentance is not a popular word in many churches today, let alone in Congress. However, the word has been familiar with true Christians from the beginning when Jesus Christ, John the Baptist, and the Apostles preached the doctrine. Repentance is essential to salvation, according to the Christian Gospel (Luke 5:32, 24:47, Acts 5:31). At the founding of this nation, this biblical idea of turning from sin was common parlance. Of course, the whole idea of repenting assumes that God is the Lawgiver and we have broken His law. When a nation sins against God's laws, that nation is then subject to the judgment of Almighty God. Because the founding fathers truly feared the judgment of God over and above the British armies, they considered repentance essential to the survival of this new nation.

After three years of conflict, things were going badly for the colonials and they were no closer to winning the war. Between the fall of 1779 and the summer of 1780, the Americans were facing the very worst of conditions. The French Navy, allied to the colonial cause, had miserably failed in its attacks on Newport, Rhode Island and Savannah, Georgia. In the most devastating setback of the war, General

Clinton had captured Charleston, South Carolina on December 26, 1779. In May 1780, the colonials suffered another tremendous loss at Waxhaws, resulting in a massacre of Virginians. Then, to make matters worse, General Gates' troops were routed by British General Tarleton, a man known for his cruelty, on August 16, 1780. In the North, George Washington was confronting the problem of mutiny among his troops. Some of his regiments were going days without food, reminiscent of the Valley Forge days. He had also just received the news of Benedict Arnold's treason. Circumstances could hardly have been worse.

During these highly critical weeks and months, we must pay particular attention to the actions taken by the Continental Congress, the body responsible for the administration of the war. Between the spring of 1780 and the spring of 1781, the Congress made three separate calls for national repentance and prayer. On April 28, 1780, the Congressional delegates issued the first call:

> "It having pleased the righteous Governor of the World, for the punishment of our manifold offenses, to permit the sword of war still to harass our country, it becomes us to endeavor, by humbling ourselves before him, and turning from every evil way, to avert his anger and obtain his favor and blessing, with one heart and one voice, to implore the sovereign Lord of Heaven and Earth to remember her mercy in his judgments; to make us sincerely penitent for our transgressions, to prepare us for deliverance, and to renounce the evils with which he is pleased to visit us."[3]

Then on October 17, 1780, the Continental Congress issued a call for another day of repentance and prayer assigned for December 7, 1780. The delegates instructed the people "to assemble on that day to celebrate the praises of our Divine Benefactor, to confess our unworthiness of the least of his favours, and to offer our fervent supplications to the God of all graces, that it may please him to pardon our heinous transgressions and incline our hearts for the future to keep all His laws and to cause the knowledge of Christianity to spread all over the earth."[4]

Expressed here in a clear statement is nothing less than the very essence of Christian government, the basis of all liberty on earth: the leaders of this nation solicited the sovereign Ruler of the universe to "incline our hearts for the future to keep all His laws." Not only did they acknowledge God's sovereignty over the hearts of men, and the necessity of regeneration, but they submitted themselves to God's sovereignty in the area of ethics. This is the complete opposite of a humanist-based democracy that recognizes only man as the source of law. This explicit recognition of God as the source of law would not be welcomed in many American churches today, let alone the legislatures. Also, the commitment to the spread of Christianity is highly important at this seminal point in the history of the country. Over the following two centuries, America became the primary source of financial support for the worldwide missionary movement. These words were both confessional and prophetic. Of course, humanism and state-endorsed polytheism (the respect of all gods and religions) would eventually dominate the American governments. During these early sessions of the Continental Congress, however, there was no interest in supporting Islam, Humanism, and the other world religions. America was born a Christian country.

America would quickly shift towards Enlightenment thinking, however, for there was an aggressive battle of ideas taking place at that very moment. The humanist Enlightenment was pressing on the entire world, but especially in Europe. Nonetheless, America was uniquely blessed by a revival of faith that came by way of the Great Awakening of the 1740s and 1750s. This was the seedbed in which men like John Witherspoon, Patrick Henry, and Samuel Adams were raised. At this time, they were far more influenced by George Whitefield than by Jean-Jacques Rousseau and his ilk.

Would these official proclamations from America's leaders at this critical juncture make any difference in the scheme of history? Is there truly a God in the heavens who presides over the destiny of nations, as these men believed and as Patrick Henry declared in his speech before the second Virginia convention? Does God take any interest in the proclamations issued by rulers He has placed in position? Is this

God as interested in nations as He is in the sparrows that fall? Is He as interested in modern nations as He was with Nineveh when Jonah called that wicked empire to repentance? Does He hold the fragile, highly vulnerable nations and armies and institutions of men between His thumb and forefinger? If this nation above all nations favored the true and living God, the God of the Bible, the Creator of heaven and earth, would He show favor to them? Would those peoples who would acknowledge God as sovereign receive His favor by His sovereign decree? Would He respond to a spirit of humble repentance as demonstrated on a national level? Obviously, the members of the Continental Congress must have held to this view of God, and believed that He might have mercy upon this nation. They must have believed Psalm 33:12, Daniel 4:17, Luke 13:3, and Acts 17:30. Indeed, God is sovereign over the nations, and He really does "call all men everywhere to repentance."

> "Blessed is the nation whose God is the Lord; and the people whom he hath chosen for his own inheritance." (Ps. 33:12)

> "This matter is by the decree of the watchers, and the demand by the word of the holy ones: to the intent that the living may know that the most High ruleth in the kingdom of men, and giveth it to whomsoever he will, and setteth up over it the basest of men." (Dan. 4:17)

> "I tell you, Nay: but, except ye repent, ye shall all likewise perish." (Luke 13:3)

> "And the times of this ignorance God winked at; but now commandeth all men every where to repent:" (Acts 17:30)

No doubt most political leaders today would scoff at these notions. When the worst hurricane in the history of this country hit the shores of New Orleans in 2005 (Hurricane Katrina), there was neither a call for national repentance nor any mention of God's judgment. There may have been a call for prayer, although this is increasingly rare. Nonetheless, the idea that the sin of New Orleans or the sin of America is of any interest whatsoever to the Almighty is rejected out of hand. American leaders, Republican and Democrat alike, tend not to allow God the right to define law or sin, let alone punish for sin.

HEAVEN'S RESPONSE

Last fall, I took my family to Colonial Williamsburg in Virginia for the first time in order that we might experience living history at the time of America's War for Independence. We spent a little time touring the large Anglican Church (where members of the Virginia Assembly attended while in legislative session). As we walked down a side street, it started to rain and we ran for cover under the eaves of an obscure, out-of-the-way building. Peering into the windows, we could see several wooden benches and a small podium crowded into a small room. I noticed an inconspicuous plaque near the entrance containing the words, "Presbyterian Meeting House." One of the resident guides explained that this was not a church, only a meeting house for Presbyterians who wished to hear the Word of God preached on occasion. The State of Virginia had restricted religious freedoms from 1607, and only the Anglican church received state sanction and financial support. What a contrast between the humble Presbyterian meeting house and the ornate Anglican Parish Church at the center of the town!

* * *

There are moments when the future sits in a very delicate balance. The prospects for liberty are tenuous. From a human perspective, the conflict appears to be a losing cause in the wake of constant setbacks and depleted resources. In this case, the answer to the appeals of America's leaders came from the Lord of Heaven and Earth...in a rather odd way.

It was in the summer of 1780 that Francis Marion, the legendary Swamp Fox of South Carolina, began his escapades. Marion was a descendant of the French Huguenots, Calvinist Protestants who were persecuted out of France in the seventeenth century. He assembled a merry band of Scots-Irish Presbyterians who gave the English no end of grief through small skirmishes throughout the Carolinas well into the spring of 1781. Marion's feats are worthy of note, but they did not turn the tide of the war.

The decisive event occurred on October 7, 1780. The British Major Patrick Ferguson had warned the South Carolinians that he was coming to "hang your leaders, and waste your country with fire and sword."[5] The threat of scorched earth warfare (as condemned in Deut. 20:19-20) became a real concern for the citizens. As Ferguson and his troops approached a place called Kings Mountain near the border of North Carolina, the Major vowed that he would be "'King of that mountain,' and…even God almighty could not remove him."[6] Now, this was a mistake. These sorts of declarations do not end well. To deny the sovereignty of God, while claiming sovereignty to oneself is hazardous business.

Meanwhile, out on the western frontier, in a town called Sycamore Shoals, Tennessee, the settlers had organized a militia to defend hearth and home from the invading force. They called themselves the "Over Mountain Men," largely consisting of "Scots-Irish Presbyterians." As the men prepared for battle, they solicited the aid of their Presbyterian pastor to preach the sermon. The little known Reverend Samuel Doak preached what may have been the most powerful sermon in the history of this country. He ended his final prayer with the passionate words from the Old Testament Scriptures, "The sword of the Lord and of Gideon!"

With that pastoral encouragement, the men marched off to the battle of Kings Mountain on the South Carolina border. It would prove to be the shortest and most decisive battle in the history of American warfare. In a single hour, the men shattered the Ferguson army. It was a total rout—the British lost 1,100 men by death or capture, as compared to the Mountain Men's twenty-eight casualties. Kings Mountain was the turning point for the colonials in the war. It was a catalytic moment in the history of freedom.

One historian summarizes the effects of the win: "The Victory at Kings Mountain was the first in a series of remarkable events that would change the direction of the war in America's favor."[7] The British General Henry Clinton himself admitted this concerning Kings Mountain in his report to King George: "Though in itself confessedly trifling, overset in a moment all the happy effects of his Lordship's glorious victory at Camden, and so encouraged the spirit of rebellion in both Carolinas that it never could be afterward humbled."[8]

General Clinton's assessment was entirely accurate. War is all about morale. The delicate balance of powers bearing such historical import will shift in wartime when the morale within the armies shifts. Ultimately, there is nothing human leadership can do to secure a certain morale. Such critical elements lie in the hand of God, and certain obscure battles may potentially shift morale in one direction or another.

Yet, this was not the end of the story. The next momentous battle occurred on January 17, 1781, also on the southern front. The British General Tarleton pursued Brigadier General Daniel Morgan with 1,100 British troops through the South Carolina back country for weeks. Finally, Morgan elected to take the stand at a road meadowland called Cowpens on January 17th. The Americans were outnumbered again, but it was another overwhelming victory in favor of the colonials. Almost the entire British force was either dead or captured by the end, and Tarleton fled the battlefield alone. This concluded a series of victories secured by the disparaged, motley band of Presbyterians. General Daniel Morgan was also a devout Presbyterian layman of Welsh background.

Reports have it that General Morgan rode across the field praising God for the victory. Later he recorded these words concerning the Battle of Cowpens: "Such was the inferiority of our numbers, that our success must be attributed under God…to the justice of our cause and the bravery of our troops!"[9] An Irish Presbyterian soldier from the Carolina back country described the battle more plainly in his prayer: "Good Lord, our God that art in heaven, we have great reason to thank Thee for the many battles we have won…the great and glorious battle of Kings Mountain, and the 'iver' glorious and memorable battle of the Cowpens, where we made the Proud Gineral Teartleton run 'doon' the road helter-skelter!"[10]

General George Washington also recognized the importance of these battles and the providential hand of God on the southern front. He wrote shortly after Cowpens: "The many remarkable interpositions of the divine government in the hours of our deepest distress and darkness have been too luminous to suffer me to doubt the happy issue of the present contest."

Following several minor setbacks for the colonials, the war was over. The Battle of Yorktown was fought just ten months after Cowpens, upon Washington's troops moving to the southern front, where the British force had already been badly weakened.

That is the story of how a few backwoods Presbyterians overcame the most powerful armies on earth, and laid another brick in the wall for freedom. Doubtless, these men carried with them memories of the killing time that had visited their forefathers a century earlier. These Scots had felt the full brunt of tyranny at the hands of the British monarchy, during the brutal Stuart reign of James I, Charles I, Charles II, and James II. Surely, the stories of the burnings, drownings, hangings, and tortures were still fresh in the minds of the patriots who came across the ocean to enjoy a little respite from that tyranny.

These are the roots of the most God-blessed nation in the world. America eventually produced over a third of the Gross World Product by the mid-2000s (although the blessing is rapidly diminishing now). Hardly any other nation has surpassed this country in terms of its economic, political, and religious freedoms. The United States is the most charitable nation in the world.[11] It is the nation that has supported the largest Christian missionary movement over the last two centuries. To this day, this nation retains the highest percentage of people who still believe God created them 6,000 to 10,000 years ago.[12] This nation spawned the creationist movements and the homeschooling and Christian schooling movements of the 1970s-1990s. European nations may mock the United States for its strong commitment to a theistic worldview, but World War II would have had an entirely different outcome had it not been for America. The godless tyrants from Germany may have wreaked even more havoc had it not been for America's involvement. Freedom does provide a net value for the kingdom of God. This nation became a tool in the hand of the Lord Jesus Christ to do much good over succeeding centuries. America was preserved by the providence of God in the winter of 1780. Since then, this nation has enjoyed great prosperity despite its many compromises with sinful practices like Unitarianism in the north and generational, chattel slavery in the south. Our history provides ample demonstrations of the longsuffering and mercy of God.

What would the world have been like had it not been for an obscure Presbyterian pastor named Samuel Doak and the little band of Over Mountain Men in Sycamore Shoals, Tennessee? What a great experiment in liberty this has been, in the history of the world! To this day, a handful of Christians have taken up the spiritual heritage of these hardy Presbyterian Mountain Men, utterly committed to the sovereign providence of God and the principles of freedom based upon the law of God. They find their roots directly connected to William Tyndale, John Knox, Samuel Rutherford, John Robinson, John Winthrop, John Cotton, Richard and Increase Mather, Samuel Davies, George Whitefield, and Jonathan Edwards. Will our God bless us with another mighty reformation that might yield one more free nation somewhere on earth? Will we see more examples of men with faith and courage to champion the cause of freedom once more for the enslaved masses in this sin-cursed world?

* * *

SAMUEL DOAK'S SERMON AT SYCAMORE SHOALS ON OCTOBER 7, 1780

The following are excerpts from Samuel Doak's famous sermon given at Sycamore Shoals on October 7, 1780, with the concluding prayer that set the course of history for the United States of America.

"My countrymen, you are about to set out on an expedition which is full of hardships and dangers, but one in which the Almighty will attend you. The Mother Country has her hand upon you, these American colonies, and takes that for which our fathers planted their homes in the wilderness—our liberty. Taxation without representation and the quartering of soldiers in the homes of our people without their consent are evidence that the crown of England would take from its American Subjects the last vestige of Freedom. Your brethren across the mountains are crying like Macedonia unto your help. God forbid that you should refuse to hear and answer their call—but the call of your brethren is not all. The enemy is marching hither to destroy your homes. Brave men, you are not unacquainted with battle. Your hands have already been taught to war and your fingers to fight. You have wrested these beautiful valleys of the Holston and Watauga from the savage hand. Will you tarry now until the other enemy carries fire and sword to your very doors? No, it shall not be. Go forth then in the strength of your manhood to the aid of your brethren, the defense of your liberty and the protection of your homes. And may the God of Justice be with you and give you victory.

"Let us pray. Almighty and gracious God! Thou hast been the refuge and strength of Thy people in all ages. In time of sorest need we have learned to come to Thee—our Rock and our Fortress. Thou knowest the dangers and snares that surround us on march and in battle. Thou knowest the dangers that constantly threaten the humble, but well beloved homes, which Thy servants have left behind them. Oh, in Thine infinite mercy, save us from the cruel hand of the savage, and of tyrant. Save the unprotected homes while fathers and husbands and sons are far away fighting for freedom and helping the oppressed. Thou, who promised to protect the sparrow in its flight, keep ceaseless watch, by day and by night, over our loved ones. The helpless women and little children, we commit to Thy care. Thou wilt not leave them or forsake them in times of loneliness and anxiety and terror. Oh, God of Battle, arise in Thy might. Avenge the slaughter of Thy people. Confound those who plot for our destruction. Crown this mighty effort with victory, and smite those who exalt themselves against liberty and justice and truth. Help us as good soldiers to wield the sword of the Lord and of Gideon. Amen."[13]

Part IV

~

LOSING FREEDOM

Chapter 13

THE MODERN
DRACONIAN STATE

"And I will walk at liberty: for I seek thy precepts." (Ps. 119:45)

There is little talk of freedom today because there is little concern about tyranny and sin. This has something to do with the fact that there is so little mention of sin in the pulpits. When Christianity fails to define law and liberty by God's Word, the political agendas are set by the secular humanists. Without fail, the policies of the humanists will only produce more tyranny, more immorality, and a curtailment of political freedoms.

The tyranny of the modern world is somewhat unique in that it really does maintain reasonable levels of comfort, at least so far. Christians in Western countries are not exactly burned at the stake these days. True, there is martyrdom and human suffering in nations like North Korea, China, Sudan, and Iran. In the post-Christian nations however, no one is walking around in leg irons, no one is starving to death, and there are no dead rats floating in the soup. Few Americans would refer to themselves or their neighbors as "slaves." The average citizen, even the average church-attending professing Christian would never describe the federal government as "tyrannical." If the social security check arrives on time, what is there to be concerned about? If a man values economic security above all else, he can hardly be troubled by the aggregate loss of freedoms in the nation.

How does one identify the loss of freedom or the rise in tyranny? Trend charts are helpful tools. The proverbial frogs who find themselves sitting in the water at 211°F are unaware of what has happened to them. If the temperature has risen a degree every year for one hundred years, they will not notice the rise...unless they have read a book like this, and have examined the charts contained in this chapter. There is benefit to asking these questions. How is life different than it was 100 years ago? Is there more government in our lives now than there was in 1776?

If slavery is defined as the superfluous and cruel servitude of men (1 Cor. 7:21), where might we find forms of servitude today? Are Christians still obligated to seek freedom? In the present context, how do believers follow through on this principle? There are two major forms of servitude and one minor form that men face in the developed countries today. The first major area is debt slavery. The Bible tells us that the "debtor is servant to the lender" (Prov. 22:7). Passages like Romans 13:8 and Deuteronomy 15:7ff clearly discourage debt (except for the very poorest in a community). Since 1900, personal debt has increased in this country by a factor of 20 (as a percentage of the GDP).[1]

This is not because Americans are impoverished through lack of opportunity or technological improvements in manufacturing and living conditions. They may be impoverishing their grandchildren and great-grandchildren by a debt-based economy, but they certainly are not forced into debt because of imminent starvation and homelessness. Over the last century, the average size of homes increased from 900 sq. ft. to 2200 sq. ft.,[2] while the birth rate has shrunk by half. That's twice the square-footage for twenty-times the debt, to accommodate half the number of kids. If the wisdom of Proverbs defines slavery accurately, then we must conclude that Americans have capitulated to a slave-based mentality and a slave-based economy over the last several generations.

The second form of servitude comes in the form of government taxation and regulation. Incredibly, government spending at all levels (federal, state, and local) in this country consumed only 8 percent of the GDP in 1900. As of 2010, government spending topped 40 percent of the GDP, an increase of five fold in a century.[3]

The third form of servitude is less tangible, and more difficult to measure. When it comes to economic servitude, there is a continuum of varying levels of enslavement. For example, hired servants are distinguished from chattel slaves in Scripture. There is a difference between contract labor and corporate salaried labor. Families have fragmented and family economies disintegrated as a result of the form of labor developed during the industrial revolution. Replacing the once ubiquitous family farms and small businesses of earlier centuries, the industrial machine steamrolled the family and restructured social systems. Conservative estimates would find seven times the self-employment in 1900 than there is today.[4]

The average American householder, therefore, is more enslaved than he was in 1900. He is tied down by a thousand Lilliputians—five times more government, twenty times more debt, and seven times more oversight from layers of bureaucratic management. Slavery has curtailed flexibility for families, churches, and the kingdom of God in general. In a materialist age, economic wealth is the only criteria of success. They "love wealth more than liberty, the tranquility of servitude better than the animating contest of freedom," as Samuel Adams would put it. They pretend to be rich, but they have little true sustainable wealth.

Of the three forms of servitude, the average family has more control over their debt and family economy, than they do over the growth of the totalitarian state. In following chapters, we will identify rays of hope for the Christian who finds value in the battle for freedom. There are islands of freedom to which we may repair, but before identifying these critical battlefronts, we shall first consider the rise of governmental tyranny in the modern world.

THE TOTALITARIAN STATE

Slowly but surely, most of the "democratic" nations in the West have accepted totalitarian forms of government. Identifying truthful and telling metrics is vitally important for understanding the present state of affairs. These charts will not be found in public school history and civics textbooks, or on the 6 o'clock news. To gain an accurate picture of the growth of the state in any nation, one particular trend chart is the most helpful of all. It is that which displays the growth of government spending, at all levels, as a percentage of the Gross National Income.

CHART 1

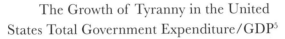

The Growth of Tyranny in the United
States Total Government Expenditure/GDP[5]

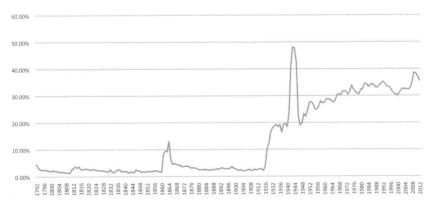

Chart 1 perfectly illustrates the encroachment of government into the life of the average American over the years. For example, government made up only 3-5 percent of the average person's life in the 1800s. Over a hundred years, that ratio has steadily increased to 40 percent. The metric is independent of population and inflation. It measures the total part government plays in our lives, by considering the proportion of the entire economy taken up by total government expenditures. Similar graphs can be produced for other countries, illustrating similar trends. With very few interludes throughout the length of this nation's history, the United States has experienced a steady increase in the size of government. Never before in history have governments played so extensive a role in the lives of the peoples of the nations. The vision of Plato's *Republic* and Orwell's Big Brother is realized in the modern world. To have brought about such a radical social change as pictured by the graph above, a society must have undergone a complete change of worldview. This has happened by way of the education system in this country, an essential element of the socialist, humanist construct.

Nonetheless, for most of the nineteenth century, America retained a high degree of freedom. The centrist powers engaged strongly in the period surrounding the Civil War. In fact, each war created the opportunity for a permanent increase in the size of government. After the war, the expenditures to GDP ratio never quite returned to pre-war levels. There were modest decreases in the size of governments in America during the 1990s under President Clinton (and in the 2000s under Barack Obama); however, most Republicans and Democrats have supported expansion of government over the last hundred years. If freedom from big government is a value to any today, the Republican party is not and has never been the party of less government (despite its pretense otherwise).

The chart above includes state government expenditures all told. However, some states are more conservative than others. The most tyrannical states in the Union as measured by state government expenditure (as a percentage of the state's product) are: West Virginia (34 percent), Alaska (24 percent), Wyoming (22 percent), Mississippi (20 percent), and Arkansas (19 percent). All five of these states are purportedly governed by "conservatives" or Republicans. Texas has the lowest state expenditures as a percentage of the gross state product (7 percent).[6] It should be pointed out that by the early part of the twenty-first century, all the states are subjected to tyrannical, centralized powers in Washington, DC.

Historically and biblically speaking, any government requiring more than a tenth of the people's income in taxation must be defined as a tyranny. Whether they call themselves Christian, Republican, or

Conservative, if they will not bind government to a standard (outside of the arbitrary whim of the democratic vote), they are no friends of freedom. Rather they contribute to the advancement of the tyrannical state.

> "And [the king] will take the tenth of your seed, and of your vineyards, and give to his officers, and to his servants…and ye shall cry out in that day because of your king which ye shall have chosen you; and the LORD will not hear you in that day." (1 Sam. 8:15,18)

Even in preparation for the worst economic disaster in Egypt's early history, the Pharaoh only taxed his people at a rate of 20 percent for seven years, under the presumption that he would collect no tax for the succeeding seven years. This was a special dispensation ordered by direct prophetic word from God (Gen. 41:34). Benjamin Franklin would have been horrified to think that America would become a tyrannical state. This founding father of our free nation wrote,

> "It would be thought a hard government that should tax its people one tenth of their time, to be employed in its service."[7]

America has presented itself to the world as the land of the free and the home of the brave, but increasingly it has forfeited that vision. America has turned itself into the most expensive tyranny in the world in total dollars. No other country comes close to this nation's total government expenditures. Three-trillion dollar federal budgets (and an additional three trillion for state and local governments), a $20 trillion debt, and a $100 trillion in unfunded liabilities is a very big empire indeed. This amounts to more money in total than any government has had to spend in the history of mankind (as far as we know)—more than Rome, more than the Soviet Union, more than Hitler's Third Reich, and more than Babylon at its zenith. If money is power, then the United State government is the most powerful in the world. George Washington would be concerned. Of course, our leaders would find him a little odd for mistrusting government with this much money and power. Washington is quoted as saying,

> "Government is not reason. Government is not eloquence. It is force. And, like fire, it is a dangerous servant and a fearful master."[8]

These expenditures are funded in three forms: direct taxation, inflation (which deflates the value of the people's money), and debt, which places a tax on future generations. The citizens are taxed at every level. Until the turn of the twentieth century, the Constitutionally secured balance of powers and the Tenth Amendment ensured a decentralized government. The expansion of the federal government after the civil war made the Tenth Amendment basically irrelevant. Simultaneously, the state and local governments adopted socialist ideologies, and expanded their powers by orders of magnitude over the last century. We are taxed if we earn income. We are taxed if we invest what we have saved after income tax. We are taxed if we sell our real estate, even if the only capital gains we have received came by way of inflation (devalued money). We are taxed if we buy anything with the money we have earned after our income is taxed. We are taxed if we own anything of value, such as property or business investments.

After a lifetime of hard labor, it is a small miracle if a family is able to scrape together a tiny inheritance for the children and grandchildren. After forfeiting 40 percent in income taxes, and paying tax on the 5 percent interest earned on savings, and watching inflation consume 3-8 percent of savings each year, a good man still hopes to leave an inheritance to his children's children (Prov. 13:22). However, the base federal tax rate on inheritance is 55 percent. Add to that an additional 10-15 percent imposed by state governments for the death tax, and there is precious little to share with the children. These taxes are adjusted rather arbitrarily at the whim of powerful forces in government; but assuming that a man saves $1,000,000 to share with his children in the year 2040, inflation has taken $400,000 of the value, leaving $600,000. At a 70 percent tax rate, he now may leave for his children a mere $180,000 in present value. It is no wonder that only 5 percent of Americans expect to receive anything substantial in inheritance from their parents. If the family is the major impediment to the growth of the state in the modern world, then disenfranchising the family by ruining inheritance is one of the most important strategies. Karl Marx's third plank in the Communist Manifesto was "Abolition of All Rights of Inheritance." If the family legacy were to grow generation by generation, eventually healthy family economies would compete with governments for power—and that would be unacceptable to the all-consuming state.

THE FUTURE TAX

The most insidious tax of all is the hidden tax of government debt. This debt is assisted by a government manipulated monetary system, in which the value of money disintegrates while certain lenders and debtors are benefited. This becomes a tax on the future. To better grasp the slow but steady move towards tyranny, the following graph follows the United States Federal Debt as a ratio of the GDP from 1792 to the present.

CHART 2

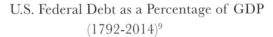

U.S. Federal Debt as a Percentage of GDP
(1792-2014)[9]

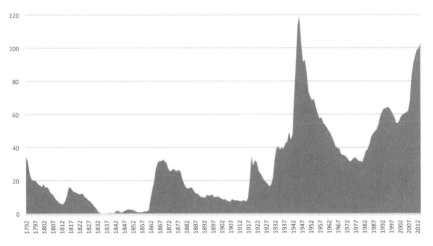

As of 2014, this country has reached a debt-to-GDP ratio of 110 percent. In 2000, America ranked as the 54th worst country in the world by debt-to-GDP, and only fourteen years later it ranked as the 10th worst country in the world (based on the same metric).[10] Worse still, this debt was racked up during a period of relative productivity and peace. The other peaks on the chart represent the Civil War,

World War I, and World War II. Debt is a hidden tax on future generations and guarantees impoverishment for the nation's grandchildren. Of the developed nations, only Italy, Portugal, Greece, and Japan are in worse shape than America. The two largest economies in the world (the United States and Japan) are among the very worst when considering the debt-to-GDP ratio. Given the international economy operating today, this scenario points to a worldwide depression of the most calamitous sort at some point in the future (the precedent of which we have never seen). If unfunded liabilities are included in the balance sheet, some believe that America's total debt exceeds $100 trillion.[11] Both Republican and Democrat administrations have added to the debt since the Clinton Administration. George W. Bush doubled the entire national debt in eight years, and Barack Obama tripled the debt in seven years.[12]

This is the work of tyrants, as defined in history and Scripture. They may be democratically elected tyrants, but they are still unprincipled leaders. The people themselves may be so corrupted that they would prefer national bankruptcy and tyranny to responsible economics and freedom. Nonetheless, the political leaders must take responsibility for this tyrannical and destructive governance.

Chapter 14
CREATING THE
SLAVE MENTALITY

"Jesus answered them, Verily, verily, I say unto you, Whosoever committeth sin is the servant of sin." (John 8:34)

A bond slave is defined as one who is entirely dependent upon the slave master. He does not earn his own living, and his activities are largely governed by the person who provides his room and board. His dependence upon the master greatly restricts his ability to make his own choices and direct his own life. Chattel slavery begins to develop when this servitude extends into the generations. One of the most egregious elements of chattel slavery occurs when the family is divided, and the husband-wife relationship is shattered. This element was seen in some instances with American slavery in the nineteenth century.[1] Something similar has played out with the majority of welfare recipients in this country since 1960. Almost 75 percent of African American children are born outside of wedlock, up from 14 percent in 1940.[2] However, it should be noted that this is not a problem inherent in a certain "race" or culture. The problem is with the breakdown of the family in the welfare state and the inner city. As of 2015, some cities in this country claim a single parent rate as high as 78 percent.[3] A Johns Hopkins University study found that the illegitimacy rate in the welfare state of Baltimore, Maryland was fifteen times higher than that in Nigeria (and the physical health of children in Baltimore was also inferior to that of African children).[4]

A slave nation is one in which the majority of the population is subservient to the government. For the first time in this nation's history, the majority of Americans receive a check from the government. Whether it be pure welfare or social security funds, Americans have become dependent on the great slave master in Washington, DC.

The Heritage Foundation's Index of Dependency on Government measures the relationship between taxpayers and tax consumers, using 1980 as its baseline year with a value of 100 and reaching back to 1962. The index has grown to 240, an increase of a whopping 31 percent since 2001.[5] According to the 2012 Economic Freedom of the World Report, America has dropped from the tenth place to the eighteenth place in just three years, falling below Denmark and Finland.[6]

Chart 3 illustrates the rise in government dependence taking into account only social security, food stamps, and Medicaid participation. Chart 4 combines the three metrics, and presents the percentage of the population beholden to government. When the ratio of those receiving government benefits exceeds 50%, socialism takes the upper hand over an economy indefinitely, and it will not be turned back short of some catastrophic collapse or revolutionary shift in governance. When the majority of the voting population has discovered that they can redistribute the wealth and vote for their own "pay raise," there is little hope for free enterprise or healthy economies in the future of the nation.

CHART 3

Growth in Government Reliance in the United States (1930-2014)[7]

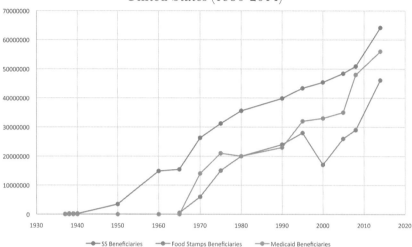

SS Beneficiaries — Food Stamps Beneficiaries — Medicaid Beneficiaries

CHART 4

The Slave Ratio—Overall Percentage of US Population Dependent on Government (1930-2014)

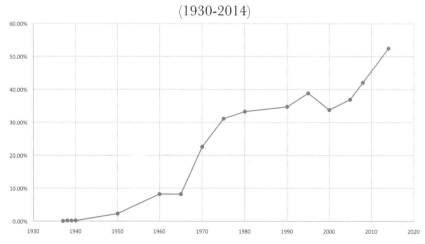

It is a contemptible condition to sink to this level of servitude. Certainly in the history of the Western world, we have never seen anything quite this catastrophic. When it comes to the integrity of the family, African nations do better on a social level than either America or Sweden. When was the last time such a high percentage of people were subjected to this level of servitude? True, not many are starving to death...yet. This presents the perfect conditions for mass starvations or heavy-handed tyranny. In this case, civil governments and various institutions have drained hundreds of millions of people of their character, family integrity, and the basic social systems that might sustain them through hard times. They have given incentive to the slave mentality, while at the same time undermining the work ethic and character for millions. Families assume very little responsibility for their own children and their own parents, and more than ever before, families are less committed to providing care for their parents in their old age.

That is why 2011 becomes a symbolic year in the history of this nation. This was the year that the Social Security Fund went into the red for the first time (and remains in the red for each successive year afterwards). Social Security was developed as a sophisticated Ponzi scheme, always relying on a positive birth replacement rate and a strong worker-to-retiree ratio. The timing for the breakdown of Social Security could not have been worse, because 2011 was also the year that the first of eighty million Baby Boomers entered their retirement years. For the following eighteen years, 80 million Baby Boomers will retire, requiring a great deal of economic support over the succeeding thirty-five years. Since 1960, the Baby Boomers began an abortion holocaust that has resulted in 80 million dead babies (by surgical abortion and various abortifacient birth control devices). Who will support these retirees in most of the developed countries around the world through the 2050s? The birth rate is imploding in 110 countries around the world, mostly affecting first world countries. This will profoundly impact worker-to-retiree (or elderly) ratios towards the middle of the twenty-first century.[8] In the United States for example, the worker-to-retiree ratio in 2040 will be 1/3 of what it was in 1950 (when social security was first implemented).[9]

But what about the character of the younger generation? Will those few young people left be able to support the heavy load of elderly retirees and a bankrupt social security system? Alas, the timing could not be worse. The character of the nation is in free fall. Over 50 percent of Americans are now supported by government mostly by welfare programs, as noted above. Over 50 percent of children born to women under thirty years of age are born out of wedlock, up from 6 percent in 1960.[10] If young men will not be the father to their own children, why would they care for the elderly?

The young men will play their computer games while the empires burn to the ground (a pattern witnessed at the fall of Rome in the 4th and 5th centuries). Also, we may ask, what lesson did the Baby Boomer generation pass on when they aborted 80 million siblings of those that will be working and voting in the year 2030? To make matters even worse, *TIME* magazine reports the Millennial generation to be the "laziest, the unluckiest, and the most narcissistic generation" ever.[11] These young people, on average, start out with less capital than any previous generation, and they are saddled with three hundred times more debt than the Gen X'ers carried in the 1970s and 1980s.[12] Meanwhile, the Baby Boomers retire with far more debt than the Silent Generation and very little, if any, inheritance to pass along.[13] This is what you get when a nation soaks in narcissism, materialism, and socialism over half a century. This experiment with socialism will not bode well for the future. What will the most narcissistic generation do to the 80 million Baby Boomers that contributed to 80 million abortions between 1970 and 2000, in the year 2040?

Mass euthanasia appears to be the only possible answer to the question, given the present economics, social conditions, and moral perspectives of this nation (and most Western developed nations). The degree to which euthanasia is employed will depend on whether the state rations medicine or not.

STATE-CONTROLLED MEDICINE

On February 7, 2009, the front page of *Newsweek* magazine announced, "We're All Socialists Now!" Of course, the article referred to the bi-partisan support for socialist medical care from both presidential candidates in the 2008 election. Republican Mitt Romney had incorporated a mandatory insurance program in Massachusetts, and

Democrat Barack Obama was eager to propose a similar program for the nation.

The history of socialist medicine in America began in the 1930s, when the first insurance programs received special tax advantages from which individuals and smaller businesses were excluded. Price and wage controls during World War II also forced corporations to compete for labor based on benefit packages rather than pay. During the mid-1960s, President Lyndon B. Johnson introduced Medicare and Medicaid, which is the primary means whereby the federal government captured 35-40 percent direct control over the medical needs of the nation. Fascism (or a government-regulated economy) increased its hold on medical care in the 1970s. The HMO Act of 1973 made grants and loans available to Health Maintenance Organizations and removed certain state restrictions if the HMO's became federally certified. Once again, government collusion created powerful systems that undermined the free market and created additional big government and big medicine. Finally, the Affordable Care Act (commonly known as Obamacare) was passed by Congress and signed by the President in 2010. This bill required medical insurance for all Americans, with several minor exclusions. Because not all Americans would be able to afford this insurance (with very stringent minimum requirements attached), federal government subsidies were inevitable and approved by the Supreme Court of the United States in a final decision handed down on June 22, 2015.[14] Fascism almost always morphs into socialism over time, as government must eventually subsidize the systems they regulate. Since implementation in 2014, problems with Obamacare have multiplied; when the smoke cleared, 86 percent of those enrolling with the insurance plan were government-subsidized.[15] That is how the scales tipped towards total socialism in one of the last free Western nations by the year 2014.

Obamacare also came with a serious marriage penalty attached. The Kaiser Family Foundation has calculated that penalty to be anywhere between $7,000 and $11,000 per family.[16] Such penalties encourage divorce and shack-ups, where men and women live together outside of the bonds of marriage. This further fractures the family and individualizes human society, as persons become more beholden to the state than to the family.

If we have learned anything from the last one-hundred-year experiment with socialism, it is this: what the government funds, the government controls. Every freedom minded man needs to understand this. When government subsidizes medical care, government can ration that care as well. Given that socialist medicine has been entrenched in a nation, suppose a young couple discovers their child in utero has Down Syndrome through an amniocentesis test. The decision concerning medical care for the child now lies in the hands of a bureaucrat in a thirty-story building in Washington, DC, who himself is constrained by 50,000 pages of regulations. The young parents receive the directive, "Abort the child, or not a dime for its medical expenses for prenatal care or the birth." In most cases, of course the child will be aborted. The most accurate reports from the United Kingdom (which has touted a socialist medical system for decades) indicate that 92 percent of children conceived with Down Syndrome are aborted.[17] Their bodies are used to provide power for the operation of the hospitals, according to other recent reports.[18] Half of all nurses in socialist Belgium admit to administering toxic drugs to kill a patient without knowledge or consent.[19] There is a word for this sort of thing—"tyranny." When medical decisions are taken away from families, there is no question that state administered infanticide and euthanasia will only increase in the modern secular states.

Stories abound concerning over-zealous bureaucrats confiscating children from their parents in hospitals and doctor's offices around the country. In 2013, a Russian family almost lost their newborn child to the bureaucracy in Sacramento when they requested a second opinion on a heart surgery.[20] Another well-publicized news story tells of a Boston family whose young daughter was caught between two hospitals that disagreed on diagnosis, and the parents lost custody for an extended period of time.[21] As of the 2010s, families who refused certain medical service for their children are already serving time in prisons across the country. Increasingly, parents are hesitant to take their children into the hospitals and doctor's offices for fear of losing custody. With socialist medicine in place, the problems will only worsen and parental authority will be further weakened.

CONCLUSION

The expansion of government will always result in less freedom for citizens who ask for more government. It also produces the slave mentality, which undermines the character of a nation. The systemic breakdown of social systems must also lead to the breakdown of economic systems. Thus, we are concerned with more than the decline of freedom. The socialists of the last four generations have created a perfect storm that will introduce unprecedented stresses on the socio-economic systems in the West.

Perhaps the most problematic statistic of all is the employment ratio. While the unemployment rate has decreased somewhat since the last recession in this country, the labor participation rate continues to decrease as well.[22] This means that Americans are not working. They do not seek work, and they have no motivation to work. This decline occurred despite a flood of women into the job market since the 1970s. Regrettably, the atomization of the nuclear family in the 1980s and 1990s did nothing to help the character or the work base of the nation.

CHART 5

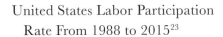

United States Labor Participation
Rate From 1988 to 2015[23]

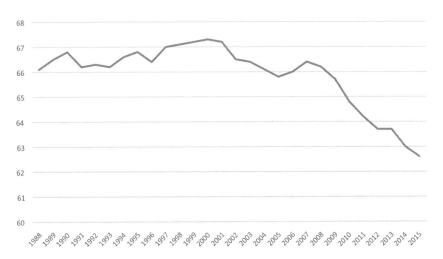

What will happen to a slave state that has run itself into massive
debt, and has broken down the character of a nation with the creation
of these huge welfare states? The next generation will bear the brunt
of the social and economic mistakes produced by the previous four
generations.

> "Nevertheless they will be his servants, that they may distinguish My
> service from the service of the kingdoms of the nations." (2 Chron.
> 12:8 NKJV)

Chapter 15

THE NEW BATTLE FRONT: FAMILY FREEDOM

"There were also that said, We have borrowed money for the king's tribute, and that upon our lands and vineyards. Yet now our flesh is as the flesh of our brethren, our children as their children: and, lo, we bring into bondage our sons and our daughters to be servants, and some of our daughters are brought unto bondage already: neither is it in our power to redeem them; for other men have our lands and vineyards." (Neh. 5:4-5)

Attacks on freedom and the persecution of innocent persons in the sixteenth and seventeenth centuries were confined mainly to the assembly of believers who wanted to worship God. This was the impetus for the first migrations to America in the seventeenth century. Since then, the tyrannical forces have shifted their attention from the church to the sphere of the family. Since it is the family jurisdiction and the family-integrated economy that represents the stronger threat to socialism, this becomes the target for tyranny in the modern state. Generally, the church jurisdiction is considered fairly irrelevant by the modern state.

The assault on the institution of the family began in the eighteenth century with Jean-Jacques Rousseau, the ideological father of the modern socialist state. After abandoning his five children on the steps of an orphanage (as soon as they were born), Rousseau proceeded to write the book on education for the modern world—a book called *Émile*. According to historian Will Durant, "Rousseau wanted a system of public instruction by the state. He prescribed many years with an unmarried tutor, who would withdraw the child as much as possible from parents and relatives."[1] Historian Paul Johnson took this to be the cornerstone for the modern totalitarian state:

> "What began as personal self-justification—hardened into convictions, into the proposition that education was the key to social and moral improvement, and this being so, it was the concern of the state. By a curious chain of infamous moral logic, Rousseau's iniquity as a parent [abandoning his children to an orphanage], was linked to his ideological offspring, the future totalitarian state."[2]

Rousseau's behavior and ideas represented socialism in its most raw form. It is a commitment to the dissolution of the family, and the incorporation of the family into the state. Some fifty years after Rousseau, the Prussian philosopher, Johann Fichte, produced his landmark speech, "An Address to the German Nation," in which he recommended that children be turned over to the state and subjected to compulsory education. Fichte's point was that "through forced schooling, everyone would learn that work makes free, and working for the State, even laying down one's life to its commands, was the greatest freedom of all."[3] Once again, he who defines key words like "freedom" wins.

Karl Marx also acknowledged his commitment to the dissolution of the family in the *Communist Manifesto*. Core to the Manifesto are the words, "Replace home education with social." These men understood the family to be the most significant threat to the all-powerful totalitarian state.

The roots of this tyrannical thinking appear first in Plato's *Republic*, in which this seminal philosopher creates a world where temporary sexual liaisons produce children and "no parent should know his child, and no child should know his parent."[4] Elsewhere, Plato specifically noted that children "belong to the state rather than to their parents."[5] The Greek philosopher would be pleased to see his vision realized in the present society. Several years ago, legislators at the Denver Capitol were considering more expansive and intrusive compulsory attendance laws for the state. A truancy judge informed the entire group of parents who had gathered to protest the bill that, "All of Colorado's children belong to us." Rousseau, Fichte, Marx, and Plato all chimed in with a hearty, "Amen!"

Those powerful ideas inspired by the Enlightenment philosophers profoundly influenced modern life, shaping new political states and institutions in Europe, America, Asia, and elsewhere. Germany adopted its first public school mandated, compulsory attendance law in 1819. America followed in 1852 when Massachusetts became the first state to adopt a compulsory school attendance law. Such revolutionary encroachments of the state into the sphere of the family on this scale was new to the world. There were no compulsory attendance laws in the 1700s in France, or the 1500s in the Netherlands, or in the 1300s in England, or in the 800s in Constantinople, or even in Rome in the 300s. For thousands of years, families were basically free to raise their own children. That all changed in the span of about eighty years, before the turn of the twentieth century.

With the transfer of education to the state came the inculcation of a uniform ideology via the state. The responsibility of parents to educate their own children was shifted to the government. Every cent of the $1.1 trillion of public monies spent on education in America teaches a worldview and a social view that prepares the next generation to be more socialist and more humanist in compliance with the state's official worldview (or religion). Every cent spent on education reminds both parents and children—"The family is not responsible. Parents are not responsible for the raising of their children—the state is responsible." Earlier in the twentieth century, governments spent one percent of the GDP on education. Now, that number has increased by six-fold, with poorer academic results and a more socialist mindset among the students.[6]

This is where our worldview clashes hard, as Scripture plainly puts the education of children in the hands of parents (Deut. 6:7, Proverbs, Eph. 6:4, 1 Thess. 2:11). Parental rights are encoded into biblical law. Regrettably, churches are afraid to teach the laws of God, and thereby they pave the way to tyranny in most Western countries. What follows is a brief summary of God's law, as pertaining to parental rights:

1. The Bible affirms the authority of the father and mother[7] in the home. Forcibly removing children from their parents' home, or kidnapping them is a capital crime (Ex. 21:16). When a young man entices a young woman to fornicate with him, the father is given the authority to determine the fate of the young man in a judicial proceeding (Ex. 22:16-17). Also, according to biblical law, the father may cancel a vow made by his daughter on the day he hears of it (Num. 30:1ff).

2. The civil magistrate may deal with abuse in the case where lasting harm ensues (Ex. 21:18-20). In serious cases involving permanent harm (including death), those inflicting the hurt, whether father or mother, should be tried for abuse. Should the father commit filicide, he is to be put to death according to God's law. In less serious cases, he would pay the medical bills to assure recovery, but he does not lose custody of the child.

Abhorrent though this may be in the view of socialists who repudiate parental rights, the Bible does not require adjudication where there is parental negligence (Ex. 21:22). For example, if a parent is guilty of academic negligence, or fails to clean the house well, the magistrate has no authority to interfere. However, the child custody case adjudicated by Solomon is relevant in the situation where parents are guilty of gross negligence in which a child's life is put at serious risk (1 Kings. 3:16-28). Not every sin is a crime as defined by Scripture. While we can be certain that God will hold all to account, the civil magistrate has limited jurisdiction, and the Bible does not allow for the tyranny of a police state. This includes the "Christian" police state where the magistrate may attempt to prosecute every moral law as defined by Scripture. A man is not to be imprisoned every time he gets drunk, nor should a mother be arrested every time she raises her voice in anger with her children. These are sins, but they are not crimes.

State confiscation of children is a mark of great tyranny and oppression. For example, King Herod's and Pharaoh's most egregious crimes had to do with the seizure and murder of children. Deuteronomy 28:32 presents one of the most terrible curses on a human society (as defined by God Himself).

> "Thy sons and thy daughters shall be given unto another people, and thine eyes shall look, and fail with longing for them all the day long: and there shall be no might in thine hand...all these curses shall come upon thee, and shall pursue thee, and overtake thee, till thou be destroyed; because thou hearkenedst not unto the voice of the Lord thy God to keep his commandments and statutes which he commanded thee." (Deut. 28:32, 45)

Tyranny is described in 1 Samuel 8:11-18 where kings commandeer children and ruin the family economies. "This will be the manner of the king that shall reign over you...He will take your sons and appoint them for himself [ruining the family economy]...and he will take your daughters to be confectionaries and to be cooks, and to be bakers...and he will take your fields, and your vineyards...and he will take the tenth of your seed, and of your vineyards, and give them to his officers, and to his servants...and ye shall cry out in that day because of your king which ye shall have chosen you."

Powerful kings and civil governments that seize control of the family will destroy both the family and the family economy. It is a very devastating thing when the family unravels in any human society. In fact, the three most horrific scenarios presented in the Bible describe a society in which the family has ceased to defend itself and protect its own—to include the cannibalism of Deuteronomy 28, Lot's behavior in Sodom in Genesis 19, and the Levite's treatment of the concubine in Judges 19. When men refuse to fight for their wives and children (Neh. 4:14), or willingly enslave their daughters and give them up to powerful interests, these families and nations represented have come under the severe curse of God. Throughout church history, we do not find the Roman Empire confiscating children from Christian parents or relatives, even when they were putting them to death in the Coliseum. Yet, this is the tactic taken by the tyrannical state in the present.

Over the last several years, Germany and Sweden have outlawed home education and have virtually expunged every remnant of it from their respective nations. I have interviewed refugees from these nations on my radio program, parents who have escaped these nations with their children. The secularists know the best way to eliminate every remnant of the Christian faith from nations like Germany. They have been working at it for twelve generations through secular humanist universities and K-12 schools. The last remnant of Christian families left in Germany are about ready to disappear. It may take another two to three generations of public schooling to completely obliterate the faith from the few Christian families remaining, but the secularists are working at it. The control of education in the hands of the state guarantees perpetual tyranny for each successive generation, and establishes socialism permanently, unless God intervenes.

In England, the Cinderella Law of 2014 carries "a maximum prison sentence of ten years for anyone who deliberately harms a child's physical, intellectual, emotional, social or behavioural development."[8] Scotland has attempted a "state guardians" program, something dangerously reminiscent of Orwell's dystopia. Under this system, parents would be reported to the state for trivial mistakes such as forgetting a medical appointment.[9]

Parental rights are disappearing at an alarming rate in this country as well. For example, in the recent Ninth Circuit Court of Appeals decision, *Fields v. Palmdale District* (in which parents objected to a psychological survey involving explicit sexual questions for eight or nine-year-old children), the court ruled that parental rights "do not extend beyond the threshold of the school door." This only confirmed decisions from other high courts in the nation, including *Brown v. Hot, Sexy, and Safer Productions* (1st Cir. 1995) or *Mozert v. Hawkins County Public Schools* (6th Cir. 1987).[10] These court decisions have greatly diminished the rights of parents whose children are educated by the state. Recently, a concerned father in Massachusetts was arrested when he asked to speak to school officials about sexually explicit material presented to his children in kindergarten and first grade.[11]

In the next chapter, we will consider islands of freedom in which some respite may be found. Nonetheless, every year millions of parents and children are harried and hassled by truancy laws, compulsory attendance laws, child-labor laws, curfew laws, social services investigations initiated on anonymous tips, spanking laws, and so on—almost all illegitimate and notorious violations of family liberties (as defined by the laws of God). The extensive network of child protective service agencies did not exist in the 1960s. Of course, all of it is presented as pretense for eliminating child abuse. But regulative systems hardly help this problem, as we can discern from biblical law. The fundamental motive for all of this has nothing to do with assuring child welfare—it is merely a working out of the conviction that children belong to the state. Year by year, this tyranny only weakens the family and strengthens the power of the state. For families who still value their children and family solidarity, these statist impositions inspire dread, discomfort, inconvenience, expense, and general discouragement.

There is serious opposition rising now against parental rights and home education in this country. A New Hampshire court ordered a homeschooling mother to cease homeschooling her daughter, despite the student's excellent academic performance. The court explained, "Amanda's vigorous defense of her religious beliefs to the counselor would strongly suggest she spends too much time with her mother and has not had the opportunity to seriously consider adopting any other religious point of view."[12]

Attempts on the part of the state to control the church is one thing, but aggressive regulation of the family creates an even more omnipresent, Orwellian state. It was a dangerous tyranny when the state sought complete control of two-hour-long church services on a Sunday morning. But when Big Brother enters every home and controls every family and every child seven days a week, we approach total government control. This is a major concern for freemen and freedom-loving people of the twenty-first century.

CENTRALIZATION OF POWER

Presidents George W. Bush and Barack Obama increased the size of the US Federal Department of Education four-fold between 2000 and 2014, and most of that increase came from the Republican administration. Increased funding implies increased control. Consequently, the nationally approved curriculum known as Common Core, produced by the Obama Administration, has been officially implemented in most of the states.[13] This is something that did not happen with Goals 2000, twenty years earlier. Without the strengthening and centralizing of power in the Federal Department of Education, federalized control of all education in America would have been impossible.

The stranglehold of total federal control of education in America is almost complete, with the exception of a few islands of freedom. There is still hope for freedom as sure as God is in the heavens. For there is still a legacy and a trust given to those who still love freedom, and that will be addressed in the last chapter.

> "Then they cried unto the Lord in their trouble, and he saved them out of their distresses. He brought them out of darkness and the shadow of death, and brake their bands in sunder." (Ps. 107:13-14)

Chapter 16
THE RISE OF FASCISM AND THE LOSS OF FREEDOM

"For the transgression of a land many are the princes thereof: but by a man of understanding and knowledge the state thereof shall be prolonged." (Prov. 28:2)

For years, America and other once free nations have been slipping on the Heritage Foundation's Index for Economic Freedom.[1] Various metrics are used for the survey, including property rights, fiscal freedom, government spending levels, business freedom, monetary freedom, trade freedom, and investment freedom. The cumulative measure of worldwide freedoms is falling fast, due in large part to the expansion of the Western governments. Either political corruption (as measured by Transparency International's Corruption Perception Index) or "legitimatized" government regulations and restrictions (or both), are choking the life out of free enterprise worldwide.

The term "fascist" is bandied around a good bit, often used as a convenient pejorative for any political group that has somehow fallen into disfavor. For those interested in the truth of the matter, fascism is defined by Benito Mussolini as government control of every aspect of business and personal life:

> "The fascist conception of life stresses the importance of the State and accepts the individual only in so far as his interests coincide with those of the State, which stands for the conscience and the universal will of man as a historic entity...The fascist conception of the State is all-embracing; outside of it no human or spiritual values can exist, much less have value."[2]

An internet search for government agencies, state and federal for this country, would identify lists of thousands of regulative systems in place to assure that every individual interest coincides with that of the State. Such massive and complex governmental systems existed only in the minds of socialist philosophers in previous centuries, and most have appeared just since World War I. This is the modern phenomenon called fascism.

Setting aside the growth of the federal government, local and state bureaucracies in this country have expanded by orders of magnitude. There were three times more state and local bureaucrats per 100 citizens in 2006 than there were sixty years earlier.[3] By the year 2011, there were twice as many people working for the government (22.5 million) as there were employees working manufacturing jobs (11.5 million).[4] The Federal Register contains the compendium of federal regulations, and provides a good metric for tyranny in this country. The Register has expanded from 9,910 pages in 1954 to some 82,580 pages in 2010.[5] "For the transgression of a land many are the princes thereof."

Almost without exception, regulations put a drag on economies. They cannot effectively harness corruption and preserve the environment. Inevitably, regulative systems favor one business over another, usually the large corporations over the small entrepreneur, and they are patently unbiblical. God's law allows for compensation for victims in cases of gross negligence (Ex. 21:28, 22:5). These fines may be assessed only when it can be proven by several witnesses that the perpetrator has hurt the person or property of another. Preemptive regulations and fines are not biblical, and violate the general equity of biblical law as laid out in the Old Testament.

Every real or perceived malady, local or national, offers new opportunities for heightened government interest and involvement in our lives. For example, the recent rise in the incidence of a sexually transmitted disease (human papilloma virus) produced a rash of bills in state legislatures across the country with the intent to mandate HPV inoculations for eleven and twelve-year-old schoolgirls.[6]

Despite wide disagreement on the causes of and extent of global warming, and the potential harm a few degrees of global warming might yield, governments worldwide (including our own) set out to regulate more of our lives in the early years of the twenty-first century. Global warming or "climate change" becomes just another ruse to add more regulations on American business. Incandescent light bulbs have been banned,[7] and more regulations on the automotive industry have been adopted.[8] This is another example of man attempting to play God by way of massive statist regulation. When neither politician nor scientist are taught the fear of God as the beginning of wisdom and knowledge in their university classes, inevitably they will turn themselves into a god. On the one hand, the politician takes on an overweening estimation of his own capacity to predict the future and to judge the relative effects of every policy he legislates over the long haul. Combine that with an overly optimistic view of the human scientist and scientific predictions, and the end result is unrelenting tyranny.

Will this massive accumulation of power and control create a better world? The political class certainly believes it will, but as the common aphorism goes, "The road to hell is paved with good intentions." It would be better to submit to the laws of God who Himself knows everything about the world He made. He understands the robustness of His physical creation. He fully comprehends the limitations of the men He made, and the laws that will properly govern sinful men in a sinful world. The underlying assumption held by the modern regulative system is that men are better controlled by hundreds of thousands of regulations and millions of regulators, and billions of dollars in preemptive fines, than they would be by God's laws. If men would humble themselves, perhaps they would realize that God knows something about justice and holding human society together. God's moral laws really do maintain the delicate balance between tyranny and anarchy, calling forth personal responsibility and imposing criminal penalties only where necessary.

Moreover, socialists believe that somehow men will do better when they have access to power, and that government officials are less likely to make unwise decisions than would the rest of the population. The citizenry is led to believe that government is by nature altruistic; that bureaucracies are less likely to give way to favoritism, engage in fraud, or produce monopolies than business operators that must work within the free market. Of course, this view is rooted in an erroneous view of human nature, and it places far too much confidence in politicians and bureaucrats than either Scripture or history would warrant.

Having rejected the salvation of Jesus Christ from the real problem of sin, the do-gooders and socialists attempt a salvation by regulation. They will not solve the problem of unloving, selfish behavior by their regulations. In fact, they only make the problem worse by creating a people that are less likely to govern themselves. The fences and the regulations only violate the liberty with which Christ has set us free, and they cannot possibly address the real problem of sin. The state has become a false Messiah, and those that support these regulations give credence to this new Messiah.

THE ABOLITION OF PROPERTY RIGHTS

> "And they covet fields, and take them by violence; and houses, and take them away: so they oppress a man and his house, even a man and his heritage." (Mic. 2:2)

The shameful history of property confiscations begins with the biblical record of King Ahab who coveted Naboth's vineyard. Naboth refused Ahab's generous offer to buy him out, and after a mock trial and execution, Ahab enacted the first case of eminent domain in biblical history. Shortly thereafter, he received a visit from Elijah the prophet, who informed him of God's judgment for his wicked treatment of Naboth.

> "Thus saith the Lord, Hast thou killed, and also taken possession? And thou shalt speak unto him, saying, Thus saith the Lord, In the place where dogs licked the blood of Naboth shall dogs lick thy blood, even thine." (1 Kings 21:19)

Thus begins the sad story of power-driven tyrants who place political interests above those of the individual. Property confiscations without benefit of trial, judge, or jury began in the 1980s and now continue to expand at the federal, state, and local levels. Journalist, Jared Wollstein summarizes the present rules that govern confiscation in this country:

> "There are more than four hundred federal offenses and thousands of state and local offenses for which your cash, car, bank accounts, and home can be seized—including shoplifting, hiring an illegal as a maid (California), playing a car stereo too loud (New York), transporting illegal fireworks, gambling, having illegal drugs on your property, and merely discussing violating any law such as underpaying your taxes."[9]

Federal agencies are given virtually unlimited authority to impose restrictions and fines on property owners by way of federal laws. These include The Peoples with Disability Act, The Endangered Species Act, The Clean Water Act, etc. Over one-half of the land west of Denver is owned and controlled by the Federal Government and its agents (the States). This includes 84 percent of Nevada, 67 percent of Alaska, 57 percent of Utah, 53 percent of Idaho, 48 percent of Arizona, and 45 percent of California.[10] The same cannot be said for the eastern half of the country, only because these states were populated well before socialism took over in the twentieth century.

Even local governments violate private property rights on a regular basis. One local government in California sentenced a man to six months in jail for building a fence and a patio without a permit and approval by the local planning commission.[11] In 2011, a Missouri family was fined $90,000 (with threats of an additional $4,000,000 in fines), when officials discovered that one of the children was raising rabbits without a permit.[12] Several years ago, the U.S. Department of Labor fined an Oregon family $73,000 when their children were caught picking strawberries at their family farm. These are just a few random examples of tyrannical actions that are taken against family businesses and private property every day. Such tyranny comes about because few of our leaders ever think about liberty, and few pastors will teach the Law of God as the basis for human ethics.

Restrictions on eminent domain are virtually non-existent in this country today. Until the *Kelo v. City of New London* (2005) case, the exercise of eminent domain was reserved for an occasional government project. This landmark case was initiated by fifteen families who refused to sell their property to a developer who planned to turn their little village on the Long Island Sound into a parking lot for Pfizer Corporation. Incredibly, Pfizer was not a party in the case and had agreed to move its development elsewhere. Nevertheless, the City of New London was determined to exercise its powers of eminent domain, in hopes that this business venture would improve tax revenues for the city. The Supreme Court of the United States sided with the city in the final ruling.

The Kelo decision was one more significant step towards tyranny in America. Now even Ahab's friends may confiscate Naboth's vineyard, as long as Ahab receives a reasonable kickback in the form of improved tax revenues for his friends' use of it. Horror stories about these property confiscations abound, and have even been covered by mainstream news sources like *Reader's Digest*. The City of Lakewood, Ohio, "recently proposed bulldozing 18 private homes and businesses and handing the land to private developers to build condominiums."[13]

At one time, "thou shalt not steal" was taken as sacrosanct because God said it, and He didn't make exceptions for government. However, the voice of the people (vox populi) has replaced the voice of God, and the people have become the source of law. They have constructed for themselves the worst tyranny of all. When government turns itself into a god, and when men cease fearing God in the university class-rooms and in the halls of Congress, they no longer consider themselves constrained by God's laws. Orwell's famed pig moseys up to the barn wall to make another slight modification: "Thou shalt not steal, unless yur the guvment."[14]

State and local governments also dispossess families every day for the failure to pay property taxes. Recently, a Pennsylvania widow lost her $240,000 home because of a failure to pay $6.30 in taxes.[15] This single county alone admitted to foreclosing on 600-1,000 properties in a year.

America has become more the land of the slave than the home of the brave. Our founders would have been appalled to see this country turned into the very nemesis of what they had envisioned. Jefferson described the essence of private property ownership as "the right to exclude everybody—even the government—from the property."[16] He would reference the famous quote from William Pitt the Elder:

"The poorest man may in his cottage bid defiance to all the forces of the crown. It may be frail, its roof may shake, the wind may blow through it, the storms enter. All of his forces dare not cross the threshold of the ruined cottage."[17]

Our forefathers fought to defend the people's rights to "life, liberty, and property!" That was the battle cry throughout the war. They would never have tolerated what we face today, conditions far worse than what the colonists faced under the British. At least the British armies would only quarter in the homes on occasion. They didn't confiscate the homes.

Property taxation put an end to private property ownership in America.[18] Of all forms of taxation, property taxes are the worst, and certainly this form of taxation has no biblical backing. The Bible forbids the confiscation of private property in passages like Proverbs 23:10 and Ezekiel 22:6-7.

"Remove not the old landmark; and enter not into the fields of the fatherless." (Prov. 23:10)

THE ALMOST TOTAL LOSS OF PRIVACY

The Fourth Amendment to the U.S. Constitution protects our person, papers, and effects from unreasonable searches, and that should form the basis for individual privacy. What does this look like in an information-submerged society? Global positioning chips are appearing on U.S. passports, cars, and cell phones. Most of our fellow citizens are willing to trade liberty for convenience or supposed security, and governments are collecting mountains of information as a result. Social networks provide minimal privacy for users, and it would not take more than an hour of sorting information for government officials to identify every Christian or every conservative in America via their online entries. Soon RFID will trace every credit card, loyalty card, and ID card in the world. Traffic cameras in most of the large cities around the country can track almost every person moving about in the city all day long. Some of the large search engines have admitted to working with the NSA, as they monitor audio and video messaging used through their systems. Biometrics, to include iris recognition, finger print analysis, and voice recognition are increasingly used for ATM's, entry control, and other systems requiring individualized signature. Facial recognition technology has already been used during certain events relating to President Obama's election campaign. England has collected blood DNA samples from babies (already in place for every person under thirty-eight years of age), and the socialists are pressing for something similar here in the United States. All of these technological advancements are either commonplace now or will be in the next ten years, but the more astounding aspect of all of this is that *none of it existed thirty years ago.*

In previous centuries, a persecuted family could escape tyranny simply because the authorities could not keep track of everybody. There were opportunities to flee to a different city or a different county. Escape from tyranny is practically impossible now, given the centralization of power and information collection and sharing across government agencies.

IMPOVERISHING THE NATION

What happens to a free nation that abandons freedom for socialism? The effects of socialist control and the breakdown of the free economy cannot but impoverish the nation. The character of a nation disintegrates first. Their social systems begin to unravel with the breakdown of the family. At some point, the economy cannot bear the weight anymore.

Over the years America has profited from economic freedom, entrepreneurial ingenuity, and technological advances in manufacturing automation and computerization. All of these factors enabled a tremendous economic boom in the mid-twentieth century. However, automation and computerization has run its course. American debt is the highest on record. 80 million Baby Boomers are in worse shape than the Silent Generation. The Social Security Fund is in the red. The worker-to-retiree ratio is fast shrinking, and the productivity of successive generations is virtually gone. America does not have the character or the strong sense of community in place where it could recover from a depression as it did in the 1930s. The majority of Americans receive a check from the government. The "good times" are over, if measured by material success. Following the "recovery" from the Great Recession of 2008, Americans are 40 percent poorer on average than they were in 2007. The average net worth fell from $135,700 to $81,400, and the median income has taken a similar tumble.[19] This is what happens when big government socialism overwhelms a free nation.

> "But it shall come to pass, if thou wilt not hearken unto the voice of the Lord thy God, to observe to do all his commandments and his statutes which I command thee this day; that all these curses shall come upon thee, and overtake thee: Cursed shalt thou be in the city, and cursed shalt thou be in the field. Cursed shall be thy basket and thy store." (Deut. 28:15-17)

Chapter 17

ERODING THE MORAL FIBER OF THE NATION

"And he shall give Israel up because of the sins of Jeroboam, who did sin, and who made Israel to sin." (1 Kings 14:16)

It is too easy to lose sight of the core issue when engaged in this tremendous struggle for freedom. In a general sense, there can be no substantial freedom for an immoral nation. There is no sense in arguing for freedom from political tyranny where the people for the most part are still slaves of sin, and they have yet to be impacted by the Gospel. The problem of political tyranny is of little consequence in comparison with the tyranny of the devil in the hearts of men. When speaking of slavery in 1 Corinthians 7:19-23, the Apostle Paul considers freedom preferential but not the primary concern. Paul says that circumcision, uncircumcision, slavery, or freedom are nothing—but what is of essence is "keeping the commandments of God" (1 Cor. 7:19). He is first concerned with how the Christian keeps God's moral laws, and somewhat less concerned with conditions in the world (slavery, poverty, debt, etc.). Ultimately, it is man's relationship with God that matters the most. Obedience to God, individually and nationally, will bring other blessings from God. And all of these good things come by the grace of God.

Thus, our primary concern is salvation from sin, the ultimate tyranny. While we would not expect every person in the world to find salvation in Jesus Christ, the influence of Christians in society does have a sanctifying effect on the rest of it. This is the principle Paul teaches in verse 14 of the same chapter. "For the unbelieving husband is sanctified by the wife, and the unbelieving wife is sanctified by the husband." If a portion of society would keep the commandments of God, this produces a preserving effect upon the rest of that society (whether it be a family or larger community).

HOW TYRANTS CREATE THE SEEDBED FOR MORE TYRANNY

For the present, however, just the opposite effect is taking place in America and in most of the rest of the developed world. Tyrants have discovered that they can create more big government tyranny by eroding the morals of a nation and opposing any and all Christian influence, street evangelism, and public address.

Over the last decade, nowhere has tyranny advanced more than by way of homosexual fascism. The German National Socialist (Nazi) party had its beginnings in the homosexual underworld of the 1920s,[1] and something similar is happening in this country now.

Under the pretense of civil rights, private enterprise in America is saddled with even more government control in hiring practices, college admission policies, property rentals, and business accommodations for those who identify themselves by a certain kind of sexual orientation. This intensive regulation of private property by these "moral" fascists (some of whom are professing Christians), is a violation of the law of God and it robs private citizens of their right to own and control property.

In the case of homosexual fascism, however, power is placed in the hands of the lowest moral element of the nation. It is nothing but the reviving of Emperor Nero's agenda from the first century AD. This Roman Caesar, universally condemned by pagan and Christian historians alike, officiated the first homosexual weddings, burned Rome to the ground, and initiated the first persecution against Christians. This is precisely the agenda that has captured most of the Western world today. Within a single decade, 98 percent of European nations, two-thirds of South America, North America, Australia, and New Zealand have capitulated to the Neronic agenda.[2] Has any social shift occurred so quickly in all of world history?

To refuse to participate in this wholly unnatural, unchristian, and immoral charade of homosexual "weddings" is akin to blasphemy or treason against the new "law order." The recent stories which testify to this fascist tyranny are too numerous to mention for this survey. However, a few will suffice. Homosexual activists sued a Christian photographer in New Mexico for refusing to participate in a "gay wedding." The homosexuals won the court battle at the New Mexico Supreme Court, and the United States Supreme Court allowed the decision to stand.[3] A baker in Denver was remanded to sensitivity classes.[4] Another bakery in Oregon was put out of business by homosexual fascists and fined $135,000 for refusing to support their "marriage."[5] A Christian gynecologist in California refused to provide in vitro fertilization to a lesbian couple, and was successfully sued. The state Supreme Court refused to consider a medical practice as protected religious speech in that case.[6]

As of this writing, pastors in Coeur d'Alene, Idaho are facing years in prison for refusing to officiate a homosexual "wedding ceremony."[7] A Methodist campground in New Jersey also lost its tax exempt status when it refused to open the facility to homosexual weddings.[8] Under these draconian controls, more Christian doctors will be forced to do in-vitro fertilizations for lesbians, attorneys will be forced to advocate homosexual adoption cases, and pharmacists will be forced to dispense abortifacients. This legal environment is turning Christian bakers, attorneys, photographers, and shop owners into outlaws.

OBERGEFELL V. HODGES

On Friday, June 26, 2015 at 10:00AM, the Supreme Court of the United States issued a decision in the *Obergefell v. Hodges* case on homosexual marriage that would shake the pillars of liberty in the Western world. In the battle between sexual license and religious liberties, it was true liberty that took the major hit. This would become the most significant move towards the wholesale persecution of Christians in the history of this country, and repercussions would be felt around the world. The decision legitimized homosexual weddings in all fifty states.

Justice Anthony Kennedy bears first responsibility for the decision as the author of the majority opinion and the swing vote on the bench. This ruling would become America's bloody Mary, James I, Charles II, and Phillip II. Simultaneously, the decision broke down all barriers for sexual and personal morality (as defined by God's laws), and opened the way for persecution and the forcible violation of the consciences of men and women of true faith. In complete contradiction to Romans 13, the Supreme Court of the United States praised the wicked, and punished the innocent. Sexual license trumped genuine liberty, freedom of religion, freedom of speech, and freedom of private enterprise.

Chief Justice John Roberts wrote in his dissent that the majority left "no comfort" for religious peoples in their decision. Justice Scalia called it a "threat to democracy," and a tool to be used "by those who are determined to stamp out every vestige of dissent." Major news commentators concluded that Christians would have to learn to live as "exiles" in their own country.[9] Millions of Christian accountants, retailers, landlords, county clerks, judges, lawyers, and pastors are now at risk of lawsuits, bankruptcy, imprisonment, and exile from the country. The Supreme Court of the United States has declared open season on Christians, unleashing persecution similar to what Nero did in the first century.

THE CURTAILMENT OF FREEDOM OF SPEECH

This is the point at which free speech and the freedom of association is curtailed for Christians and God-fearing citizens as well. On October 10, 2004, eleven men and women were arrested by police, as they read the Bible in the vicinity of a publicly-funded, homosexual event on the streets of Philadelphia. Upon their acquittal, attorneys from the Alliance Defense Fund pursued a suit for wrongful arrest. On January 19, 2007, a United State District Judge dismissed the case, concluding that a "permit granted by the city to homosexuals allowed police to silence the Christian activist message on the streets."[10]

In 2008, a Colorado bill (SB-200), required all public toilets (including those in private establishments) to be made available to sexual deviants of all sorts. Signed into law by then Governor Bill Ritter, the bill required prison time for any person who should publish or publicly speak anything that may be perceived as "offensive" to homosexuals in the context of public accommodations.[11] Another California bill passed in 2004 expanded hate crimes to include speech interpreted as "threats, intimidations, or coercion." If the victim testifies that the speech made him "feel intimidated" the violator could be liable to fines up to $25,000 and a year in jail.[12]

The erosion of the right to free speech is working its way through the Western nations, and homosexual fascism is the mode by which this freedom will be curtailed. On February 27, 2013, Canada's Supreme Court released a unanimous decision to enforce a fine "that could amount to hundreds of thousands of dollars" against a pro-family activist who had distributed literature opposing homosexuality. The court would not allow a distinction between "hating the sin" and "loving the sinner," stating, "Courts have recognized a strong connection between sexual orientation and sexual conduct and where the conduct targeted by speech is a crucial aspect of the identity of a vulnerable group. Attacks on this conduct stand as proxy for attacks on the group itself."[13]

Thus, the secular courts equate public condemnation of sin to hate speech, and any attempt to define sin on God's terms and call people to salvation from that sin will result in prosecution, fines, and possibly imprisonment. True Christians must prepare for real persecution in Western countries for the first time in 300 years. An extraordinary enthusiasm for the ultimate abomination (homosexual marriage) on the part of Western governments, combined with the weakening opposition from mainstream Christians, portends difficult days ahead for the thin minority of Christians that still take the higher moral stand against it.

PERSECUTION

Of course, persecution is nothing new for Christians. It has been the ultimate manifestation of tyranny many times throughout history, if we were to define tyranny biblically (Rev. 6:8-10, 17:6, 18:24). Our brothers and sisters in China and the Soviet Union have felt the heavy hand of the beastly state over the last 80 years. That this tyrannical force should revert to the materialistic and atheistic West will come as no surprise to Christians.

Material comforts have dulled our senses to what is of essence. We have lost appreciation for the higher values in life. The Christian church has lost its edge, and it fails to challenge the world for its evils. Perhaps it is time for a little persecution in that this is God's special means to wake up an anemic church. We know that God is sovereign over the rise of the Western tyrannies. We know that God has His purposes working through all of these historical events, foremost of which is to produce a stronger church. If these fiery trials should strengthen the voice of the church more than weaken it, then why should we fear them? We will declare even more strongly the sins of the nations, and demand that they bow the knee to the living Christ. We shall point out the bankruptcy of sin and tyranny, and lead people back to the Savior of the world that sets all men free. We shall appreciate more the freedom that Christ gives when we recognize that the pseudo-freedom of a materialist culture was only the slavery of idolatry.

Persecution may very well become the route to freedom for us, as it has been for others. Would there be an America without the bloody persecutions of the sixteenth and seventeenth centuries in France,

Scotland, and England? Without the martyrdoms of the Reformation that included Puritans, Pilgrims, Huguenots, Baptists, and Presbyterians, there would have been no America.

GOVERNMENT-FINANCED PERVERSIONS

During the early 2010s, our church rented space from a local K-6 grade school in Douglas County, Colorado—one of the most conservative counties in the state. Posted in prominent view of the children attending the school was a sign produced by an organization called the "GLSEN." It is the Gay Lesbian Straight Education Network, an organization that has spread across the country through the work of a man named Kevin Jennings, who was appointed by President Obama to the position of School Safety Czar.[14] It is the intent of this federal government that every six-year-old child attending the schools is indoctrinated in the acceptance of the homosexual lifestyle. How does this early education in homosexuality affect a child? What will it produce when these children are raised in this milieu? Of the 80-90 percent of the evangelical parents whose children attend these schools, how many support this indoctrination in sexual deviance? Are these Christian parents fully on board with their children coming out of the closet at sixteen or seventeen years of age? The Lord Jesus Christ spoke to this issue directly, when He said:

> "But whoever causes one of these little ones who believe in Me to sin, it would be better for him if a millstone were hung around his neck, and he were drowned in the depth of the sea." (Matt. 18:6 NKJV).

As early as 1994, Virginia school districts conducted a sex survey with 12-year-old children, suggesting that some children will have sex as early as nine years of age with three or more people.[15] The interest of the progressives to sexualize children and pervert them continues without restraint. In the first decades of the 21st century, homosexual adoptions have come to be preferred by state bureaucracies over Christian adoptions.

We could talk about the Darwinian evolution, atheistic materialism, existentialism, pluralistic polytheism, and all the rest of the ideology that slips into the school textbooks, but nothing is as opposed to biblical truth, morality, and social health as the promotion of homosexuality and transgenderism.

GODLESS EDUCATION

State control of education requires indoctrination in the state religion of humanism. That is why Supreme Court decisions *Engel v. Vitale* (1962), *Wallace v. Jaffree* (1985), and *Stone v. Graham* (1980), were so critical to the radicalization of the schools. By Supreme Court mandate, it is illegal to worship and praise and fear the true and living God (as the beginning of knowledge) in American public schools. No teacher may legally pray aloud, or otherwise express the fear of Almighty God as he teaches the works of God in science and history in this country. Only if the instructor teaches humanist autonomy in ethics, and speaks approvingly of homosexuality will he comply with the law. In fact, as of 2012, California law (SB 1172) forbids any school counselor or other counselor to provide a teen with Christian counsel concerning homosexuality, especially if he appears given to that disposition.[16] Additionally, the State of California requires training in homosexuality for every student attending public schools as of 2011.[17] Homosexual and lesbian teachers and coaches are spreading through the public schools. News reports concerning the homosexual molestation of students on the part of their teachers have become increasingly commonplace as well. When will the progressive schools require mandatory laboratory experience in homosexuality, in keeping with the humanist vision maintained by the old Greek gymnasiums?

It was only a generation ago that President Eisenhower issued an executive order requiring the discharge of homosexual workers from federal employment including military service.[18] Forty years later, President Clinton initiated a "Don't Ask, Don't Tell" policy (on June 24, 1994). The United States Supreme Court overruled a Texas sodomy law on June 26, 2003 (*Lawrence v. Texas*). In another significant move towards the adoption of the Neronic agenda, President George W. Bush signed legislation allowing death benefits for "domestic partners" in 2002.[19] President Obama repealed the "Don't Ask, Don't Tell" policy on September 20, 2012, providing full approval for homosexuals in the military. When Joint Chiefs Chairman Mike Mullen was asked by a group of chaplains, "Will those of us who hold biblical orthodox views concerning homosexuality be protected in this new environment to speak about those views?" Mullen responded, "Chaplain, if you can't get in line with this policy, resign your commission."[20] Freedom for Christians is null and void, and Nero is on the loose. Much has changed since 1953.

Our governments today are bent on focusing a great amount of power and money on the promotion of immorality. From the perspective of this country's founding fathers, this is the only way that tyrants and slave states can further expand their powers. Only an immoral people can be enslaved by powerful governments. The best way to anesthetize the frogs in the boiling pot is to encourage the abandonment of responsibility, the breakdown of the family, and general moral dissoluteness.

To this, the Scriptures speak:

"Woe to him that buildeth a town with blood, and stablisheth a city by iniquity!…Woe unto him that giveth his neighbor drink, that puttest thy bottle to him, and makest him drunken also, that thou mayest look on their nakedness!" (Hab. 2:12-15)

"Wherefore thus saith the Holy One of Israel, Because ye despise this word, and trust in oppression and perverseness, and stay thereon: Therefore this iniquity shall be to you as a branch ready to fall, swelling out in a high wall, whose breaking cometh suddenly at an instant." (Isa. 30:12-13)

"Woe unto them that are mighty to drink wine, and men of strength to mingle strong drink: Which justify the wicked for reward, and take away the righteousness of the righteous from him! Therefore as the fire devoureth the stubble, and the flame consumeth the chaff, so their root shall be as rottenness, and their blossom shall go up as dust: because they have cast away the law of the LORD of hosts, and despised the word of the Holy One of Israel!" (Isa. 5:22-24)

As sure as God is still in the heavens, He yet presides over the destiny of nations. He is very much attuned to the shameless rebellion of these Western countries. A careful study of the Old Testament prophetic statements issued towards the pagan nations of Moab, Assyria, Tyre, Sidon, Sodom, and others, would identify two reasons for temporal judgments against the nations—sexual sin and the shedding of innocent blood. The Apostle Paul reminds us that God winked at much of the wickedness committed by the pagans before Christ came, but now "He calls all men everywhere to repentance" (Acts 17:30). If anything, these apostate nations (in the Western world) will be held to an even tighter account than the ancient city states of Sodom and Gomorrah.

Those nations in Europe, North America, and South America which have approved of homosexuality and turned the practice into a social norm are actually experiencing God's judgment right now. According to Romans 1:27-32, the sin of homosexuality carries within itself the judgment of God. Sexual nihilism is just another manifestation of a rotted-out social system. Christians must form new socio-economic systems based on biblical principle—a subject to be addressed in the final chapter.

GOVERNMENT-FINANCED MURDER

Yet, the most chilling aspect of tyranny will be witnessed when innocent citizens are subjected to mass slaughter. While we have not experienced forced starvations or mass murder such as what the Soviet Union and China went through in the twentieth century, something just as insidious is happening in America, Sweden, England, and elsewhere now. It is government-funded abortion and infanticide. For some reason, pro-abortion organizations are always supported by government money, and pro-life organizations and pregnancy counseling centers are supported by private dollars. Immorality is backed by the support of wicked and tyrannical governments. In this country, at least 60 million babies have been murdered by surgical abortion, and another 60-200 million by abortifacient drugs. Since 1960, at least two billion babies have been killed worldwide by chemical abortions and abortifacients—perhaps the largest mass slaughter in the history of the world.

Societies that kill their children and spend their great-grandchildren into debt are living the existentialist life—consuming all resources on themselves in the present at the expense of the future. They use up the financial and character capital of previous generations for their own benefit, and they leave nothing to sustain their empires.

The Supreme Court decision *Roe v. Wade* (1973) legitimized convenience abortion in all fifty states in 1973. On December 1, 1992, the High Court nullified a Guam law which would have prohibited abortion in that territory. Justices Sandra Day O'Connor, Anthony Kennedy, David Souter, and Clarence Thomas (all Republican nominees to the court) supported the majority opinion to kill the law. Justice White, a Democrat appointee from the 1960s dissented from the majority vote.[21]

Although several states have provided some restrictions to abortion, national government funding for abortion continues under both Republican and Democratic administrations. This is the most egregious form of tyranny, in that government funding implies government force in the slaughter of innocents. Planned Parenthood receives hundreds of millions of dollars each year from the Federal Government Title X funding. The total amount of money the organization has collected from taxpayers since 1987 exceeds $4 billion.[22] Having performed 327,000 abortions in 2014, Planned Parenthood remains the largest abortion provider in the country.[23] The organization contributes to millions more abortions each year, if the numbers were to include the distribution of emergency contraceptives and other abortifacient forms of birth control. Recent reports indicate that the organization earns additional income from harvesting body parts from aborted babies and marketing them to businesses and universities.[24]

Adding up the annual budgets of all of the major pro-family organizations in the country (including Focus on the Family, Family Research Council, Alliance Defending Freedom, American Family Association, etc.), altogether they do not exceed $270 million in annual operations, only one-quarter of Planned Parenthood's annual budget, and one-half of what Planned Parenthood receives from Title X each year. That single example accounts for only one leftist organization out of hundreds of others that receive significant support from federal tax dollars. Judicial Watch recently reported on an additional $16.6 billion (collected from a lawsuit from Bank of America) distributed to leftist organizations around the country.[25] Thus, any conservative pro-family opposition is dwarfed by the redistribution of trillions of dollars of tax monies towards pro-socialist, anti-freedom causes.

In addition, the socialist medicine program called "Obamacare" has added many more opportunities for government-enforced and government-funded abortion and abortifacient forms of contraceptives. In some cases, even churches are being compelled to fund abortion via their insurance coverage.[26] Recently, the Seventh Circuit required a Christian college to provide abortifacient coverage for their students and employees.[27] In the State of New Jersey, pharmacists are required to provide abortifacient drugs to their customers regardless of their "moral, religious or ethical" convictions.[28] The Ninth Circuit Court recently upheld this requirement for Washington State pharmacies as well.[29] The removal of a copay requirement for abortifacients in the Obamacare program has increased access to harmful, deadly chemicals to millions of women.

Although some state legislatures will advance a pro-life, pro-family, and pro-freedom policy on occasion, it is doubtful that the nation will shift direction any time soon. On June 29, 2015, the United States Supreme Court stopped a Texas law that would have shut down the majority of abortion clinics in that state.[30] As the single most enthusiastic supporter of infanticide in the country among the most powerful, national politicians, Barack Obama was elected president of the United States in 2008 and again in 2012. Previously, Obama had successfully defended policies that permitted infanticide while he was a member of the Illinois legislature.[31]

WHEN OTHERS LOSE THEIR FREEDOMS

Perhaps some would be motivated to defend their own freedoms and their own lives and property, but few are interested in defending the lives of others. Thus, conservatives often defend their cause on the basis of self-interest. If the nation will murder babies by the millions, perhaps they will one day kill the elderly, or Christians, and then they will come after you. Would this provide sufficient motivation to the elderly and to Christians to defend the lives of others? More often than not, personal interest does not provide sufficient motive to engage the masses in the cause of freedom. This battle is far too challenging, and requires far too much personal sacrifice at the front end. After all, the authorities are not knocking on the door yet, so why should one act now? As an active member of the pro-life community in Colorado for twenty-two years, it seems there is only a handful of people who stay in the fight, year after year, election after election. Most of us know each other on a first-name basis. Since I ran as the pro-life candidate for governor in 1994, and the pro-life candidate for U.S. Senate in 1998, I know how difficult it is to secure any votes for the right to life and liberty. The Republican and Democratic candidates I ran against were committed to supporting abortion and the funding of Planned Parenthood. I secured four percent of the vote in 1994, and one percent in 1998. The majority of citizens simply do not care about the right to life enough to cast their vote for principle. The Personhood Amendment appeared on the ballot three times in Colorado, none of which gained more than 35 percent of the vote.

Several years ago, I had a conversation with a pro-family activist about the upcoming legislative agenda. I mentioned the right to life issue, and he quickly responded, "Oh, that issue doesn't get any traction anymore. We're going to leave that one on the back burner."

The defense of the life of the unborn is an inglorious and unpopular task. There is much spiritual opposition to this work, and not a very high probability of immediate success. We have to be willing to stay in the battle for fifty years, perhaps even for multiple generations. This is the essence of the freedom fighter. Principled men and women do not care about glory, and they do not fight for themselves. They do not seek anyone's praise; certainly they do not expect thanks from the babies whose lives they save. Their reason for starting the battle is enough of a reason to continue in the battle for fifty years. They act out of pure love for neighbor and love for God, and they do it in obedience to God.

244 ~ THE STORY OF FREEDOM

This is the highest motive of all: a love for God and a love for His righteousness. If we do not fight for justice and the freedoms associated with God's standard of justice (as defined by biblical law), then God will.

> "Thus saith the LORD; Execute ye judgment and righteousness, and deliver the spoiled out of the hand of the oppressor; and do no wrong, do no violence to the stranger, the fatherless, nor the widow, neither shed innocent blood in this place...but if ye will not hear these words, I swear by Myself, saith the LORD, that this house shall become a desolation." (Jer. 22:3, 5)

The voices of the helpless innocents killed by the millions scream out to God from the ground for blood justice (Gen. 4:10, Num. 35:33). He is a God of both mercy and justice; and as Christians we are committed to both principles. In fact, Jesus Christ calls us to the weightier matters of the law, which are faith, mercy, and judgment (Matt. 23:23). We show men and women the mercy of God in Christ, while we insist upon protecting the life and liberty of babies and all citizens (according to the standard of God's law). To separate forgiveness from obedience, or justification from sanctification presents a false picture of the Gospel. To preach grace and mercy for thieves and murderers, while ignoring the slaughter of the innocents and the confiscation of widows' property in no way reflects the ministry of Jesus Christ (Matt. 23:24). Ultimately, the fight for freedom is rooted in a commitment to the righteous standards of God's laws. The right to our property is based in the eighth commandment, "Thou shalt not steal." The right to life is based in the sixth commandment, "Thou shalt not murder." The Bible further defines these laws throughout the Old and New Testaments, especially as far as they apply to the civil magistrate. We fight for freedom because we are committed to righteousness. Our first commitment is to see that our own obedience to these commandments is matured, and then we are ready to "avenge all disobedience" according to God's ordinances (2 Cor. 10:4-6). First, we love our neighbors as ourselves and we engage all lawful endeavors to preserve his person and property. We are then qualified to make judgments in church and civil courts to see that others do not violate the person and property of their neighbors.[32]

Does God really care about the great travesty of abortion in this country and most other countries around the world? What would happen if God sat at the head of the conference table as the Christian coalitions discussed their public policy issues? What would God put near the top of the agenda in 48 point font?

> "If thou forbear to deliver them that are drawn unto death, and those that are ready to be slain; If thou sayest, Behold, we knew it not; doth not He that pondereth the heart consider it? and He that keepeth thy soul, doth not He know it? and shall not He render to every man according to his works?" (Prov. 24:11-12)

Part V

~

FREEDOM!

Chapter 18

SEEKING FREEDOM

"Art thou called being a servant? care not for it: but if thou mayest be made free, use it rather." (1 Cor. 7:21)

What the world needs are more freemen—freedom loving men and women who would rather die than consign themselves to a life of slavery. They would rather die to their flesh than to be a slave of sin. They would rather be beaten to death by tyrants than relinquish their liberty by denying the Lord that sets them free. They would rather die in a bloody war with tyrannical, evil powers than subject themselves to these systems that would destroy their faith, family, and freedoms through successive generations. The tyranny described in the previous chapters would make a freeman sick to his stomach. He would instantly recognize the evil character of this state of affairs in the West.

Slaves must be cured of their slave-mindedness if they would ever play a part in this battle. Otherwise they will perpetually trade one form of slavery for another at the hands of every new charlatan politician and political philosopher that comes along.

Men are blinded to truth by nature. They are irrational, inconsistent, and imbalanced; and they wrongly assess good and evil. The most radical revolutionary thinkers, known as "leftists," by their own admission have rejected God's laws as the basis for their ethics. They will fight for the rights of rats, child molesters, and abortionists, and they yawn at the massacres of hundreds of millions of innocent people at the hands of communist governments. They would put an innocent person in prison for twenty years for destroying an eagle's egg, and then award some woman with $1000 of federal funds if she will murder her child. This is the very essence of demonic blindness. All men are hypocrites by nature because they are sinners, and they will not ordinarily admit to it. Leftists build monuments to hypocrisy. They revel in their hypocrisy. Of course, they will never do anything to stop child sex slavery and child murder, while they boast in their "charitable" welfare programs that destroy millions of inner city families. They will murder ten thousand babies in the womb in the morning, and argue for more welfare money for children in the afternoon. They mourn the "trail of blood" and promise the Native Americans reparations for Andrew Jackson's broken treaties, while ushering more of them into the welfare reservations with each successive generation. After all of their programs and projects, they have nothing but *more* slavery and misery to show for it.

That we might gain a vision for freedom ourselves, it would be well to define the idea in God's terms and ask how we might recognize it in the life of the free man or free woman. What is the mindset of the freeman? The all-important question is this: Are *we* acting as freemen and are we raising our children to be free men and free women?

THE FREEMAN SEEKS SUBSTANTIVE FREEDOMS

When the freeman thinks of freedom, he doesn't take the word to mean he can do whatever he wants to do. He isn't thinking about the freedom to get high, get drunk, get addicted, and die in a ditch curled up in the fetal position. He doesn't want the freedom to enslave himself to God's good gifts of plants, food, and sexuality. It should be obvious that subjection of oneself to slavery is not freedom.

Actually, the Bible does not recommend an intricate system of regulations whereby the church and the civil government come to dominate our lives. Paul goes so far as to say "all things are lawful for me," and he includes every substance that God has created, including marijuana. However, he follows that up quickly with a qualification:

> "All things are lawful unto me, but all things are not expedient: all things are lawful for me, but I will not be brought under the power of any." (1 Cor. 6:12)

Hemp is useful for making rope and super absorbent diapers. Intoxication that displaces Spirit filling is unacceptable for the Christian (Eph. 5:18), although the Bible does allow strong drink for the dying (Prov. 31:6).

Paul points out in the book of Colossians that Jesus Christ has set us free from the "rudiments of the world," which denote the highly externalistic, regulative systems usually administered by religious and political institutions. Paul explains that these regulations extend to material things that people will touch or taste (Col. 2:21). For example, God's law forbids intoxication and self-murder, but it does not forbid touching or possessing alcohol, drugs, guns, swords, television sets, and so on. These are the substances that highly controlling governments and churches want to fence off by regulation. Their efforts to purify society by these means always prove futile. Thankfully, the powerful work of the Lord Jesus Christ on the cross has rendered these externalistic regulations unnecessary. By His sacrifice, He brought down principalities and powers, "making a show of them openly, triumphing over them in it" (Col. 2:15)—this in order that he might blot out the handwriting of ordinances, those regulative programs that forbid tasting, touching, and handling (vs. 16-21). Of course, this does not legitimize an antinomian world where people break the Ten Commandments at will. Rather, it removes the fences and regulations that enforce empty externalisms.

The freeman therefore, seeks freedom from all forms of idolatry and addiction which are always limiting for him. Only the worship and service of the true and living God can provide maximum freedom for him. If he had a choice between the freedom to worship the true

God and the freedom to use hallucinogenic drugs, of course he would choose the former. He seeks substantive freedoms. He would rather live in a country where he could educate his children in the fear of the true God according to the dictates of his conscience, than live in a country that gives him the freedom to have sexual relations with anything and murder his child anytime he wants to (as long as the child is still in the womb).

A MAN OF FAITH

In this war against tyranny, the enemies are far too formidable, the tyrants are too ubiquitous, and the loyal opposition usually too few in number for it to be turned over to weak and faithless men. The battle for freedom is always that described by Pastor Doak in his sermon preached at Sycamore Shoals. It is always the picture of Gideon with his 300 men and their lamps and clay pots opposing 150,000 Midianites in the valley of Moreh. It is the cosmic war between good and evil. But why faith? Of course, we must have faith because we are involved in a spiritual war. "We wrestle not against flesh and blood, but against principalities, against powers, against the rulers of the darkness of this world" (Eph. 6:12). This war cannot be won by mere male bravado, self-confidence, superior intelligence, winning strategies, and humanist platitudes. What enslaves men is the devil and sin, which cannot be opposed by men who are already bound hand and foot by the devil himself. Faith in the Christ who took our sin upon Himself and overcame the devil at the cross is the necessary constituent in this war. We have to believe the words of Christ, "If the Son will set you free, you will be free indeed." We follow this Christ, and we believe in His Person and work. We declare His Lordship, and submit to it. We find strength in Him. We answer the accuser with the words of liberty, "There is therefore now no condemnation to them which are in Christ Jesus, who walk not after the flesh, but after the Spirit" (Rom. 8:1).

The Old Testament leader Nehemiah serves as a terrific example of a man committed to freedom, obedience to God, and the rebuilding of a shattered nation. He is a man of intrepid faith and bold action. He trusts in God's sovereignty, prays in faith, and acts out of a strong sense of moral responsibility to God. His faith in an all-powerful sovereign God yields great confidence and resilience against all opposition. When the King of Persia (Artaxerxes) supported the return of the exiles with Nehemiah, he plainly attributed the king's decision to the "good hand of my God upon me" (Neh. 4:8). From the outset his motto is full of faith: "The God of heaven, he will prosper us, therefore we his servants will arise and build" (Neh. 2:20). Nehemiah is constant in prayer to God throughout (Neh. 1:5-11, 2:4, 4:4-5, 9, 6:9, etc.). He is dogged in his defense of the people against the opposition, always responding with wisdom, watchfulness, and steady courage. He is passionate about his commitments to the point of pulling beards, weeping, rebuking, confronting leaders, and shaking out his garments in disgust.

At one point in the story, Nehemiah becomes incensed with these people that they have enslaved their sons and daughters, and mortgaged their lands (Neh. 5:4-6). After their redemption from the hands of the Babylonian tyranny, he cannot believe that the people would so quickly revert to slavery upon return to Jerusalem. He calls for an instant release of lands and persons from slavery, and the people comply (Neh. 5:11-13).

There is no man more courageous and faithful than the one who maintains indomitable trust in God's sovereignty with an undying sense of responsibility to God, to the point of laying down his life. As long as he knows for certain that his life is in God's hands, he is willing to risk it for a good cause—for God's cause. Freedom simply will not be fought for nor won without this kind of faith. Neither the pagans who believe that all is in the hands of fate, nor those humanists that believe all is in their own hands will achieve anything substantial in the war against tyranny in the long run.

A SELF-GOVERNING MAN

The most crucial point in this consideration of freedom is this: core freedom is freedom from sin. Jesus promised an absolute freedom because it is not superficial or merely temporal. It is an essential freedom. Therefore political or economic freedom is meaningless, temporary, and vacuous without Christ's freedom at the core. That is why Paul admonishes the freeman in Romans 6:12, to shake off these chains of sin: "Let not sin therefore reign in your mortal body, that ye should obey it in the lusts thereof." He goes on to say, "For sin shall not have dominion over you: for ye are not under the law, but under grace." These eighteen words contain tremendous wisdom, worthy of much contemplation. Since sin is the transgression of the law (1 John 3:4), the promise is freedom from the problem of transgressing the law of God—fundamental, core freedom.

As it turns out, the means by which this comes about is the Gospel. We are free to keep the law (and not break the law), while the principle which motivates us is grace (and not law). Law is no longer a task-master for the Christian. We are not slaves to the law because we are friends of grace. The motive of love is always much stronger than the motive of fear of punishment. Misunderstandings concerning these verses usually yield a faulty religion, and have contributed to a break-down of the Christian faith. It is critical that Christians not separate faith and love from obedience to the commands of Christ. It is just as critical that the Christian not create a long list of extra-scriptural rules that displace God's laws. This extra-scriptural legalism creates more religious forms of bondage, and usually separates grace and law, rules and relationships.

The person who is principally opposed to obeying the commands of God is still a slave of sin. Generally, these people are called antino-mians. They will separate faith from works, and claim that obedience to Christ is a burden. While sin is burdensome (as defined by Scrip-ture), the commands of God are not: "For this is the love of God, that we keep His commandments. And His commandments are not burdensome" (1 John 5:3 NKJV).

The man who is enslaved to the dragon of pornography is hard-ly the man to join the battle for freedom. So Christian pastors who appreciate political and economic freedom, must first seek to set the captives free from sin (through faith in Jesus Christ). This is ultimate freedom, and it will yield other forms of freedom eventually.

The breakdown of manhood and fatherhood also undermines

freedom for any society. One of the largest socialist voting blocs in America is single women. Over 50 percent of children born to women under thirty years of age are born out of wedlock, up from 6 percent in the 1960s. Neither President Obama nor President Clinton (both raised by single mothers), would have been elected had it not been for the single women vote.[1] These were the most socialistic presidents to serve since Lyndon B. Johnson and Franklin D. Roosevelt. Single women will mostly turn to the security and benefits found with the socialist welfare programs if they have no husbands and fathers to provide for them. Therefore, socialism must rely upon the breakdown of the family and fatherhood. The same pattern has been repeated in England, Scotland, Sweden, and elsewhere. As long as the majority of fathers refuse to take responsibility for their own households (which begins with marrying the woman that bears their children), there is no hope for a return to freedom for the nation. Karl Marx's commitment to abolish the family made considerable progress in the Soviet Union during the twentieth century, and now those countries are paying for it. America is experiencing the same thing in the twenty-first century. If strong families are a constituent part of free and self-governing societies, then strong marriages, healthy fatherhood, and biblical roles in marriage will be important.

The freeman rules his family well, "having his children in subjection with all gravity" (1 Tim. 3:4-5). He develops a family economy for his wife and daughters (Prov. 31:11), and he takes the time to disciple his sons in faith, industry, honor, and purity. These things don't come naturally for most young men, and without careful discipleship in these areas, self-government disappears. These are the basic building blocks of freedom. The faith and character of each successive generation is the fruit produced by those who did the evangelism and discipleship work. Without hundreds of thousands of fathers willing to invest millions of hours in the lives of young men, there will be very little substantive character left in the following generation.

This father is concerned about the spiritual well-being of his family, and will do his utmost to protect his children from unsavory influences that enter by way of education, media, or certain social situations. He will train his children to filter their inputs by the Word of God.

Self-governing fathers provide the only real solution to the rise of big government and the destruction of freedom. When fathers take responsibility for their families, they will naturally pay attention to the physical safety of the home, and that will usually include the possession of defensive weapons. Fundamentally, commitment to this freedom will not be sustained through the generations on the basis of a self-defense motive alone. The individualist self-orientation will never produce enough force to defend the cause of freedom. Family-defense introduces an altruism or a self-sacrificial love motive producing a more substantial commitment to freedom. Also, there is a stronger biblical basis for family defense than for individual self-defense (Gen. 14:14ff, 2 Sam. 3:23ff, Neh. 4:14, John 15:13). Too much of the pro-gun lobby still rests on male machismo and individualistic libertarians, the sort that sport the bumper stickers on their cars that shout out: "They can take away my gun when they pry it from my cold dead fingers." This is weaker than the motive that drove Patrick Henry, Robert FitzWalter, and William Wallace, and it will not sustain in the battle for freedom.

Without a restoration of fatherhood, there will never be a recovery of the family. The rise in homosexuality follows the breakdown of father-child relationships. The rise in divorce rates in the 1960s and 1970s inevitably resulted in the increase of uncommitted shack-ups and illegitimacy in the 2000s with the millennial generation. Although it is always expected to find some percentage of young women emancipating from the family at 18-20 years of age, this is now the norm. Almost 100 percent of young women emancipate, and the average marriage age approaches 30. These changes gradually loosen the bonds of family life, and create a more socialist mindset in the younger generation.

Until fatherhood and family shepherding is restored, we will never see a restoration of the church. Faithful family shepherds become church shepherds. As the Apostle puts it, "If a man know not how to rule his own house, how shall he take care of the church of God?"

(1 Tim. 3:5). This is the heart and soul of a biblical social theory. The state is of lesser importance, although necessary. Both family and church are basic constituent parts, and the former rests upon the latter. All of it rests on healthy fathering.

A society where 64 percent of children under six years of age are latchkey will never be a healthy society. Mary Eberstadt makes this point strongly in her book, *Home Alone America*.[2] Scripture calls women to the position of the "Home Manager" (1 Tim. 5:14). Where families are the strongest, there are women governing their homes with wisdom, self-denying love, and grace. Discontented, disconnected mothering is another sign of the breakdown of family life and the self-orientation of the present generation. Freedom-minded women will understand the importance of building strong marriages and families, because they know that this is what stands in the way of socialism and political tyranny. By faith, they will make the tough choices and do the hard work. They won't turn their children over to a government-subsidized daycare at two years of age. They would sooner build the family economy than some boss's corporate dream. Her heart is at home, and "The heart of her husband safely trusts her; so he will have no lack of gain" (Prov. 31:11 NKJV).

It takes freemen to create the productive economies developed in early America, England, the Netherlands, and Switzerland. Transparency International conducts its Corruption Perception Index each year, and invariably the most corrupt nations are atheist, communist, Muslim, Animist, and Roman Catholic countries. Of the sixteen least corrupt nations, thirteen were predominantly Protestant nations, one was half Catholic and half Protestant, and the other two were nations colonized by Protestants.[3] These nations were formed through the generations by men and women who were taught the Christian faith and the commandments of God (Rev. 14:12). By God's grace, and by careful discipleship they learned to keep the eighth and tenth commandments. A free country by definition must be populated by freemen who conduct their business with a high degree of integrity and honesty. Nations like Mexico and Uganda are still impoverished simply because there are not enough honest men living there. They have yet to hear the Gospel of Christ that will set them free (from breaking the eighth and tenth commandments).

Free enterprise systems are corrupted when greed dominates in the hearts of men and they begin to cheat, lie, and steal. This is the story of capitalism in the twentieth century. Labor-management relations broke down by oppression, envy, mistrust, lying, sexual intimidation, and economic inequity. The principles of the Bible are basic to the maintenance of free enterprise: "Masters, give unto your servants that which is just and equal, knowing that ye also have a Master in heaven" (Col. 4:1).

THE DEBT-FREE MINDSET

Perhaps the reader felt a bit of frustration over the rising tyranny described in the previous section of the book. There is much happening in the world that cannot be remedied by a small minority of frustrated conservatives. However, there are some areas in which the freeman can still seek freedom and obtain it. According to the principle found in 1 Corinthians 7:21, we are to take advantage of the opportunities for freedom available to us. We may not have control over $18 trillion dollars of federal debt, but we do have control over our own financial choices. There is no sense in arguing against the rise in government debt, if we are unwilling to deal with personal debt. For these reasons and others, the freeman must seek after the debt-free life.

The Bible speaks of debt as a form of slavery (Prov. 22:7), and limits debt for God's people to seven years (Deut. 15:1ff). The New Testament language on debt is even more restrictive (Rom. 13:8). With longer term debt, men will tend to adopt the slave mindset. When men are constrained by long term debt and large monthly payments, they will be more dependent on the steady paycheck, and the security of big government (or large corporations). As with all forms of servitude, debt restricts a man's control over his own time and resources.

Because most of the world follows John Maynard Keynes' debt-based economic model, these biblical principles come across as old-fashioned and irrelevant. All of our major economic and political institutions favor debt and put the debt-free man at a disadvantage.

Of course, investors expect profits obtained from leveraging in an inflating economy, as long as fractional banking can keep inflation at an even keel (and recession is averted). Meanwhile, the average person who files taxes in America will want to take advantage of the interest write-offs on Attachment A of the 1040 form. These write-offs that include mortgage interest on a home well exceeds the standard deduction. Capital gains taxes on real estate sales kick in, unless the investor is rolling the investment into more debt. And nobody wants to pay capital gains taxes on 3 percent per year increases on value which barely keeps up with inflation. Zoning commissions enforce certain minimal standards, forcing millions of families into more debt. Entire communities are tied up in municipal bonds used to build sewer systems, sidewalks, roads, and parks, driving costs upwards for those who wish to purchase a home. These costs are passed along to thousands of families who then must obtain heavy thirty-year mortgages to afford them. Debt is then accepted as a way of life in America. Against all of these powerful influences, the Word of God says plainly, "Owe no man anything."

The decline in the character of the nation is obvious when viewing the exponential increase of governmental, corporate, and personal debt, especially over the last fifty years. Easy bankruptcy has ruined the integrity of millions of men and women. Debt has fueled much greed, stealing, instant gratification, idolatry, irresponsibility, and slavery across the nation. Not many will consider the intangible impact of debt as it affects character, personal integrity, risk-taking, confidence, and freedom-mindedness. When people think about the value of debt, these losses are seldom considered against the gains on the balance sheet.

Political freedom may be difficult to regain when the majority have embraced the security of their chains over the "animating contest of freedom." However, economic freedom is well within reach of many Christian families. Some will gladly sacrifice material comforts for freedom. In early America, men like Patrick Henry raised 6-8 children in a 400 square foot house. Throughout the nineteenth century, families raised as many as 6-8 children in 800 square foot homes (on average). How many middle-income families today are willing to live in an 800 square foot home (valued at $100,000), paid in full rather than living in a 2400 square foot home with a $250,000 mortgage? Americans have come to appreciate their material comfort more than the blessings of freedom.

There are many blessings attending the debt-free, mortgage free life. The risk of losing all equity to foreclosure is gone. Should a three-bedroom, two-bath home valued at $200,000, (where the owner invests $50,000 in equity) deflate to $150,000, the debtor loses all of his equity if he is forced to sell it. On the other hand, the debt-free man in the same situation still owns the same house with three bedrooms and two baths. He still owns the same amount of drywall he owned when he bought the place. Moreover, the debt-free man can absorb job loss and fluctuations in income (if self-employed) much better than the debtor. Without a regular, dependable job, the debtor could default on his loans, lose his home, and face bankruptcy. The debt-free man who has saved a little has the margin to absorb losses and survive the famine years should the crops fail. Also, the debt-free man will take less interest in charitable write-offs on Internal Revenue Service Form 1040-Attachment A, even if the state removes tax exemptions from churches and other Christian charitable work.

Since many families are caught in the vortex of mortgage debt, personal debt, and credit card debt, they cannot imagine what the free life would look like. To begin the journey towards a debt-free life, I suggest the following steps.

1. The freeman must first repent of the consumerism and materialism that characterizes much of modern life. Perhaps a shopping fast might be in order from time to time. Go without shopping (for all but food and toilet paper) for a month or two and see if you can live on less or make do with what you already have.

2. Develop a family economy with multiple income streams. Replace almost all of your entertainment or discretionary time with fruitful work and charitable service. Some families may wish to schedule a total entertainment fast for several months at a time. This is a one good way to discover the hold that entertainment has over you.

3. Lay out long term goals, and think in terms of a generational vision. Raise your children with a vision for freedom. If a fifteen-year-old young man gets a vision for the debt-free life, he could very well realize that vision by marital age. Suppose he forfeited his computer games, and dedicated twenty hours a week that would typically be given to entertainment, and worked at a sandwich shop for $10.00 per hour. Of ninety-six waking hours in a six-day week, twenty hours is not very many. But if he worked those twenty hours and saved every dime, he could own a small home debt-free at twenty-five years of age.

Healthy economies will never sustain where the majority of the people are infatuated with leisure, and where men work for the chief purpose of recreation and retirement. Freedom cannot survive under this mentality. When the Pilgrims came to America, there weren't any jobs, but there was a lot of work to do. They had a vision, a purpose, and a kingdom motive that brought a free, prosperous nation out of a wilderness (ever so fleeting though that freedom might have been). It was a great experiment in freedom, and it can happen again.

THE COMPASSIONATE MAN

The problem of the poor will never be solved or even helped by socialism. The thieving schemes of socialism have only served to rot out the inner cities, increase illegitimacy rates, ruin the character of the youth, increase prison populations, reinforce the slave mindset, and destroy the relevance of family and church relationships. God will never bless the socialist form of charity where bureaucrats are merely redistributing the wealth. These immoral Marxist scams involve the poor as accomplices in what can only be described as highly organized criminal activity. This is how an atheist humanist disciples the poor, further perverts their character, and robs them of their dignity. Inner city churches that refuse to encourage repentance in this area are only contributing to the problem, and their efforts to disciple families will prove largely fruitless.

The freeman is fully committed to the eventual elimination of government welfare, including farm and housing subsidies, international aid, public school funding, educational vouchers for homeschools, food stamps, health care funding, and even social security. Realistically, this may not happen overnight. Nonetheless, the freeman must set a new direction for assisting the poor through family charity and church charity, one person at a time, one relationship at a time.

The freeman will look first to his own use of government funds. The person reliant upon social security can hardly condemn another who relies on food stamps, especially if the social security recipient is receiving more than he put into it. The argument always comes back, "Yes, but I pay my taxes." Here we are left with an irresolvable stand off. The government won't lower taxes (and increase our freedom) until we agree to get off of the programs; yet no one will quit the programs until governments lower taxes. As long as the most freedom-minded of the nation play this game, there is no hope for a reduction in the size of government. When it comes to avoiding government programs, we must hold ourselves to a tighter account than we would require of others. This is the principle Christ lays out in Matthew 7:3—We first pull the log out of our own eye, in order to see clearly as we help others wean themselves off of welfare.

How might we extricate ourselves from this hopeless morass of misplaced intentions? The longer the present course is pursued, the worse it gets. When you discover you are digging yourself deeper into a hole, the first thing to do is to stop digging. At this point, we must reject humanist wisdom for God's wisdom. What does God's Word tell us about the poor and our duties to the poor?

The most fundamental biblical injunction is love and personal involvement. This is entirely antithetical to Jean-Jacques Rousseau, the father of the modern socialist state. The man who deposited his own children when they were born on the steps of the orphanage, regularly referred to himself as "the most loving man who ever lived."[4] Rousseau was the prototype liberal (progressive socialist). The socialist sitting in his legislative committee room really does believe that he is the most generous of all…as he redistributes other people's money. Jesus Christ, however, considered personal involvement and the altruistic love motive essential for true charity. He soundly condemned the "benefactors" of the Gentiles, whose motive is not love, but power

(Luke 22:25-26). No doubt, most socialists would be reluctant to admit this power motive, but we will let Jesus Christ discern the motive that characterizes Gentile leadership.

The motive of self-sacrificial love is fundamental to Christian charity. That love must be followed up with personal, local, and relational action. There is a vast difference between reaching for your own wallet and reaching for somebody else's wallet. Jesus' Parable of the Good Samaritan brings this lesson to the forefront. When by God's providence, the Samaritan comes across the man left for dead on the side of the road, he gets personally involved (Luke 10:25-37). He does not refer the matter to the "Department of Accosted Strangers." He personally attends to the needs of the man even to the point of paying the innkeeper out of his own purse. Our Lord finishes the story with the words, "go and do likewise." That's the simple admonition for every freeman in the world. Get involved in the lives of the poor who come into your circles. If God brings a poor man before you, He has presented you with an opportunity to act.

If we will restore freedom and recover privatized, personal, local, and relational charity, we must begin in the family. Jesus Christ severely condemned the Pharisees for their system of Corban in Mark 7:10-13. They had developed a program whereby grown children were relieved of their responsibility to care for their elderly parents as long as they assigned their assets to the temple (in something similar to the modern Social Security system). These were the classic liberals. They put on a great religious show, revealing the best of intentions, all the while aggrandizing the power of their institutions. Meanwhile, God's laws were ignored, and families ceased to care for their own. From the beginning, it was God's intent that families take care of their own. Should a man refuse to care for his own mother or grandmother, the Apostle calls him "worse than an unbeliever" (1 Tim. 5:4, 8; verse four describes the widow as a mother or grandmother). Is Paul resorting to hyperbole here? Does the Apostle come across a little too harsh in his imprecations? Taken at face value, these words describe one fundamental trait for the true Christian man. He is the responsible family man...the freeman. The church cannot permit in its membership a single irresponsible man who refuses to provide for his widowed mother or grandmother. Ongoing abdication of responsibility in this area is a sin warranting dis-fellowship (or excommunication) from the church (2 Thess. 3:14-17). It is true that many aging parents are not interested in receiving care from their own children. Relationships across the generations can be a little stiff, and those raised with the socialist mindset usually prefer socialist programs to the care of their own family. Nonetheless, every man with the freedom mindset should be more than willing to take on this responsibility.

When social security fails, when the worker-to-retiree ratio implodes, when half the aged patients in the hospital are euthanized, and when the elderly from America are shipped off to Vietnam or Guatemala (for less expensive accommodations), some may finally realize something of the benefits of freedom. Those who wish something better for themselves thirty years from now, would do well to live out the vision for freedom now. If this generation would set a better example for their children by taking special care of their elderly parents, they may expect better treatment for themselves in their waning years. Now is the time to take meaningful steps towards less reliance on social security, government-funded medical care, and institutional care. While there are limitations to what can be done in the present and some may still need to rely on social security for now, families should work towards preserving inheritance and providing more family-based care for elderly parents or grandparents.

In a situation where a woman is widowed or divorced, the extended family will be called upon to look after her needs. In Leviticus 22:13, we learn that this was a biblical normative for the wife who loses her husband: "She returns to her father's house, as in the days of her youth." Thus, the family is the first line of defense in economic crisis. Instead of seeking security in the state, our mothers, wives, and daughters should find more security in the sphere of the family. The security of the state is more dangerous, more insecure and far less free in the end.

If the burgeoning State Departments of Welfare and Human Services will ever be defunded, every free family must establish their own "Department of Charity." The "third year poor tithe" ordered by God in Deuteronomy 26 was local, voluntary, and relational. This tithe is not to be enforced by the state, but that does not negate God's requirement. This 3.3 percent annual poor tithe on income was in addition to the regular 10 percent tithe given to the church (or temple).

> "When thou hast made an end of tithing all the tithes of thine increase the third year, which is the year of tithing, and hast given it unto the Levite, the stranger, the fatherless, and the widow, that they may eat within thy gates, and be filled...Look down from thy holy habitation from heaven and bless thy people Israel." (Deut. 26:12-15)

This is a tithe distributed by the family to the poor in the local area. Although, Christians may differ on the exact application of Old Testament law, few would negate the principles contained here. If modern Christians would reject the 3.3 percent per year requirement in favor of the law of Christ, we should ask whether Christ is more or less generous than Old Testament law. Shall we give less now after Christ has given us His life? Would New Testament Christians give less than Old Testament Jews who conformed themselves to the law? If we can surrender 50 percent of our income to government, would we be willing to give something over 13 percent of our income for charitable purposes, and reverse the tyranny of government?

An important phrase included in the above passage, is "within thy gates." Biblical charity is local and relational. Certainly, the redistribution of $1.5 trillion every year by a faceless bureaucracy in Washington and the state capitals does not capture this principle. The recipients of charity need to know the names of the people who provide for their needs. Often, the poor will seek that anonymity in order to avoid accountability. The systems cultivate an expectation mentality, and gratitude is almost entirely lost. Obviously, this is unhealthy for the character of the poor. Instead of inspiring gratitude, socialism does just the opposite. It always tends to foment class envy or an entitlement mentality, vices that can bring entire economies down (Prov. 27:4).

Another biblical form of charity is found in the gleaning law—allowing the poor to glean from the edges of the fields (Deut. 24:19-21). According to biblical law, farmers should allow the poor to harvest a little from the edges of their fields. Some effort is required on the part of the poor to harvest the crops, and there may be a small degree of anonymity in the gleaning. However, in the case of Boaz's fields (in the book of Ruth), the farmers were aware of the gleaners and knew them by name (Ruth 2:7). In application to the present day, almost every business can provide some gleaning opportunities for the poor (whether it be farms, manufacturers, publishers, stores, or restaurants). Many stores and restaurants now provide day-old food to the poor. Manufacturers may also allow the poor to refurbish their scratch-and-dent product (and otherwise slightly defective merchandise).

THE RESTORATION OF THE CHURCH

The restoration of the church as a relevant social unit is also critical for the salvaging of Christian freedom (in a socialist world). From the turn of the twentieth century, the church diaconate has been made irrelevant. For almost 2000 years, the office of the deacon would take care of the widows and orphans in a church community (reference Acts 6:1-6). This author is unaware of any widow in America who relies on the church (instead of the government) for her economic well-being at the present time. Almost every church would turn their widows over to the state, voluntarily. At this rate, how will the church be prepared to handle the breakdown of the social security system? Socialism simply cannot survive, especially when 60-90 percent of the population is dependent on welfare (provided for by a small number of economic producers). Will the church stand against mass euthanasia in the year 2045?

According to clear biblical dictate, the church is the second source of provision for the destitute widow. Her first source of support is her father, her sons, her nephews, or her grandsons (1 Tim. 5:3-8,16). If she has family, we read, "let not the church be charged." Nonetheless, the church is the second line of defense for the poor widow. Only those widows over 60 years of age receive a regular stipend or regular guaranteed support from the church (1 Tim. 5:9). The church may still assist the young widows and the poor during times of crisis (given that there is no family helping them).

Historically, the church gave one-fourth of its income to the poor. We find this tradition first recorded in a letter from Gregory I, repeated in Bede's *Ecclesiastical History of the English People*, and referred to in John Calvin's *Institutes of the Christian Religion*. Given this ratio for budgeting, a modern church with $600,000 of annual income (accounting for one hundred middle income American families), would allocate around $150,000 for the poor widows. This should provide sufficient income for at least ten widows in the church (accounting for as much as ten percent of the congregation). However, a modern survey of church budgeting would find far less than 25 percent allocated to the widows. It would be surprising to find a church budget of $600,000 allocating more than $6,000 per year (or 1 percent) to the poor. As long as evangelical churches restrict their charitable provisions to nothing more than an annual can drive during the Christmas season, there will be little hope for reversing the trends towards socialism in this country. Ten thousand "conservative" politicians will do nothing to reduce government, salvage the inner-city family, and restore freedom, if the church is disengaged. Only an active, relevant diaconate can lead the way towards restoring a biblical approach to charity. The billions of dollars that pour into government systems, United Way, and other large non-local charities (where there are no long-term accountable relationships operating), will only exasperate our social problems. By the power of the Holy Spirit working in the hearts of Christians everywhere, we must rebuild the diaconate in tens of thousands of local churches capable of supporting hundreds of thousands of widows in an honest, loving, accountable, biblical, charitable system.

This calls for a change of heart with the poor as well. There must be a humility, and a faith, and an appreciation for relationships with the poor among us, that they would repudiate the anonymous, bureaucratic approach to charity. These men and women of faith must voluntarily seek out fruitful, long-term, accountable relationships in the local church. Of course, it is much easier for them to take the handout in the relationship-free context.

Only a powerful work of God can produce the faith to reject the dreary, dystopian world of the modern slave state. Both the giver and receiver must come to passionately pursue the freedom found in God's design for charity as well as reject a system based on government-sponsored larceny, the breakdown of the family, and the moral degradation of the poor.

Given that we are already taxed to over 40 percent of our income to cover welfare, social security, and a hundred other programs, this challenge seems an impossible undertaking. Under such oppressive conditions, how could a family voluntarily provide for the medical care, shelter, and food for the widows and orphans? Actually, this is not the first time Christian families have faced such overwhelming difficulties. During the 1980s and 1990s, millions of families of faith reassumed the responsibility for the education of their children, while rejecting government aid in the form of vouchers. They did it in spite of the oppressive tax system levied by the modern socialist education system. How would the care of the widows and elderly parents be any different? If Christians must wait for tax credits and the defunding of the welfare system before they begin to construct a more principled, privatized approach then it will never happen or it will come too late. Without men of faith who are willing to take the first step towards freedom, there would be no hope for restoring a more biblical approach to charity...and liberty.

The transfer of education back to the family also reordered the economics of education. Mom and the kids at the kitchen table replaced expensive administrative bureaucracies, state-of-the-art million dollar buildings, and professional staff. What costs the federal, state, and county governments upwards of $12,000 per student per year can be handled by a family for less than $400 per child per year with much better results.[5] Recent research indicates a growing percentage of minorities home educating their children—African American participation increased from 4 percent to 8 percent in four years, and Hispanic participation increased from 9.8 percent to 15 percent over the same time period.[6] The reintegration of the family and the freeman mindset is a hopeful sign for the future of freedom and socio-economic stability among these cultural groups.

There is no "perfect system" for the distribution of funds to the poor. Of course, we will never "fix" poverty by our voluntary distributions, but this is not the Christian objective. Primarily, we are interested in the souls of our poor brothers and sisters. We want to see their relationships with God and with their own families and churches improved. We want to see them contributing in the body of the church with their own gifts even if they cannot contribute much to the offering plate. The expectation mindset of the poor has done more to damage private charity than anything else. If charity will be received rightly in the Galatians 6:2-5 spirit, the recipient will be surprised and thankful because he never expected to receive the gift in the first place. He had planned to bear his own burdens, and now here is a brother who has offered to carry a portion of that burden for him, and he therefore receives it with gratitude.

Private, voluntary charity falls apart quickly by several fallacious assumptions. Much could be said about this, however, I would issue the following cautionary notes when it comes to distributing charity in family and church.

1. It is fallacious that the poor must always demonstrate improvement in character *before* they receive any charity.

2. It is fallacious that the poor must always work for charitable contributions.

3. It is fallacious that the poor need only financial assistance. Often, the larger problem with the poor is isolation, depression, spiritual needs, etc.

4. It is fallacious that the poor are only to receive assistance if they are starving to death.

5. It is fallacious to prioritize the needs of those outside of our communities, and outside of the local, relational context. This does not prevent involvement with other churches or nations that are struggling through crises, however the day-to-day priority needs are closest to home.

THE FREEMAN IS COMMITTED TO STRENGTHENING FAMILY AND CHURCH

Both political and economic forces have devastated family solidarity in almost every country around the world. In the opening paragraphs in his famous autobiography written in 1888, the missionary John Paton commented that the destruction of the family farm and the family economy in Scotland did not need to happen, but that "the loss to the nation as a whole is vital, if not irreparable."[7] When dad left the home for his corporate job and mom left the home for her job, initially the children were turned over to the capitalist corporation. Subsequently, the children were then passed off to the state by way of child labor laws and compulsory attendance laws. The same thing is happening to the women now, as their medical insurance and social security are moved from the corporation to the state by way of Obamacare. One hundred years ago, Hilaire Belloc and G.K. Chesterton argued for a "third way" in place of capitalism and communism. They insisted that a family-based economy with a widespread ownership of property (debt-free) would protect "primal family relations and the home economy."[8] They warned that "measures such as unemployment insurance, a minimum wage, and national health insurance constituted a dangerous new form of servitude."[9]

The strongest external force that has worked to separate the oneness of the family is the education-economic institutional complex. For 6,000 years, families had worked together; David, Rachel, and Joseph would feed their father's sheep, and Aquila and Priscilla worked together as tentmakers (Gen. 29:10, 1 Sam. 17:15, Acts 18:3). Following the family-fragmenting industrial revolution and the rise of socialism, family economies have virtually disappeared. The children plug into the state as early as their pre-school or kindergarten years. They eventually wander away from the family, with ever decreasing odds that they will ever start their own family. David enrolls in college two thousand miles from home, gets an apartment, plays computer games until he's twenty-nine, hooks up with Rachel for three months, and thinks about having kids when he's forty-eight. Meanwhile Rachel goes off to college, gets her career going, tries not to get pregnant, and

270 ~ The Story of Freedom

bears 1.2 kids by the time she's forty-five years old (with or without a husband). Women are freezing their eggs, in hopes they might have children later in their forties.[10] Rachel doesn't need a husband because she has her corporate job and besides, the President will take care of her in her retirement years. That is the new socialist economy of the twentieth and twenty-first centuries. But what happens to a society where the nuclear family is in the minority, and dysfunctional families become the norm? Dysfunctionality will give rise to more dysfunctionality—that is inevitable for now.

Without the radical reintegration of the family economy and family education, we will fail to restore family freedoms, or salvage a civilization for that matter. The vision for family-based economics is growing. Especially during a period of economic downturn, we will begin to see families pulling together and developing income streams. The family economy may work together on a single stream (as in a family farm), or multiple streams. Everyone pulls together. Each player is vital to the team, and everyone works. We are not speaking of the "traditional" family here, where the father works and the mother stays home. Nor is it the latchkey family where children are raised by the state to play their part in the individuated, statist economy. The word "economics" is taken from the Greek word *oikonomia*, which translates as "household law." From the beginning, the basic economic unit was not the individual, but the family. Proverbs 31 was clear: "The heart of her husband safely trusts her; so he will have no lack of gain" (NKJV). In modern life, this verse must be read differently: "The heart of her corporate boss and seven layers of bureaucracy does safely trust in her."

According to recent reports, about 70 percent of young men are not "grown up" by thirty years of age (a rate that has risen from 30 percent in 1970).[11] They do not have steady work, they are not married, and they are not ready to raise children. Young men are still playing computer games at twenty-nine, and they are the only demographic group making less money than they did in 1970, because they were not trained to work when they were young boys. For the last three generations at least, fewer boys have been mentored by their own fathers.

"School," as traditionally configured, does not train a boy to work. To wait until a boy is sixteen or eighteen years of age before putting him to work is a grave error, and many developed nations are suffering the consequences of it. We must train our sons and daughters to contribute to the household economy from the beginning. Then we will have an inheritance to give them, and they will take care of their parents in their old age. With the family economy, we have more opportunity for discipleship, family integration, and the preparation of our daughters for their own family economies.

Writing in the early part of the twentieth century, Hilaire Belloc considered both capitalism (of the modern form) and socialism as inherently unstable economic systems, especially given the inherent tendency in both systems to disintegrate the family. What happens to a society where the young thirty-year-old men are playing computer games, while the sixty-five-year-old men are playing golf? What happens to a society where there are far more retirees than birth-imploded Generation Z's in the work force, especially if the social security system is approaching bankruptcy? Unless we change the way we educate, the way we do our economics, and the way we integrate the family, we will be ill-prepared to meet the collapse of a socio-economic system. Now is the time to redefine a biblical economy based upon the reintegration of the family.

When Barack Obama was elected president of the United States in 2008, he committed himself to restoring the federal inheritance tax.[12] Previously, George W. Bush had allowed the elimination of the tax for a single year, but the Democrats committed themselves to bringing it back. Rousseau's ideological children are committed to disempowering the family, generation by generation. Almost all of our institutions (whether economic, educational, or political), are dedicated to the enrichment of the state at the expense of the family. Inheritance taxation is one of the most blatant attacks on family solidarity. In some states, this tax (federal and state combined) can exceed 75 percent of the total inheritance. The freeman must find a way to empower the family in spite of these strong opposing forces. At least for now, we can expect socialism to continue to grow. Who knows what the next socialist president will do to tax inheritance four years from now, or twelve years from now? Will the government confiscate Individual Retirement Accounts? Would future administrations move to tax inheritance at a 90 percent rate in order to salvage a bankrupt government?

In direct opposition to the ideas of Rousseau and Marx, the Word of God places a strong value on the family and freedom. When it comes to a man's inheritance, the confiscatory powers of government are strongly condemned in Scripture (1 Kings 21:3, Mic. 2:2). The freeman is the "good man" described in Proverbs 13:22: "A good man leaveth an inheritance to his children's children." The first heritage which we bequeath to our children will be faith and truth. Then, we want to pass on a vision for freedom. Life is more than making money and buying toys. We want to pass along a vision for the kingdom of God, and the formation of more healthy families and churches. Finances play a part in this. A financial inheritance can also help to provide stronger generational connections, especially where there is true faith and love operating in the family, rather than the fleshly works of greed and covetousness that characterize the world.

Many families are taking advantage of gift tax exemptions, living trusts, and other "islands of freedom" to protect their families from the death tax. By combining the lifetime gift tax exemption of $1,000,000 with a $12,000 annual, per child gift allowance, families may exempt several million dollars from the estate tax. Keep in mind that inheritance tax laws may become more egregious in the next thirty years. So if God gives us the freedom to pass along an inheritance in the form of gifts to our children, we may be able to protect ourselves from confiscatory taxation later.

Recent surveys indicate that the church receives an average of a two-percent tithe from congregants.[13] Meanwhile, federal, state, and local governments take closer to 50 percent of the people's income. This clearly demonstrates the irrelevance of the church in most communities around the world. In modern society, the public schools and social security programs are ten times more important to the lives of the people than the local church. Thus, socialism breaks down the church community and the love of brethren. Socialism is another form of Christian apostasy. Such conditions are completely unacceptable in the mind of the freeman.

If there are Christians who love Christ and value the church over heartless, socialist systems, of course they will contribute to the church community by leaving their inheritance to these ministries instead of handing it over to the government.

When social security fails and euthanasia is wiping out thousands, if not millions, of the elderly, Christian families and churches will find their relevance in human society again. Now is the time for Christian families to consider caring for the elderly seniors within their churches.[14] Some families will add an additional wing of bedrooms to their homes to accommodate their own parents or other elderly in their communities. Churches with foresight are preparing to provide funds to elderly widows living with member families in the congregation. This will create a better cross-generational context for the church community in the future.

CONCLUSION

Those who have adopted the humanist social view will not resonate with this message or understand the urgency of it. When the only significant relationship left in human society is the relationship of the individual to the state, other human relationships began to diminish in importance. Those who have recaptured the vision for freedom will more and more renounce government control and funding of the education of their children. They will save an inheritance for their children and provide for their aging parents. Thus, the renewal of family and freedom will come simultaneously.

If there is anything we can glean from history's great battle for freedom, it is this: freedom will never be won without generations of struggle and sacrifice. If the massive educational, economic, and political forces are geared towards enslaving the masses and disintegrating the family, of course it will take great faith to oppose these forces. The battle for freedom is long and difficult, but it is not an impossible battle if it is waged every day in homes everywhere. Each family that seeks freedom must map out their own unique plan for applying this vision.

They must seek God's wisdom through prayer and study of the Word.

What follows is a summary of some of the practical steps that may be taken as families work towards the goal of more freedom and less dependence upon the state. Each one of these strategies is geared to maximize freedom and empower the family in the areas where the modern world has weakened it.

1. Pay for your own children's food, clothing, and education.

2. Work towards a debt-free life.

3. Incorporate your family into your economic vision. Build family businesses and ministries.

4. Raise your sons and daughters with the idea that the family is an economic team (Gen. 2:18, Prov. 31:11). Do not raise a child with the objective that he or she will become his or her own independent economic unit.

5. Take advantage of every opportunity to care for your parents and grandparents in their waning years.

6. Opt out of social security if possible. Be careful not to rely upon social security, and consider money invested in the fund as money thrown away.

7. Opt out of government-funded socialist medicine.

8. Save an inheritance for your children.

9. Do not plan on retirement in the modern definition of the word. There is much to be done in service, ministry, and economic endeavor for Christ until He calls you home.

10. Be generous towards the poor in your community. Be faithful with the tithe and other offerings to the church. Consider taking elderly widows from the church into your own home.

Chapter 19

IN SEARCH OF THE
SECOND MAYFLOWER

"For the Lord will not cast off his people, neither will he forsake his inheritance. But judgment shall return unto righteousness: and all the upright in heart shall follow it. Who will rise up for me against the evildoers? Or who will stand up for me against the workers of iniquity?" (Ps. 94:14-16)

The second *Mayflower* was launched in 1993. It wasn't a real ship, but it was an idea that had formed during the latter half of the twentieth century in the United States. During these years, there was a rising minority to be found who were still committed to liberty as defined by God's laws. The second *Mayflower* was a vision, a blueprint, or a movement for those who wanted another free nation somewhere in the world. It makes the most sense to start where we live, especially if there are any like-minded persons who value freedom here. Since that time, the national scene has changed significantly. The former political movements known as the "Christian Coalition" and the "Moral Majority" have disappeared, and the millennial generation is more committed to a leftist agenda than ever before. Evangelicalism has developed more of a sour taste for politics, and it is doubtful most evangelicals would oppose the tyrannical state (unless their tax exemptions were threatened). Most of the mainline church is either apolitical or supportive of the progressive socialist agenda. At the present, a movement of conservatives called the "Tea Party" gained some national recognition. In the 800th year following the publication of the Magna Carta, there is a concerted minority still interested in freedom.

To abandon the possibility of a return to freedom somewhere in the world is to deny the influence of the Lord Jesus Christ in history. He must reign until all his enemies are under His footstool (Acts 2:34-35), and that must include every anti-Christ tyranny in the world. It is an indisputable fact of history that Christian men have fought some successful battles and made a mark for freedom in times past. It can happen again. As long as Christ is conquering His enemies we can hope that the principle of political freedom will return somewhere, sometime in the future.[1]

Given that most nations will continue pursuing big government, what strategy might freedom-minded people take to the next stage of the battle? If we are called to secure what freedoms we can, where do we begin?

PERSECUTION

Christians hold a wide range of eschatological perspectives today. Some believe an antichrist is coming in this generation, some believe he came in the first century. Some believe things will get worse while others believe things will get better. Regardless of eschatological views, true Christians will always stand for justice and truth, as defined biblically. *Christians must always oppose tyranny.* To our dying breath, we will oppose tyrants who violate God's laws in their policies and actions.

Yet, persecution for Christians works much like the fertilizer that speeds the growth of crops in the fields. Therefore, the leaders of the church must use every instance of persecution to strengthen faith in God amongst their people, to steel their commitment to liberty, and to cause them to cry out to Christ, "How long?" (Rev. 6:10). As persecution of Christians by wily tyrants and the homosexual fascists increases, every Christian radio station, magazine, and church should publicize the stories of persecution and defend these believers. We do take comfort in the fact that all tyrannical persecution of the Christian church will strengthen it. That is the way God ordains it. Nonetheless, this does not absolve the tyrants of their sinful actions. Indeed, Judas' betrayal and Jesus' death yielded a good effect. But, Jesus said, "Woe to the man by which the offense comes" (Luke. 17:1). Of course, the authorities will use trumped-up charges, media propaganda, and slander within the church community to castigate the persecuted. We do not want to be on the wrong side of this battle (Rev. 14:9-12).

When it comes to civil governments, there will always be Christians in strategic positions. In the very worst of times, when God's people were inches away from annihilation, God raised up Joseph and Esther to stand in the gap. God put these leaders in place to preserve His people. When Christian influence declines in the political sphere, and the cause of freedom loses on the various battlefronts of taxation, abortion (the right to life), property ownership, and so on, we stay on full court press against the tyrants. At times, we may be pushed to a defensive posture on our own five yard line. The role of civil government in Romans 13 and Genesis 9:6 is clearly to punish the evildoers, and the top priority for the magistrate should be to put the murderer to death. Thus, the highest priority for a righteous government is to execute justice with abortion and murder. However, when godly influence wanes to the point that this cannot be accomplished (which is happening now), we return back to the example of Esther and Joseph. They used their civil influence to preserve the lives of God's people. We do not find the Apostle Paul advocating pro-life bills in the Roman senate, because Christians had very little political influence at this seminal stage of the church. Yet we still find Paul appealing to Caesar in Acts 25:11 in order to preserve his own life (from almost certain death in Jerusalem). Any Christian who finds himself in a position of influence, therefore, will first defend the liberties of God's people who minister the Gospel in the church or in the family. Christians will do their best to keep Christians out of jail for witnessing, evangelizing, teaching, preaching, writing, or discipling (whether on the streets, in the home, or in the church building).

ISLANDS OF FREEDOM

We do not completely abandon the struggle for freedom at any level. However, we must be realistic. America will not be won back to the principles of freedom as contained in the original intent of the Constitution any time soon. The trends are moving in the opposite direction. It is time to be strategic. By God's all-wise providence, He has provided islands of freedom everywhere for those who are looking for them. I will give a number of examples of these islands in the remaining pages. Those who have a heart for freedom will be thrilled at these opportunities. They represent beacons of hope in an otherwise dystopian world (as described in the previous section of the book). Although the islands are not actual geographical locations, these opportunities are not to be ignored. Let us not despise "the day of small things" (Zech. 4:10). The boundaries of this liberty are more fluid and less universally applied to every person in a particular nation. "Where the Spirit of the Lord is, there is liberty" (2 Cor. 3:17). It is still the duty of every Christian to seek this liberty wherever they are. We take the more accessible islands first, and someday we may see more liberty on a wider, institutional level. Act the freeman, disciple others in the Gospel of liberty, and one day God may bless our entire nation with more freedom.

Not everyone who believes in freedom will agree on the best strategy for recovering it. Some believe the Titanic may be salvaged, to use a metaphor. Others are more interested in the life-raft manufacturing centers, in hopes that this will produce more long term success. Some will be more involved in Washington, DC, sending young, promising freedom fighters into the engine room of the Titanic before the nation hits the iceberg. Or perhaps we have already hit the iceberg. There will always be disagreements concerning strategy, but it is often the case that both approaches have merit. There is "Joseph" in the engine room of the large ship, while others work the life-raft manufacturing centers on the deck. These various battle fronts attract different persons with differing gifts, and we must respect God's calling on each person's life.

GEOGRAPHY

Geography does play into the strategy. Certain battles are more effectively waged in some states than others. A bill that works in the Texas legislature would be dead on arrival in Washington, for example. Some states provide more liberty than others when it comes to laws affecting homeschooling, abortion, guns, and taxes. At the time of this writing, Texas remains near the top of the list on most accounts. However, the City of Houston in southeast Texas recently proved itself to be one of the most tyrannical cities in the country, when its lesbian mayor advocated persecution against Christian pastors in the city. Thus, "red states" (more favorable to freedom), are often controlled by large "blue cities" (less favorable to freedom). The most leftist cities in the country are usually either university towns or the largest cities in the respective states.

Concerning restrictions on self-defense or family-defense, a flurry of gun laws over the last thirty years have created more freedom in some states and less in others. Right to Carry laws have been adopted in thirteen states without restrictions, and about thirty states allow ordinary citizens to carry with a permit. Between 2013 and 2015, state legislatures passed sixty-four bills that restrict guns, and seventy that lessen restrictions.[2] The worst states for gun laws are Connecticut, California, Illinois, New Jersey, New York, Delaware, Hawaii, Massachusetts, Colorado, and Maryland. The best states include Arizona, Alaska, Louisiana, Mississippi, Kentucky, Missouri, Wyoming, Texas, and South Dakota.[3]

Families who cherish their freedoms will often raise their children in red states, and fight for what freedoms they can get. If their children attend the blue universities, they must send them there in battle mode. Otherwise they will repeat the mistake that millions of families have made for 200 years, paving the way towards progressive socialist agendas, generation by generation. Wherever God directs our families, one thing is certain: we must always be aware of the battle lines and fight tooth and nail on those lines. We employ what freedoms are available in order to press for more freedom. This is the modus operandi of the man who is free in Christ.

Even the poor man cast away in a communist prison in China may exercise his freedom in Christ. The story of Brother Yun testifies of a man who was more free to share the message of the Gospel within prison walls than outside of it.[4] Hundreds of hardened criminals were marvelously saved when this man was incarcerated in both Chinese and Burmese prisons during the 1990s. When he was through working with the prisoners inside, he walked out of a high security prison past thirty to forty guards apparently oblivious to his escape. Eventually, Yun found more freedom in the West, as he was sure his life was at risk within China. The Christian acts a freeman wherever he finds himself. "For he that is called in the Lord, being a servant, is the Lord's freeman" (1 Cor. 7:22). Prison ministries can be highly fruitful, because these are the highways and byways from which Christ calls men and women to the great wedding feast (Matt. 22:1-14). There are murderers and rapists who find freedom from sin in maximum security prisons. A man who was perhaps the worst criminal ever prosecuted in America testified of his faith in Jesus Christ on national television, the day before he died. The staggering report of Jeffrey Dahmer's baptism and change of life will remain forever a testimony to what Christ can do, as He sets the prisoners free from the bondage of their sin.[5]

AN ISLAND OF FREEDOM IN EDUCATION

According to Karl Marx, the author of the Communist Manifesto, the core value of communism is "public education for all." His objective was to "replace home education with social." When it comes to preparing the next generation of citizens, the humanist state cannot tolerate competition from the family. Socialists must always prepare the next generation of socialists by remanding the children to socialist schools for at least twelve years.

Since the 1980s, an island of freedom formed in education for millions of families. By the first part of the twentieth century, home education had disappeared almost entirely in this country. State-certified teachers who had attended state-certified schools had been installed in the schools. This assured that state-certified methods and content would dominate both public and private schools. Accreditation was jealously sought after by private schools, but home education constituted a radical departure from this. Uncertified parents teaching their children in their homes was antithetical to the socialist ideal. At a time when Orwell's *1984* agenda seemed inevitable, something very opposite to this dystopian construct emerged. By God's providence, some families extricated themselves from the socialist "matrix" through this new movement called "homeschooling." In a series of remarkable events taking place in legislatures and courtrooms, home education became legal in all fifty states.[6] While public schooling families were losing freedoms to exempt their kids from sex-ed classes, and other similar programs (in court cases like the Brown case and the Palmdale case), millions of homeschooling families were gaining freedoms through the 1990s, 2000s, and 2010s. An otherwise liberal media was also generally friendly to homeschooling during the same period. For some reason, homeschoolers wielded surprising political influence when it came to this particular issue. It was an island of freedom, in an otherwise dismal period of time in Western history.

Throughout the twentieth century, Rousseau's devotees worked hard to expand the compulsory attendance laws around the country. The State of Colorado expanded its compulsory attendance law several times over the last decade. However, homeschool families argued vehemently against these more onerous restrictions. To accommodate their requests, the legislature exempted them from both bills. Home educators maintain that parents know their children's needs and abilities better than the bureaucracy, and the one-size-fits-all system of education touted by large centralized governments is tyrannical and ineffective. These bills represented a gross violation of family freedoms. Only a handful of families showed up at the committee meetings to protest these intrusions on liberty. No doubt, the other 98 percent of the population considers such efforts a waste of time, a symbolic protest in defense of unnecessary liberties. That is why the majority will never do anything to defend freedom. Most of England did not support the Pilgrims at the turn of the seventeenth century. Few understood why they should make such a big deal over state-approved ordinations of pastors and state-enforced accouterments like candles in the worship service. For the Pilgrims, it was a matter of principle, and they were willing to give their lives for it. Almost half of them died the first year in America, but they were glad they came. And we are glad they came.

Today's Pilgrims are those who have the foresight and principle to fight for substantial freedoms—to carve out an island of freedom wherever they can find it. They will do it for the benefit of future generations that will live 400 years from now, should Christ tarry. The problem in 1620 was the State's interference with the church, but that is not so much the concern to freedom-minded people today. We are more concerned by the state's interference with the sphere of family. A vast majority of the population will not show up in the state government committee meetings to argue for these freedoms because they do not see the value in it. They have grown accustomed to governmental control of every part of their lives. Basically, they do not think like freemen.

There it is. The island is available for the taking. Of course, when parents take the controls of their children's education, they will need great faith, much hard work, the cultivation of good relationships, and faithful prayer to make it work. These constitute the building blocks of freedom for ourselves and our children. Every day, we lay another brick. After a generation or two, we will find that by God's grace we have made some progress.

AN ISLAND OF FREEDOM IN FAMILY MEDICINE

Turning over medical decisions and medical rationing to the hands of powerful bureaucrats is not a good idea, and that will become increasingly obvious during bad economic times. Freedom-minded people will take note of the rising involvement of government in medical care. The rapid expansion of "physician assisted" suicide and euthanasia in the United States, Belgium, and other Western nations portend even more trouble, especially since the decisions rest more in the hands of government bureaucracies. As of January 2014, Belgium lawmakers have even approved euthanasia for children.[7] These trends are troubling to say the least, especially when the government-controlled medical establishment is so eager to provide euthanasia to their patients. Already, children with birth defects like Trisomy 18 are regularly denied routine medical care, and parents have to fight hard for the lives of these precious children.[8]

Christian families must fight for every inch in the battle for freedom in medical care. Thus far, most Western nations have not seen the gross tyranny of forced abortions and infanticides which have plagued China for almost three decades now. Considering the fact that England and America have surrendered their Christian heritage and destroyed the nuclear family, this scenario is not entirely out of the question. As birth rates fall amongst the majority population, government-enforced birth control and birth rationing may very well be imposed on those communities that do not contribute to the birth implosions. Within the Christian, Mormon, and Roman Catholic populations, there are some who still find reason for carrying on their civilization and their faith.

Another island of freedom was formed on March 23, 2010, when Barack Obama signed the "Patient Protection and Affordable Care Act" into law. This landmark legislation intended to extend government-subsidized medical insurance to 30 million uninsured persons in America.

However, many Christian families did not want to provide support for the government-mandated abortion and abortifacient drug insurance funding. They did not want to revert to government-subsidized insurance. They did not want to sign up for the $11,000 a year marriage penalty hardwired into the Obamacare package. They wanted the freedom to make their own medical decisions for their families. Moreover, the exorbitant costs of these federally-mandated insurance programs (with estimates exceeding $23,000 per year for a family of four), would only further impoverish families and the larger economy.[9]

Sensible people, Christian people, free people, needed an island of freedom in the socialist dystopia that was forming. That is what God provided by the exemption on Page 128 of the Affordable Care Act. Those participating in health care sharing ministries were exempted from participating in the Obamacare program. The three tiny medical sharing ministries had no lobby to speak of in Washington, only a few friends in strategic locations (and the God of Daniel, Esther, and Joseph). It was nothing short of God's good providence that this exception was permitted.[10]

This is yet another testimony to the faithfulness of God. The tiny embers of freedom will not die out completely. Somehow, small islands of freedom will still survive during the dark era of the modern Orwellian states—freedom for those who want it.

The Christian medical sharing ministries do not provide total security (which is just another word for "tyranny"). They are not bottomless coffers of debt-based government funding. Those who participate must not trust in princes. They must trust in God, and they must love their brothers and sisters who have medical needs. Participants share medical needs, they write personal checks each month directly to a family in need, and they are expected to pray for these needs.

There are a few other fledgling, free-market expressions in medical care still available in the world, including cash-only services and medical tourism. These may very well grow as socialism proves a failure. Throughout Western history, medical care was mostly a charitable service provided through the church. Many hospitals in America are still named for the denomination that formed them (Presbyterian, Catholic, Baptist, and Adventist). However, the government coup that has brought about socialist control of medicine in America has destroyed charity and the influence of the church. Nonetheless, true churches must work to circumvent these government programs. Retired Christian doctors may choose to volunteer their services in church clinics. All of these efforts are important to the enlargement of the islands of freedom. As the islands grow and socialism wreaks havoc on the mainland, God in His good providence may very well supply another opportunity to establish a free country somewhere in the world.

SMALL COMPANIES

The Obamacare Employer Mandate also opened up an island of freedom for small companies with fewer than fifty employees. With these small companies, the employer could allow its employees to rely on the "individual mandate." As already mentioned, Christian families under the individual mandate may exempt themselves from this draconian beast through the medical sharing ministries. Therefore, a Christian company with forty-nine employees could offer bonus pay for those who are willing to register with one of these sharing ministries. This would be a savings of $750,000 per year (over what a competing company of fifty-one employees would have to pay for insurance). The average small business receives an average annual revenue of $3.6 million per year, with a net profit of $540,000. The savings that a small company that exempts itself from Obamacare receives exceeds the entire average net profit of a similar small company. Thus, an island of freedom in this fascist world gave the small company an edge in the market.

Moreover, many Christians report persecution in the workplace for their opposition to the homosexual lifestyle (and refusal to participate in the "gay" celebration week imposed on them by the large corporate offices). Over time, these Christians will be forced into smaller companies that do not enforce the politically-correct agenda. Small companies become the refuge, the island of freedom for those recalcitrant Christians who refuse to submit to the "beastly" agenda.

Since the *Obergefell v. Hodges* ruling in 2015, large companies and even schools will be increasingly held to the requirements laid out in Title VII, governing hiring practices extended to sexual orientation. However, Title VII requirements are restricted to companies with fifteen or more employees.[11] Once again, Christians will have to seek out these islands of freedom if they are to bear up under the present rash of persecutions.

FAMILY ECONOMIES

Interest is growing fast in the area of the family economy.

Opportunities for a more decentralized family-based economy are burgeoning. The technology that enabled the development of large corporations, could very well decentralize economies as well. The internet has opened up a trillion dollar market for niche businesses. For example, one family who lives off the grid in Idaho developed an on-line business selling refurbished 1930s sewing machine parts. Earlier in the 1980s, a physical shop in the Boise, Idaho business district would never have been successful (with such a niche product line). The market has changed dramatically, with the advent of the internet. Moreover, basement operations are now producing films and music mp3s and competing with powerful Hollywood and Nashville producers. What used to require millions of dollars of equipment can now be done in a basement with a few thousand dollars of capital investment. Moreover, distribution is made possible through the Internet. This author's online radio podcast competes with NBC, CBS, ABC, and *The New York Times*. Also, the pet breeding and pet care industry has grown from $32 billion to $62 billion in just the last ten years. Then there is the multi-trillion dollar elderly care market that will provide huge opportunities for business and ministry over the next 30 years. Could Christian family economies take something of a market share, and thereby salvage inheritance, and siphon some of the retirement funds from large institutions and the death tax? The large elderly care institution cannot provide what the family can give, such as relationships and cross-generational contact. The institutions will tend to drain the family resources and increase dependence on the state. The opportunities for the family economy in the twenty-first century are endless. The island of freedom is there for the taking.

DEFENDING THE ISLANDS

Now that we have identified several islands of freedom that have formed in this country and in other countries around the world, the question remains how free men and women will defend them. Legal defense organizations and special interest lobbying groups stand in the gap for gun-owners, homeschoolers, and Christians. Most of these organizations have been in operation for less than thirty years.

Pro-life organizations have been marginally effective at restricting abortion, within the constraints of *Roe v. Wade*. However, they have been incapable of stopping the federal tyranny from funding Planned Parenthood and legalizing the trafficking of baby body parts. Moreover, the increased use of contraceptives, Plan B, and RU-486 abortifacients far transcends the use of surgical abortion in this country. In fact, the federal government has even imposed abortifacients on Christian colleges and organizations since the incorporation of Obamacare.[12]

Nonetheless, the battles will continue in order to protect religious liberties, homeschooling, gun-ownership, adoption rights, and healthcare freedoms for Christians, as well as to protect Christian families from forced abortion and infanticide. Christians will always need a Joseph, Daniel, Esther, and Erastus at every level of government to stand in the way of tyranny. The level to which a Christian will be involved in politics depends upon opportunities, calling, gifting, and preparation. God does not call us all to the same involvement. Since a biblical social system is not based on socialism and government cannot do much to change the behavior of men, Christians must be careful not to over-emphasize politics. Yet, every Christian has a duty before God to do justly and to love mercy (Mic. 6:8). We still have a responsibility to defend the lives of the orphans in the face of tyrants. Political force may be used to restrain the most wicked men who are likely to rape, steal, and murder the innocent.

Therefore, freemen will seek principled men who fear God, hate covetousness, and love the truth to serve in the civil magistrate (Ex. 18:21). It is better to prefer one principled man who fears God over a hundred unprincipled "conservatives" or "liberals" for the office of the magistrate. One $200 check to the campaign of a God-fearing statesman, who stands on the basic principles of God's Word, is worth more than a hundred votes for an unprincipled "conservative" Republican. Liberty will not be defended or won without the sacrifice of life, fortune, and sacred honor. Too many of our leaders are unwilling to risk their reelection (sacred honor) for the cause of principle, and this will never secure liberty.

The Son who sets us free, our Lord Jesus Christ, is on the right hand of the Father, and He is ruling until all of His enemies are under His footstool. The kings of the earth should be reminded from time to time to "kiss the Son, lest he be angry, and ye perish from the way" (Ps. 2:12, Acts 4:25-26). They really should be instructed to "serve the Lord with fear, and rejoice with trembling" (Ps. 2:11). To claim anything less concerning Christ's involvement with the civil magistrate is to render Him discredit and to risk His disfavor, something Peter and the Apostles would never have done. Indeed, Jesus Christ is Lord of all.

HOPEFUL SIGNS

While there are windows of opportunity still open for those who seek freedom, the vulnerability to greater tyranny has never been higher. The millennial generation is more pro-socialist than ever.[13] Privacy is practically nonexistent, and it wouldn't take the federal government more than five minutes to identify almost every committed Christian, homeschooler, or gun owner who used e-mail or Facebook over the last ten years. The immediate trends towards more socialism and more persecution do not look good.

As the battle for freedom continues into the twenty-first century, there is a wild card in the deck that must not be missed—the exponential growth of the homeschooling population. This author has been part of the homeschooling movement since 1968, and has served as a leader in a state homeschooling organization for almost twenty years. Recently, Generations, in association with the National Home Education Research Institute, conducted a survey of 10,000 homeschool graduates and the results of the study were very encouraging. Assuming the rate of growth provided by the Department of Education of 8 percent per year over the next fifteen years[14] (and adding in second generation growth),[15] the homeschool population in America is expected to break out from 2.5 million to 10 million students over the next fifteen years. That will account for about 15 percent of the school-aged population in this country. Most of this interest group are freedom-minded, and according to a recent study from the National Home Education Research Institute, graduates are fourteen times more likely to be involved in political leadership than their counterparts from public and private schools.[16] From the historical narrative, we have learned that it only takes a principled minority to stand in the gap, and make a lasting impact for liberty. This is the story of the Magna Carta, William Wallace, William the Silent, Patrick Henry, and the Pilgrims. The animating contest of freedom is left to a handful of courageous men and women who plant the seeds of liberty. Millions will enjoy the fruits of it, but few do anything to produce it.

From this eight-hundred-year survey of Western freedom, one strategic lesson is clear: if liberties will be gained, it will be through interposition. Without Robert FitzWalter, there would have been no Magna Carta. Without William Wallace and Robert the Bruce, there would have been no independence for Scotland. Without William the Silent, there would have been no independence for the Netherlands and no relief from the Spanish Inquisition. And, without Patrick Henry, Samuel Adams, and George Mason, there would have been no independence for America and no Bill of Rights. Any substantial progress towards political liberty must come by the lower magistrates. It will not come from Washington, DC. It will come from Texas, Alabama, or Nebraska. Most importantly, it will come from principled leaders with great faith who are willing to sacrifice their lives, their fortunes, and their sacred honor for the cause of liberty.

The next forty years will be interesting. Socio-economic systems in developed nations are cracking. The nuclear family has mostly disintegrated and the moral character of the nation is in free-fall. Sexual nihilism and revolutionary social perspectives have more or less guaranteed birth implosions in every developed nation. When "the women have no more children and the men lose reason and faith,"[17] you can be sure these nations will not survive. New nations will rise up in their place.

Over the next forty years we will better understand why God in His good providence established islands of freedom and culture for us. We will see families and churches sustained through the postmodern revolutionary storms. Should the Lord tarry, once again we will lay foundations of faith upon which a civilization can grow and freedom can prosper…somewhere in the world.

NOTES

Preface

1. "Walter E. Williams on welfare: As gov't plays 'father,' 'black males have become dispensable,' http://dailycaller.com/2011/06/04/walter-e-williams-on-welfare-as-govt-plays-father-black-males-have-become-dispensable/.

2. Reference George Orwell, *1984* (London: Secker & Warburg, 1949).

PART I - FREEDOM

Chapter 1: Freedom Defined

1. www.google.com.

2. "Google Books Ngram Viewer," https://books.google.com/ngrams.

3. Dr. Keith Ablow, "America is Drunk," January 14, 2012. http://www.foxnews.com/opinion/2012/01/14/america-is-drunk/.

4. National Institute on Drug Abuse, "DrugFacts: Nationwide Trends," http://www.drugabuse.gov/publications/drugfacts/nationwide-trends.

5. CovenantEyes, "Get the Latest Pornography Statistics," http://www.covenanteyes.com/2013/02/19/pornography-statistics/.

6. William Penn, Letter to Peter the Great, Tsar of Russia, 1688.

7. Heritage Foundation, "Index for Economic Freedom," http://www.heritage.org/index/.

PART II - TYRANNY

Chapter 2: A Brief History of Tyranny

1. Noah Webster, *An American Dictionary of the English Language: Exhibiting the Origin, Orthography, Pronunciation, and Definition of Words*, 1828.

2. John of Salisbury, Policraticus: The Statesman's Book of John of Salisbury, trans. John Dickinson (New York: Russell and Russell, 1963), 4.

3. Salisbury, 258.

4. Martin Luther, "The Diet of Worms, 1521. Luther's Final Answer," *Documents of the Christian Church*, ed. Henry Bettenson & Chris Maunder (New York: Oxford University Press, 2011).

5. Martin Luther, "Secular Authority: To What Extent It Should Be Obeyed," *Martin Luther: Selections from His Writings*, ed. John Dillenberger (New York: Anchor Books, 1962).

6. Ibid.

7. John Calvin, *Institutes of the Christian Religion*, trans. Henry Beveridge (Peabody: Hendrickson, 2008), Book IV, 20:30.

8. Ibid., Book IV, 20:31.

9. Ibid.

10. Pierre Viret, *The Christian and the Magistrate: Roles, Responsibilities, and Jurisdictions*, trans. R.A. Sheats (Psalm 78 Ministries, 2015), 61.

11. Ibid., 73.

12. Ibid., 100.

13. John Knox, *The Works of John Knox* (Edinburgh: Banner of Truth Trust, 2014), 4:495.

14. Ibid., 504.

15. Samuel Rutherford, *Lex Rex, or The Law and the Prince: A Dispute for the Just Prerogative of King and People* (Edinburgh: Robert Ogle, 1844), 34.

16. Ibid.

17. Ibid., 47.

18. Ibid., 73.

19. Ibid., 142.

20. Ibid., 141.

21. reference Kevin Swanson, *Apostate: The Men Who Destroyed the Christian West,* 2nd Ed. (Parker, CO: Generations, 2018).

22. Friedrich Nietzsche, *Beyond Good and Evil: A Prelude to a Philosophy of the Future,* trans. Walter Kaufmann (New York, Vintage Books, 1966), 9.42.

23. G.W.F. Hegel, quoted in Hegel: Selections, ed. Jacob Loewenberg (New York: Charles Scribner & Sons, 1929), 443-444, 447.

24. The Venerable Bede, *Ecclesiastical History of the English People: With Bede's Letter to Egbert and Cuthbert's Letter on the Death of Bede,* trans. Leo Sherley-Price (New York: Penguin, 1990), Book III, Chapter 26.

25. Terence P. Jeffrey, "Census: 49% of Americans Get Gov't Benefits; 82M in Households on Medicaid," http://cnsnews.com/news/article/terence-p-jeffrey/census-49-americans-get-gov-t-benefits-82m-households-medicaid, Lymari Morales, "Gov't Employment Ranges From 38% in D.C. to 12% in Ohio," http://www.gallup.com/poll/141785/gov-employment-ranges-ohio.aspx.

26. Keith Hopkins, "On the Political Economy of the Roman Empire," Cambridge University, http://www.sshi.standford.edu/conferences/1999-2000/empires/hopkins. PDF.

27. David Daniell, *William Tyndale: A Biography* (New Haven: Yale University Press, 1994), 79.

PART III - A BRIEF HISTORY OF FREEDOM

Chapter 4: Freedom Breaks Into the Western World: Christians Redeem the Slaves

1. Aristotle, *The Politics of Aristotle,* trans. B. Jowett (Clarendon: Oxford, 1885), 1:5.

2. Friedrich Nietzsche, *Beyond Good and Evil: A Prelude to a Philosophy of the Future,* trans. Walter Kaufmann (New York, Vintage Books, 1966), 9.259-260.

3. Augustine, *The City of God,* trans. Marcus Dods (Edinburgh: T&T Clark), 19:15.

4. "Constitutions of the Holy Apostles," *The Ante-Nicene Fathers,* ed. Alexander Roberts and James Donaldson (New York: Charles Scribner's Sons, 1905), Book IV, Section 9.

5. Saint Augustine, "Letter 10: To Alypius," Letters, Volume 6 (1*–29*) (The Fathers of the Church, Volume 81), ed. Robert B. Eno, S.S. and Wilfrid Sister Parsons et. al. (Washington: The Catholic University of America Press, 2010.)

6. Ibid

7. J. Wylie, *History of the Scottish Nation* (London: Hamilton, Adams, and Co., 1886), 2:162-165.

8. Thomas Cahill, *How the Irish Saved Civilization* (New York: Anchor, 1995), 82.

9. Patrick, "Letter to the Soldiers of Coroticus," *The Confession of Saint Patrick,* trans. John Skinner (New York: Image, 1998), Paragraph 5.

10. Ibid., Paragraph 14.

11. Ibid., Paragraph 7.

12. Ibid., Paragraph 10.

13. Ibid., Paragraph 21.

14. Patrick, *The Confession of Saint Patrick.*

Chapter 5: 1215: Freedom Conceived

1. David Carpenter, *The Struggle for Mastery: The Penguin History of Britain, 1066–1284* (New York: Penguin, 2005), 84.

2. "Coronation Charter of Henry I," *England in the Early Middle Ages*, ed. Derek Baker (Dallas: Academia, 1993), 123.

3. Danny Danziger and John Gillingham, *1215: The Year of Magna Carta* (New York: Touchstone, 2003), 217.

4. Winston Churchill, *A History of the English-Speaking People* (New York: Skyhorse Publishing, 2011), 87.

5. Danziger and Gillingham, 89.

6. Ibid., 92.

7. Ibid., 93.

8. Roger of Wendover, *Flowers of History: Comprising the History of England from the Descent of the Saxons to AD 1235*, trans. J.A. Giles (London: Henry G. Bohn, 1849), 2:283.

9. Danziger and Gillingham, 171.

10. Darien B. Jacobson, Brian G. Raub, and Barry W. Johnson, "The Estate Tax: Ninety Years and Counting," http://www.irs.gov/pub/irs-soi/ninetyestate.pdf

11. Churchill, 103.

12. Danziger and Gillingham, 50.

13. Ibid.

14. Ibid., 253.

15. Ibid., 264.

16. Churchill, 107.

Chapter 6: Freedom Engrained: The Swiss Heritage of Freedom and How It Was Achieved

1. The story of William Tell was first popularized by Friedrich Schiller's play. Schiller drew from Aegidius Tschudi's *Chronicon Helveticum*, written around 1550 AD, and the *White Book of Sarnen*, composed in 1474 AD by Hans Schriber. Both sources serve as the best ancient records available, validating the events which took place during this period of Swiss history as Swiss independence was formed under a confederacy. This account relies heavily upon the Friedrich Schiller telling of the story.

Chapter 7: Freedom Birthed: The Battle for Scotland's Independence

1. William Hamilton of Gilberfield, *Blind Harry's Wallace* (Edinburgh: Luath Press, 1998), 64.

2. J. Wylie, *History of the Scottish Nation* (London: Hamilton, Adams, and Co., 1886), Volume 3, Chapter 6.

3. Ibid., Chapter 21.

4. Ibid.

5. Ronald McNair Scott, *Robert the Bruce: King of Scots* (New York: Peter Bedrick Books, 1982), 21.

6. Ibid., 24.

7. *Chronica Wilelmi Rishanger et Annales in Chronica Monasterii S. Albani*, ed. H.T. Riley (Rolls Series, 1865), 241.

8. Scott, 37.

9. *The Chronicle of Walter Guisborough*, ed. H. Rothwell (Camden Series, 1957), 10.

10. William Hamilton of Gilberfield, 4.

11. Ibid., 6.

12. A.F. Morison, *Sir William Wallace* (New Lanark, Scotland: Geddes & Grosset, 2000), 52.

13. Ibid., 55.

14. Ibid., 52.

15. Ibid., 54.

16. Andrew Fisher, *William Wallace* (Edinburgh: Birlinn, 2002), 12.

17. Hamilton, 87.

18. Ibid., 204, 222.

19. Ibid., 206, 207.

20. Ibid., 106.

21. Ibid., 201.

22. Winston Churchill, *A History of the English-Speaking People* (New York: Skyhorse Publishing, 2011), 129.

23. Scott, 146.

24. Ibid., 48.

25. reference Ibid., 71.

26. Ibid., 88.

27. Ibid., 99.

28. Ibid., 109.

29. Ibid., 120.

30. Ibid.

31. J. Barbour, *The Brus*, ed. and trans. G. Eyre Todd (1907), 205-208.

32. Scott, 158.

33. J. Barbour, 237.

34. "The Declaration of Arbroath," The National Archives of Scotland, http://www.nas.gov.uk/downloads/declarationarbroath.pdf

Chapter 8: William the Silent: Freedom Won by Unmitigated Sacrifice

1. John Lothrop Motley, *The Rise of the Dutch Republic* (London: Strahan and Co., 1964), 172.

2. Ibid.

3. Ibid.

4. Jonathan Kirsch, *The Grand Inquisitor's Manual: A History of Terror in the Name of God* (New York: Harper Collins, 2008), 154.

5. Cecil Roth, *The Spanish Inquisition* (New York: Norton, 1964), 170.

6. Petrus Johannes Blok, *History of the People of the Netherlands: Part II*, trans. Ruth Putnam (New York: G.P. Putnam and Sons, 1899), 255.

7. Ruth Putnam, *William the Silent, Prince of Orange, the Moderate Man of the 16th Century* (New York: Knickerbocker Press, 1894), 1:75.

8. Kirsch, 154.

9. Sophie Arie, "Historians say Inquisition wasn't that bad," http://www.theguardian.com/world/2004/jun/16/artsandhumanities.internationaleducationnews.

10. *William the Silent's Apology*, trans. Frederic Harrison, 1897. https://en.wikisource.org/wiki/William_the_Silent%27s_Apology.

11. Putnam, 34.

12. Ibid., 71.

13. *William the Silent's Apology*

14. Ibid.

15. Motley.

16. Alexander G. Cardew, *A Short History of the Inquisition* (New York: The Truth Seeker, 1913), 202.

17. Ibid.

18. Putnam, 183-184.

19. Ibid., 184.

20. Ibid.

21. Ibid., 221.

22. Ibid., 266.

23. Ibid., 280.

24. C.V. Wedgwood, *William the Silent* (London: Jonathan Cape, 1944), 114.

25. Putnam, 285.

26. Ruth Putnam, *Prince of Orange: The Moderate Man of the Sixteenth Century*, vol. 2 (New York: Knickerbocker Press, 1895), 5.

27. Ibid., 12.

28. Ibid., 33.

29. W.G. Van de Hulst, *William of Orange: The Silent Prince* (Pella: Inheritance Publications, 1992), 81.

30. Van de Hulst, 104.

31. Putnam, vol. 2, 318.

32. "The Dutch Declaration of Independence, 1581," http://legacy.fordham.edu/halsall/mod/1581dutch.asp

33. Wedgwood, 231.

34. Wedgwood, 250.

Chapter 9: Freedom Sought: The Courage of the Pilgrims

1. John Robinson, *The Works of John Robinson* (Harrisburg: Sprinkle, 2009), 3:162.

2. As far as the Pilgrims' theological commitment is concerned, Pastor John Robinson took the side of the Calvinists in the debates at the Synod of Dort. Their theological distinctives were the same as most reformed Christians. They believed in household (infant) baptism, yet disagreed with state control of the church. They were congregational in their church government.

3. "Mayflower Compact, 1620," http://www.pilgrimhallmuseum.org/mayflower_compact_text.htm.

4. Robinson, 1:xxxvi.

5. William Bradford, *Of Plymouth Plantation* (Bulverde: Mantle Ministries, 1998), 19-20.

6. Robinson, 2:304.

7. "William Brewster, 17th Century Documents," http://www.pilgrimhallmuseum.org/pdf/William_Brewster_17th_Century_Documents.pdf.

8. Robinson, 1:lv.

9. Michael G. Hall, *The Last American Puritan: The Life of Increase Mather* (Hanover: Wesleyan University Press, 1988), 347.

10. Will Durant, *The Story of Civilization*, vol. 6 (New York: N.Y.: Simon and Schuster,

1957), 190.

11. W.H. Carslaw, *Exiles of the Covenant* (Paisley Alexander Gardner by Appointment to the late Queen Victoria, 1908).

Chapter 10: Oliver Cromwell: The Great War Against Tyranny and a Legacy for Liberty

1. J.H. Merle D'Aubigne, *The Protector* (Harrisburg: Sprinkle, 1847 Edition), 85.

2. Ibid, 39.

3. Otto Scott, *The Great Christian Revolution* (Vallecito: Ross House, 1991), 248.

4. D'Aubigne, 51.

5. Robert Southey, *Life of Cromwell* (New York: Appleton and Co., 1845), 76.

6. D'Aubigne 161.

7. Ibid., 160.

8. "Congress shall make no law respecting an establishment of religion, or prohibiting the free exercise thereof," United States Constitution, First Amendment.

9. United States Constitution, Article I, Section 8, Clause 11.

10. Thomas Carlyle, *Oliver Cromwell's Letters and Speeches with Elucidations*, vol. 3 (London: Chapman and Hall, 1886), 18.

11. Ibid., 138.

12. D'Aubigne, 193

13. Ibid., 162.

14. Ibid., 163-164.

15. Ibid.

16. Ibid., 24-25.

17. Ibid., 53-54.

18. Ibid., 59.

Chapter 11: Freedom Espoused: The Passion of Patrick Henry

1. Michael G. Hall, *The Last American Puritan: The Life of Increase Mather* (Hanover: Wesleyan University Press, 1988), 212ff.

2. *The Demosthenes of His Age: Accounts of Patrick Henry's Oratory by His Contemporaries*, ed. Mark Couvillon (Red Hill: Patrick Henry Memorial Foundation, 2013), 31.

3. Ibid., 94.

4. Ibid., 74.

5. Edmund S. Morgan, *The Birth of the Republic, 1763-89.* (Chicago: University of Chicago Press, 1956), 111.

6. Norine Dickson Campbell, *Patrick Henry, Patriot and Statesman* (Old Greenwich:

Devon-Adair Company, 1975), 343.

7. Stephen Ambrose, *Undaunted Courage: Meriwether Lewis, Thomas Jefferson, and the Opening of the American West* (New York: Simon and Schuster, 2002), 56.

8. George Washington writing to James Madison, "The edicts of Mr. H- (in the assembly) are enregistered with less opposition by the majority of that body, than by those of the Grand Monarch that are in Parliament or France. He has only to say let this be Law, and it is Law."

9. *The World's Best Orations: From the Earliest Period to the Present,* vol. 7 (Nubu Press, 2012), 2485.

10. It is important to note that the two colleges left in America that still retain some commitment to the vision of American liberties are named after Patrick Henry and George Mason.

11. Campbell, 352.

12. Campbell, 350.

13. Walter E. Williams, *The Washington Times,* June 10, 1992.

14. "Letter to Mrs. Anne Christian, May 15th 1786," in William Wirt Henry, *Patrick Henry: Life, Correspondence and Speeches,* vol. 2 (New York: Scribner, 1891), 287.

15. From eyewitnesses Patrick Henry Fontaine and Moses Coit Tyler, *Patrick Henry* (Houghton Mifflin and Co, 1887), 422.

Chapter 12: Freedom Secured: The Blessing of God's Providence

1. Pat Alderman, "Samuel Doak's Famous Sermon and Prayer," *One Heroic Hour at King's Mountain* (Overmountain Press, 1968), 21.

2. David McCullough, *John Adams* (New York: Simon and Schuster, 2001),160.

3. Rod Gragg, *By the Hand of Providence* (New York: Howard Books, 2011), 160.

4. Ibid., 165.

5. Nat Hillborn and Sam Hillborn, *Battleground of Freedom: South Carolina in the Revolution* (Columbia: Sandlapper, 1970), 145-55.

6. Ibid.

7. Gragg, 169.

8. Claude H. Van Tyne, *The American Revolution 1776-1783* (New York: Harper, 1905), 323.

9. Gragg, 171.

10. Ibid.

11. Jessica Durando, "Which country is most charitable? The USA – and Myanmar," http://www.usatoday.com/story/news/nation-now/2014/11/20/giving-index-charity-united-states-myanmar/70008604/.

12. Tia Ghose, "4 in 10 Americans Believe God Created Earth 10,000 Years Ago," http://www.livescience.com/46123-many-americans-creationists.html.

13. Alderman, 21.

PART IV - LOSING FREEDOM

Chapter 13: The Modern Draconian State

1. In 1900, there were approximately $1 billion in home mortgages, according to the Statistical Abstract of the United States (1969, p. 705). Given that the GDP was $20 billion in 1900 (http://www.usgovernmentspending.com), the debt to GDP ratio stood at 5%. According to the Federal Reserve Bank, 2010 Mortgage Debt in the United States stands at $14 trillion or 95% of the GDP (as of 2010). see "Mortgage Debt Outstanding," http://www.federalreserve.gov/econresdata/releases/mortoutstand/current.htm, and "US GDP 2010," http://econpost.com/gdp/us-gdp-2010. The debt-load ratio has increased by a factor of almost twenty times in a hundred years.

2. Steve Kerch, "1900 to 2010: Evolution of the American Home Today: Fun Housing Facts," http://articles.chicagotribune.com/2000-06-18/business/0006180063_1_single-family-homes-two-or-three-bedrooms-new-housing-units.

3. Government spending at all levels (Federal, State, and Local) in 2010 added up to about $7.3 Trillion (including $1.3 Trillion in the Federal Deficit) (http://www.usgovernmentspending.com/breakdown_2010USrt_14rs5n). This accounts for 52.1% of the GDP. In 1900, government spending stood at $1.608 billion (http://www.usgovernmentspending.com/total_spending_1902), or 8% of the GDP. This represents an increase in government tyranny of a full 650% since 1900. Moreover, there are 30 times more government regulations (as determined by pages of Federal Register) now than there was in 1936 (http://www.llsdc.org/attachments/wysiwyg/544/fed-reg-pages.pdf).

4. According to Wikipedia, there were 22 million farms in 1880 (reference "History of Agriculture in the United States," http://en.wikipedia.org/wiki/History_of_agriculture_in_the_United_States). This accounts for about 45% of the population (since the population was 50,200,000 per the 1880 census). Reference "1880 United States Census," http://en.wikipedia.org/wiki/1880_United_States_Census. As of 2008, only 2% were employed in agriculture (http://www.csrees.usda.gov/qlinks/extension.html), with the national self-employment ratio hovering around 11% (http://www.csrees.usda.gov/qlinks/extension.html).

5. Sources: Michael Schuyler, "A Short History of Government Taxing and Spending in the United States," http://taxfoundation.org/article/short-history-government-taxing-and-spending-united-states, "Receipts and Outlays of the Federal Government, 1789-2013," http://www.infoplease.com/ipa/A0104753.html, "Government Spending Chart," http://www.usgovernmentspending.com/spending_chart_1900_1920USb_16s2li011mcn_F0f.

6. Kurumi Fukushima, "The 10 Most 'Socialist' States in America," http://www.thestreet.com/story/12783796/19/the-10-most-socialist-states-in-america.html.

7. Benjamin Franklin, *The Way of Wealth* (Bedford: Applewood Books, 1986), 11.

8. *The Cry for Justice: An Anthology of the Literature of Social Protest*, ed. Upton Sinclair et

al. (1915).

9. "Accumulated Gross Federal Debt," http://www.usgovernmentdebt.us/ spending_chart_1792_2016USp_XXs1li011mcn_H0f_Accumulated_Gross_Federal_ Debt#copypaste.

10. "List of countries by public debt," http://en.wikipedia.org/wiki/List_of_ countries_by_public_debt.

11. Keith Weiner, "Unfunded Liabilities are Fraudulent Promises," http://www.forbes. com/sites/keithweiner/2014/03/19/unfunded-liabilities-are-fraudulent-promises/.

12. Terence P. Jeffrey, "+106%: Obama Has More Than Doubled Marketable U.S. Debt," http://cnsnews.com/news/article/terence-p-jeffrey/106-obama-has-more-doubled-marketable-us-debt.

Chapter 14: Creating the Slave Mentality

1. Wilma Dunaway, *The African-American Family in Slavery and Emancipation* (New York: Cambridge University Press, 2003), 53ff.

2. Walter E. Williams, "The True Black Tragedy: Illegitimacy Rate of Nearly 75%," http://cnsnews.com/commentary/walter-e-williams/true-black-tragedy-illegitimacy-rate-nearly-75.

3. "Top 101 cities with the highest percentage of single-parent households, population 5000+," http://www.city-data.com/top2/h6.html.

4. "Poor teens in Baltimore face worse conditions than those in Nigeria – study," http://rt.com/usa/210607-baltimore-study-nigeria-health/.

5. William Teach, "Dependence On Government Spikes 23% Under Obama," http://rightwingnews.com/democrats/dependence-on-government-spikes-23-under-obama/.

6. "Economic Freedom of the World: 2012 Annual Report," www.freetheworld. com/2012/EFW2012-complete.pdf.

7. Social Security data obtained from www.ssa.gov/briefhistory3.html, Medicaid data obtained from www.cms.gov, Food Stamps data obtained from www.fns.usda.gov/ snap/short-history-snap.

8. "List of sovereign states and dependent territories by fertility rate," https:// en.wikipedia.org/wiki/List_of_sovereign_states_and_dependent_territories_by_ fertility_rate.

9. www.populationpyramid.com

10. Jason DeParle and Sabrina Tavernise, "For Women Under 30, Most Births Occur Outside Marriage," http://www.nytimes.com/2012/02/18/us/for-women-under-30-most-births-occur-outside-marriage.html?_r=0.

11. "The Me Me Me Generation," http://nation.time.com/millennials/.

12. Nicholas Rayfield, "National student loan debt reaches a bonkers $1.2 trillion," http://college.usatoday.com/2015/04/08/national-student-loan-debt-reaches-a-bonkers-1-2-trillion/, Sandy Baum, "The Evolution of Student Debt in the U.S.: An

Overview," http://www.upjohn.org/stuloanconf/Baum.pdf.

13. Rodney Brooks, "Retirement Living: Debt holds many Boomers back," http://www.usatoday.com/story/money/columnist/brooks/2013/01/28/retire-debt-crisis-retirement-boomers/1840225/.

14. "Supreme Court Upholds Obamacare Subsidies, President Says ACA 'Is Here to Stay'," http://abcnews.go.com/Politics/supreme-court-upholds-obama-health-care-subsidies/story?id=31931412.

15. Dan Mangan, "Subsidy, what subsidy? Millions unaware of their Obamacare aid," http://www.cnbc.com/id/101872265#.

16. Hans Bader, "Obamacare Provides $7,200 'Divorce Incentive,' $11,000 for Older Couples," http://www.cnsnews.com/commentary/hans-bader/obamacare-provides-7200-divorce-incentive-11000-older-couples.

17. Cora Sherlock, "92% of Babies with Down Syndrome in England are Killed in Abortions," http://www.lifenews.com/2014/06/10/92-of-babies-with-down-syndrome-in-england-are-killed-in-abortions/.

18. Sarah Knapton, "Aborted babies incinerated to heat UK hospitals," http://www.telegraph.co.uk/news/health/news/10717566/Aborted-babies-incinerated-to-heat-UK-hospitals.html.

19. Simon Caldwell, "Warning to Britain as almost half of Belgium's euthanasia nurses admit to killing without consent," http://www.dailymail.co.uk/news/article-1285423/Half-Belgiums-euthanasia-nurses-admit-killing-consent.html.

20. "US court returns five-month-old baby to Russian couple in custody case," http://sputniknews.com/voiceofrussia/2013_04_30/US-court-returns-five-month-old-baby-to-Russian-couple-in-custody-case-070/.

21. "Hospital Holds West Hartford Girl for 9 Months After Parents Argue Diagnosis," http://foxct.com/2013/11/19/hospital-holds-west-hartford-girl-for-9-months-after-parents-argue-diagnosis/.

22. "Bureau of Labor Statistics," http://data.bls.gov/timeseries/LNS11300000.

23. Ibid.

Chapter 15: The New Battle Front: Family Freedom

1. Will and Ariel Durant, *Rousseau and Revolution* (Simon and Schuster: New York, 1967), 179.

2. Paul Johnson, *Intellectuals* (Harper and Row: New York, 1988), 23.

3. John Taylor Gatto, *The Underground History of American Education* (Odysseus Group, 2000).

4. Plato, *The Republic*, Book 5, Section 2, Part 6.

5. quoted in A.M. Adam, *Plato: Moral and Political Ideals* (Cambridge: University of Cambridge Press, 1913), 152.

6. "US Education Spending History from 1900," http://www.usgovernmentspending.

com/education_spending.

7. reference Ruth 4:9-10.

8. "Parents could be criminalized under new law," www.christian.org/religious_parents_could_be_criminalized_under_new_law.

9. www.christian.org.

10. Michael Farris, "Has American Abandoned Parental Rights," http://www.hslda.org/courtreport/V22N4/V22N401.asp.

11. "Father Faces Trial Over School's 'Pro-Gay' Book," http://www.wnd.com/2005/08/31618/.

12. Bob Unruh, "Court Orders Christian Child Into Government Education," http://www.wnd.com/2009/08/108084/.

13. "Standards in Your State," http://www.corestandards.org/standards-in-your-state/.

Chapter 16: The Rise of Fascism and the Loss of Freedom

1. "2015 Index of Economic Freedom," http://www.heritage.org/index/about.

2. Benito Mussolini, *Fascism: Doctrine and Institutions* (Rome: Ardita Publishers, 1935).

3. www.mwhodges.home.att.net/state_local.htm#Person

4. Stephen Moore, "We've Become a Nation of Takers, Not Makers," http://www.wsj.com/articles/SB10001424052748704050204576219073867182108.

5. "Federal Register Pages," http://www.llsdc.org/attachments/wysiwyg/544/fed-reg-pages.pdf.

6. "Texas is First State to Require Pre-Teen HPV Immunization," http://www.healthinschools.org/News-Room/EJournals/Volume-7/Number-11/Texas-HPV-Vaccination-Requirement.aspx.

7. "Lights out for the incandescent light bulb as of Jan. 1, 2014," http://www.foxnews.com/tech/2013/12/31/end-road-for-incandescent-light-bulb/.

8. "Regulations & Standards: Light-Duty," http://epa.gov/otaq/climate/regs-light-duty.htm#new1.

9. Jared Wollstein, "Government Property Seizures Out of Control," http:www.newsmax.com/archives/articles/2001/6/27/191414.shtml.

10. "The States With the Most Land Owned By The Federal Government," http://247wallst.com/investing/2011/05/16/the-states-with-the-most-land-owned-by-the-federal-government/2/.

11. "RHE man gets jail time for property fines," *The Daily Breeze*, August 27, 2007.

12. "Nanny State Agents Out to Kill Raw Food Industry," http://bobmccarty.com/2010/11/19/nanny-state-agents-out-to-kill-raw-food-industry/.

13. Tucker Carlson, "Home Wreckers," *Reader's Digest*, August 2003.

14. reference *Animal Farm*, by George Orwell.

15. Kelly Phillips, "Widow Loses House Over $6.30 Tax Bill," http://www.forbes.com/sites/kellyphillipserb/2014/04/29/widow-loses-house-over-6-30-tax-bill/.

16. Andrew P. Napolitano, Senior Judicial Analyst, Fox News Channel, "Property Rights After the Kelo Decision," Imprimis, January, 2007.

17. Ibid.

18. Some of the early state constitutions exempted widows from property forfeiture. Reference Constitution of the State of Arkansas of 1874, Article 10, Section 5 (Rights of Widows and Children).

19. Quentin Fottrell, "Obama renews focus on the still struggling middle class," http://www.marketwatch.com/story/americans-are-40-poorer-than-before-the-recession-2014-12-12?reflink=MW_GoogleNews&google_editors_picks=true.

Chapter 17: Eroding the Moral Fiber of the Nation

1. Scott Lively and Kevin Abrams, *The Pink Swastika: Homosexuality in the Nazi Party* (Keizer: Founders Publishing, 1996).

2. "Same-sex marriage in the United States," http://en.wikipedia.org/wiki/Same-sex_marriage_in_the_United_States.

3. Jeri Clausing, "Supreme Court Declines to Hear New Mexico Gay Wedding Photography Case," Supreme http://www.huffingtonpost.com/2014/04/07/supreme-court-gay-wedding-photography_n_5104699.html.

4. Todd Starnes, "Baker forced to make gay wedding cakes, undergo sensitivity training, after losing lawsuit," http://www.foxnews.com/opinion/2014/06/03/baker-forced-to-make-gay-wedding-cakes-undergo-sensitivity-training-after/.

5. http://www.foxnews.com/opinion/2014/01/21/christian-bakery-guilty-violating-civil-rights-lesbian-couple/http://www.katu.com/news/local/Final-order-Oregon-Bureau-of-Labor-and-Industries-BOLI-Gresham-Sweet-Cakes-Melissa-bakery-must-pay-135000-to-lesbian-couple-311494301.html.

6. "Calif. Court: Fertility doctor must treat gays," http://www.christianexaminer.com/article/calif.court.fertility.doctor.must.treat.gays/43979.htm.

7. Cheryl K. Chumley, "Idaho city's ordinance tells pastors to marry gays or go to jail," http://www.washingtontimes.com/news/2014/oct/20/idaho-citys-ordinance-tells-pastors-to-marry-gays-/.

8. "Judge rules Christian facility cannot ban same-sex civil union ceremony on its own premises," https://www.lifesitenews.com/news/judge-rules-christian-facility-cannot-ban-same-sex-civil-union-ceremony-on.

9. Rod Dreher, "Orthodox Christians Must Now Learn to Live as Exiles in Our Own Country," http://time.com/3938050/orthodox-christians-must-now-learn-to-live-as-exiles-in-our-own-country/.

10. "Philadelphia 11 Appeal Free Speech Limits," http://www.wnd.com/news/article.asp?ARTICLE_ID=54276.

11. "Legislator: Law Allows Banishment of Bible," http://www.wnd.

com/2008/07/68542/.

12. Family Research Council, http://www.frc.org/get.cfm?i=PW07B03.

13. "Supreme Court muzzles free speech in Canada, rules against Christian pro-family activist," http://www.lifesitenews.com/news/supreme-court-muzzles-free-speech-in-canada-crushes-born-again-christian-ac#sthash.HCjAMfzO.dpuf.

14. "Kevin Jennings," http://en.wikipedia.org/wiki/Kevin_Jennings#GLSEN_and_writing.

15. *The Washington Times*, October 6, 1994, A1.

16. "California Reparative Therapy Ban," http://www.huffingtonpost.com/news/california-reparative-therapy-ban/.

17. "California governor signs bill requiring schools to teach gay history," http://www.cnn.com/2011/US/07/14/california.lgbt.education/.

18. "Executive Order 10450," https://en.wikipedia.org/wiki/Executive_Order_10450. 1953 was the year Executive Order 10450 was issued.

19. "Equal benefits in death," http://articles.chicagotribune.com/2002-07-13/news/0207130177_1_domestic-partners-group-of-gay-republicans-equal-rights.

20. Chad Groening, "Report: Military to chaplains – resign or conform," http://onenewsnow.com/culture/2011/08/24/report-military-to-chaplains-resign-or-conform#.VLRVuyvF-V0.

21. *The Washington Post*, December 4, 1992, A1.

22. Gundron Schultz, "Planned Parenthood Reports Record $882 Million Income, $63 Million Profit," http://www.lifesite.net/ldn/2006/jun/06060805.html.

23. Douglas Ernst, "Planned Parenthood performed 327K abortions in fiscal 2014: 'We've come a long way'," http://www.washingtontimes.com/news/2015/jan/1/planned-parenthood-327k-abortions-fiscal-2014/.

24. Cheryl Wetzstein, "4th Planned Parenthood video: Selling fetal body parts deemed 'research' for legal protection," http://www.washingtontimes.com/news/2015/jul/30/4th-planned-parenthood-video-selling-fetal-body-pa/.

25. "DOJ to Give Leftist Groups Cut of B Settlement," http://www.judicialwatch.org/blog/2014/08/doj-give-leftist-groups-cut-b-settlement/.

26. Chuck Norris, "California Forces Churches to Fund Abortions," http://townhall.com/columnists/chucknorris/2014/10/28/california-forces-churches-to-fund-abortions-n1910553/page/full.

27. Jack Bouboushian, "Christian College Loses Challenge to Obamacare," http://www.courthousenews.com/2015/07/06/christian-college-loses-challenge-to-obamacare.htm.

28. Fr. Roger J. Landry, "Trampling or Upholding the Conscience of Pharmicists," http://catholicpreaching.com/trampling-or-upholding-the-conscience-of-pharmacists-the-anchor-november-16-2007/.

29. "Ruling: Washington can require pharmacies to dispense Plan B," http://www.

seattletimes.com/seattle-news/ruling-washington-can-require-pharmacies-to-dispense-plan-b/.

30. Natalie Villacorta and Jennifer Haberkorn, "Supreme Court blocks Texas abortion law ruling," http://www.politico.com/story/2015/06/supreme-court-texas-abortion-law-blocked-119550.html.

31. "Links to Barack Obama's votes on Illinois' Born Alive Infant Protection Act," http://www.jillstanek.com/2008/02/links-to-barack-obamas-votes-on-illinois-born-alive-infant-protection-act/.

32. For a complete defense of the Christian's responsibility to engage the battle for the right to life (on the abortion issue), reference Kevin Swanson, *Keep the Faith: On Family & Sexuality* (Parker: Generations with Vision, 2014).

PART V - FREEDOM!

Chapter 18: Seeking Freedom

1. Maggie Fox, "New voter bloc emerges: single women," http://www.today.com/health/new-voter-bloc-emerges-single-women-1C6904321.

2. Mary Eberstadt, *Home Alone America: The Hidden Toll of Day Care, Behavioral Drugs, and Other Parent Substitutes* (New York: Penguin, 2004).

3. transparencyinternational.org.

4. J.H. Huizinga, *The Making of a Saint: The Tragi-Comedy of Jean-Jacques Rousseau* (London: H. Hamilton, 1976).

5. For many studies performed on home education, reference www.nheri.org.

6. HSLDA Court Report, First Quarter, 2015, 8-9.

7. John Paton, *Missionary to the New Hebrides: An Autobiography* (London: Hodder & Stoughton, 1889), 5.

8. Quoted in Allan C. Carlson, *Third Ways: How Bulgarian Greens, Swedish Housewives, and Beer-Swilling Englishmen Created Family-Centered Economies* (Wilmington: ISI Books, 2007), 176-177.

9. Quoted in Ibid.

10. Charlotte Alter, "Working Women are Planning More, Which is Why Some Are Freezing Their Eggs," http://time.com/3969601/working-women-are-planning-more-which-is-why-some-are-freezing-their-eggs/.

11. Why Young Men Delay Adulthood to Stay in 'Guyland'," http://www.newsweek.com/id/156372.

12. Robert W. Wood, "Obama's proposed 68% Death Tax Would Be Highest in World," http://www.forbes.com/sites/robertwood/2015/02/03/obamas-proposed-68-death-tax-would-be-highest-in-world/, Jonathan Weisman, "Obama Plans to Keep Estate Tax," http://www.wsj.com/articles/SB123172020818472279.

13. "Tithing Hits Record Low; Churches Spend More to Make Congregants Happy,"

http://www.christianpost.com/news/tithing-hits-record-low-churches-spend-more-to-make-congregants-happy-58237/.

14. reference www.ChristianFamilyEldercare.org to find out more of what Christian families are doing to help these precious folks.

Chapter 19: In Search of the Second Mayflower

1. A fuller description of this vision of the "Second Mayflower" is laid out Kevin Swanson, *The Second Mayflower* (Parker, CO: Generations with Vision, 2009).

2. "Law Center to Prevent Gun Violence," smartgunlaws.org

3. "Annual Gun Law State Scorecard 2014," http://gunlawscorecard.org.

4. Paul Hattaway and Brother Yun, *The Heavenly Man: The Remarkable True Story of Chinese Christian Brother Yun* (Grand Rapids: Kregel Publications, 2002).

5. Roy Ratcliff, *Dark Journey, Deep Grace: Jeffrey Dahmer's Story of Faith* (Leafwood Publishers, 2006).

6. This remarkable series of events and legal shifts are chronicled in Christopher Klicka's book *Homeschool Heroes: The Struggle & Triumph of Home Schooling in America* (Nashville: B&H, 2006).

7. "Belgian lawmakers vote on euthanasia for kids," http://www.dw.de/belgian-lawmakers-vote-on-euthanasia-for-kids/a-17245525.

8. "Labeled: The Movie," https://www.facebook.com/labeledthemovie/info?tab=page_info.

9. Chris Conover, "Obamacare Will Increase Health Spending by $7,450 For a Typical Family of Four," http://www.forbes.com/sites/theapothecary/2013/09/23/its-official-obamacare-will-increase-health-spending-by-7450-for-a-typical-family-of-four/.

10. Participation in the Health Care Sharing Ministries represented huge cost savings over the Obamacare requirements for insurance. Samaritan Ministries, for example charged families between $3,000 and $5,000 per year; a savings that would amount to $200,000 in ten years. President and Founder Ted Pittenger formed this non-profit ministry in 1993, and the organization has grown to over 40,000 member families.

11. "Federal Laws Prohibiting Job Discrimination Questions and Answers," http://www.eeoc.gov/facts/qanda.html.

12. Jack Bouboushian, "Christian College Loses Challenge to Obamacare," http://www.courthousenews.com/2015/07/06/christian-college-loses-challenge-to-obamacare.htm, Abby Broyles, "Local Christian universities lose case over Obamacare birth control exemption," http://kfor.com/2015/07/15/local-christian-universities-lose-case-over-obamacare-birth-control-exemption/, "Timothy C. Morgan, "Christian Pharmacists and Pharmacy Owners Lose Emergency Contraceptive Appeal," http://www.christianitytoday.com/gleanings/2015/july/christian-pharmacists-lose-emergency-contraceptive-appeal.html.

13. "Pew Research Center," www.pewresearch.com.

14. Michael Tennant, "Homeschooling Up 62 Percent Over a Decade," http://www.thenewamerican.com/culture/education/item/20926-homeschooling-up-62-percent-over-a-decade.

15. www.generations.org

16. www.nheri.org, reference "Homeschooling Grows Up" study.

17. Reference Rudyard Kipling's "Gods of the Copybook Headings"